MW00720498

Vinegar on the Cross

Terry Stocker

Tula Press, Inc.
Pensacola, Florida

Printed in the United States of America
First Edition
Library of Congress Catalog Card Number: 96-090662
ISBN: 0-9654427-0-5

Cover design by KOMACOM Seoul, Korea

TULA PRESS, INC.
P.O. Box 36275
Pensacola, Florida 32516

That which is to be escaped is pain yet to come. We cannot escape pain past, for it is gone. And present pain is happening now, thus it is a current experience. So only pain which is yet to come can be escaped. It is only the pain yet to come which can hinder a person. Only this pain can be changed and escaped.

Adapted from *The Yoga-System of Patanjali*

CONTENTS

1

DIGGING UP DEAD GODS

*All subjects should be open for
ongoing reconsideration. In other
words, we need a reality check
every now and then.*
                        -my father

INQUIRY AND CHANGE

My mind tuned to its programmed silence when my trowel partially exposed the yellow face of another small clay figurine. As my soft paint brush cleared the dirt from the painted face, I asked my never-ending question, "Who are you?" Its static, elliptical eyes stared back at me with the same question.

I switched back to the living world as a truck with no muffler barreled down the Mexican road not far off. For a moment of relief, I glanced at the sacred mountain of Jicuco. As an archaeologist, I have excavated thousands of figurines, images of gods and goddesses no longer in existence. Each one prompted me to ask, "How many religions have there been since the beginning of time?" But this one time, I also inquired of myself, "And how many more religions will there be until the end of time?"

My archaeological specialization is ancient extinct religions. Excavating dead goddesses and gods for a living does have an exotic image. But trying to understand ancient religions no longer practiced and the ongoing change in religions is, for me, an energy-consuming endeavor.

I was raised a Christian, but went on to explore many religions around the world. Being mystified by individuals purporting to "have the truth" while condemning others as heathens made me want to investigate the "truths" espoused by others.

I practiced Zen Buddhism for awhile because the daily meditation helped me fight stress and control my mental well being--somewhat. Zen Buddhists also have very different attitudes toward death than do most Christians. The Zen don't have the view of a burning hell that I had instilled in me as a youth. Furthermore, they don't believe in personal immortality. One of the qualities I like about Buddhism is that one must find one's own salvation. Doing that requires questioning of the world around one.

Yet, I do not consider myself a Zen Buddhist. I regard myself as an animist. I believe that everything in the universe has a spirit, even rocks. Where do we go when we die? I don't know, but I like to think that we are recycled into some type of spiritual energy pool that permeates the universe. I don't know how the good and the bad aspects of our spirits interact or are separated. There is something powerful beyond the boundaries of our solar system. I'll leave it at that, "something."

Through the eyes of Zen and animism, I saw a different Jesus than the one Christians presented to me. The more I analyzed the Gospels, the more incomplete was the Jesus presented to me by the Christian world. I saw a man much like Buddha, a man who knew there was suffering in the human desire to possess. Jesus saw materialism as the great corrupter.

My main personal religious concern is how to balance materialism and spirituality. Jesus was adamant on this matter. He didn't suggest a balance but an entire focus on spirituality. He told his disciples, "It will be difficult for a rich person to enter the kingdom of heaven." (MT 19:23)

I don't think materialism necessarily corrupts. I think more along the lines of Confucius: One can be rich and still be a moral person. But I also believe that the more one is consumed by the material world, the more one is restricted from fully experiencing the spiritual realm surrounding us and within us. Thus I am constantly faced with the questions: Which direction to go? How much of the spiritual realm do I really want to experience? And why? And equally important: What is the spiritual realm?

THE FUTURE

After Jesus fasted 40 days, Satan "appeared" to him and made three propositions. As a child, I was mesmerized by one temptation of Jesus. Satan took Jesus onto a high mountain and "...shewed unto him all the kingdoms of the world in a moment of time." Satan proposed, "All these I will give to you if you kneel and worship me." (MT 4:9)

As a child, I was intrigued by Satan showing Jesus all the kingdoms of the world in a moment of time. I constantly conjured images of a sky full of kingdoms, wondering *what* did Jesus see? Did the vision occur in the sky? Or since Satan and Jesus went up on a mountain, did they see the kingdoms on the ground? Or all around them? Or below them?

The few people I talked with about my interest in this vision simply said, "So what difference does it make?" The difference was I really wanted to, and still do want to, understand what Jesus experienced.

Growing up in Ohio didn't leave me much latitude to figure out the difference between looking down from the mountains and looking up. There weren't any mountains for me to go to. I continued to wonder if the kingdoms surrounded Jesus. Everywhere he turned was there another kingdom? But he is said to have seen them all in a moment of time. Maybe he had to turn around fast. I know if it were I, I'd be staring into one kingdom for a long time. Like so many of us, I just wish the Bible gave more details.

For almost 40 years, I have contemplated Jesus peering into all the kingdoms of the world. Was Jesus actually having the vision; or was Jesus sharing Satan's vision? As I grew older, I thought about that vision in great detail. What did Jesus see? Temporal or spiritual kingdoms? Real or imagined kingdoms? Just those kingdoms then existing? If the latter were the case, the Hawaiian islands would still be uninhabited. Teotihuacan outside of Mexico City was then a grandiose metropolis boasting the Pyramid of the Sun.

Or did he see all of the kingdoms existing up to that point? If so, Jesus might have seen the great city of Persepolis when Alexander the Great rode into it after his routing of Darius. Maybe he looked into China and saw Ssuma Ch'ien writing his apocryphal biography, *Shih chi*, of the life of Confucius 200 years before Jesus' own birth.

Or maybe Jesus' vision was of all the kingdoms that have existed, do exist, and will exist. How many kingdoms have there been since the beginning of time? Perhaps Jesus looked in on the Korean potters of the Choson Dynasty as they were making their wares in hues of white. Possibly he saw the crusades of the Christians to liberate the Holy Lands from the Muslims. Or was the year 1578, and Jesus saw Altan Khan of the Mongols confer Bsod-nams-rgya-mtsho with the title of Dalai Lama?

There are internal temporal problems with my thoughts of all the kingdoms of the world in a moment of time. The day Alexander the Great rode into Persepolis was just that, an entire day. At what point would Jesus look in? Would he look in when Alexander first arrived in Persepolis or in the end when he finally settled into his new kingdom?

The temporal constraints of the "kingdoms vision" are not limited to just a day. I mentioned Jesus might have looked into the Choson Dynasty of Korea. That dynasty lasted from 1392 to 1910. Toward the end of the dynasty, the royalty were dying off at an alarming rate, and there were great numbers of people wearing the white attire required during mourning. How would Jesus interpret this?

I'm no closer to understanding the vision now than I was as a child. But in the process, I have come to understand other aspects of Christianity quite well. I created a rather finite framework for viewing Christianity. Imagine a three tube telescope. The tiny lens for viewing is my cultural values. The first small tube is Jesus, the second tube is the Bible, and the third tube is the global society in which all of us exist. The large lens is history, and beyond that is the future. I am the one peering in the tiny lens.

The large lens--history--at the end of my metaphorical telescope rendered my wonderment about Jesus' vision a thing of never-ending complexity. There is a constant question in my head: "What was he seeing?"

Maybe he saw certain individuals or ongoing acts, like the invention of plate glass in 1688. Maybe he looked into the White House as President Theodore Roosevelt entertained Dr. Louis Klopsch, the designer of the first red letter Bible. Maybe he saw the construction of Interstate 80 across the United States. Maybe the visions Satan presented Jesus had everyday people just walking down streets like extras in a movie.

Of course we are stuck with the basic question: "What was a moment of time for Satan and Jesus?" Further, would a moment in time be different after a 40-day fast? Doing a 40-day fast might tell us.

There are also spatial problems. Even if the vision were only of all the kingdoms existing during the time of Jesus, how would those kingdoms fit into one vision? Actually, that's the beauty of visions. They aren't confined to the present boundaries of space and time. They are rather like passing the event horizon of a black hole. Time and space have different qualities from what we now experience. I've only had a few visions in my life. When I looked out at the sky, the sky wasn't there; my visions were. That's a lot of space to fill.

I am most fascinated by where the telescope is aimed--the future. The Bible is about one phenomenological endeavor. It is about knowing, seeing, and prophesying an apparently predictable future. Of course, this gives the practitioners of Christianity confidence in the future that is promised to them in the end of the Bible. The last book in the Bible, Revelation, is about a future yet to come. It is about a future presumably revealed to John the Apostle.

THE PAST

My fascination with predicting futures ironically was a result of studying the past. I became an archaeologist. I'm sometimes entranced by the thought of ancient kingdoms like the Aztecs. Of all the aspects of ancient kingdoms I studied, I was especially drawn to soothsayers--those apparently wizened individuals who predicted the future. Soothsayers and soothsaying are mentioned in the Bible several times. (In some renditions of the Bible, soothsayers are called wizards or diviners.) The Old Testament makes clear that the Israelites believed in knowing the future, but they rejected the soothsaying of other people in favor of their own prophets.

So, the Jews believed the future could be foretold. But they had their own readers of the future called prophets, and the readers of the future from other cultures were called soothsayers. How soothsayers or prophets were to understand the future is not well known. Nevertheless, viewing soothsayers of other religions, I began to have a larger context for understanding Jesus and Christianity. Christianity is a manifestation of human desire to control the future. Jesus' message was precise. He would return at some point in the future and we would enter a new phase of existence.

EXPERIENCE

In many groups from around the world, fasting is a technique for prophesying. I began fasting in 1975. At first, my fasting was only physical experimentation. However, the experience changed my life as a spiritual component slipped into my being. Not too soon after my first fast, one of my ambitions was to do a 40-day fast in hopes of discovering more about myself and maybe answering some of my questions about the temptations of Jesus.

Building up to my 40-day fast in isolation, I began to look more fully into the life of Jesus. I squinted with new eyes, and I saw a reality much different than traditional Christian thinking. As I studied, I quickly found myself embroiled in a world of controversy about the life of Jesus and the Bible. But a good friend, Glen Van Ingen, suggested to me, "Don't worry, any fool can give you answers; the trick is learning to ask the right questions." I know this to be a paraphrase of Voltaire, "Judge a man by his questions, rather than his answers." Regardless of asking or answering, the quality depends upon available facts.

While the Bible doesn't tell us much about Jesus' fast or his vision of kingdoms, there is one fact: Jesus had the vision while doing his 40-day fast. Of course, when I mentioned doing a 40-day fast, I was often met with laughter and remarks such as,

> "Terry, if you fast 40 days, you'd hallucinate and probably see more than a bunch of kingdoms."

> "I bet Jesus saw kingdoms full of food."

> "Why didn't Jesus just say he didn't want to go with Satan and see kingdoms? He had to be tired, right?"

I never much appreciated remarks like these, especially since most people have never fasted for even a couple of days.

Regardless, I wanted to do a 40-day fast to determine what it was like. Until 1994, my longest fast was 20 days. At the age of 47, I finally managed the time for 40 days. It's not easy to do a 40-day fast in our high-speed society. Most people think a four-week vacation is a luxury. A 40-day fast is six weeks. As for the luxury of time, I keep asking myself, "How does anyone achieve that delicate, ongoing balance between the material and the spiritual worlds?"

For our own mental health, I think it would be good if we as society, we as families, we as parents took our children on retreats, retreats where we do nothing for four or five days but reflect in isolation upon our being. It would also be beneficial to instill in them the idea of fasting. It might only be for a day or two, but a brief fast might help our children reflect upon how they are being conditioned to consume, consume, consume.

Globalization is a buzz word these days. Where are we going as a global society? There are diverse opinions. One is: consume more, consume more, consume more. While finishing this book in 1994-1996, I lived in the Republic of Korea. The emerging vision of its society was globalization. Economic productivity was the underlying theme, and that can only ever translate as consumption.

Globalization is about the future, and I ask, "Why do we believe what we believe about any subject, including what the future holds?" Above all, is the future knowable? If not, then we can't control it. That is a scary thought. In my quest to control my future, I seek a balance between materialism and spirituality. I think to know the future we have to somehow detach ourselves from the present. Or as phenomenologists say, we have to suspend presuppositions we have about the present situation to see the world in an alternative way.

That is one reason why I wanted to do a 40-day fast. During that time, I hoped my presuppositions would break down. Furthermore, by accomplishing a 40-day fast, I might also come to know more about Jesus the man through experiencing some of what he experienced.

2

ME PEERING IN

I grew up in a small-town, Midwestern, Methodist environment. Is that different than a big-city Methodist environment? Oh yes! There were no black people in Bradford, Ohio. Still aren't. So, as part of my upbringing, prejudiced Protestants talked about Catholics the way white bigots elsewhere talked about black people. (Remember, this was a small town in the 1950s.) Many Protestants in my small rural town developed the saying, "I don't have anything against Catholics." In the heat of an argument, someone might point out that an individual's rantings and ravings about another individual were religious persecution. Then would pop up the saying, "I don't have anything against Catholics." Sometimes there was an additional sentiment, "I even have a few Catholic friends."

My parents did not have Catholic "friends." I even saw as an adolescent that my friendship circle was defined for the most part by individuals I interacted with in church on Sundays. Out of this religious isolationism, I became curious. Resenting the put-downs others received just because of their religious interpretations, I became sensitive to different cultures and religions.

Why, I would wonder, is it that each society and even each branch of Christianity seems to have a built-in ideological belief that it has the right way and everyone else is wrong? That wondering encompassed a decade long process. From the age of 5 to 15, each Sunday I was presented with little tidbits about an individual named Jesus. He seemed to be the type of individual who would be tolerant of another's religion--as long as one led a morally decent life.

WHAT'S IN A DIFFERENCE?

Trying to see the world through the eyes of others is somehow my compulsion. The best way to see the world as people from different times and places did or do is by experiencing what they did or do. At times, this can be tough. I'm certainly not going to be crucified to feel what Jesus did.

However, if I could accomplish a 40-day fast, I might understand more about Jesus. Cross-cultural knowledge and experience help us understand who someone else is and likewise help us understand ourselves. I fell into this thinking by luck. Considering my background, one would think I might have become a bigot.

The only industry in Bradford, Ohio, was a factory for canning tomatoes. Migrant Mexican laborers came to town to pick the tomatoes. The town elders were good at keeping the Mexicans hidden at the edge of town in the defunct railroad roundhouses. They were hidden so well that I never saw the workers until I was a senior in high school in 1963. When I relate this story, many friends say they find it hard to believe I didn't know about the migrant workers in a town so small. But our town of 2000 covered quite a bit of territory since it was a railroad center before the Depression. Also during a greater part of the summers, I was away fishing on Lake Erie with my grandfather. I found out about the workers when our new Methodist minister stood up outraged in front of the congregation and began haranguing the congregation about the spiritual injustice of forbidding the Mexicans from attending church.

But during my senior year, the churches opened their doors. At this point, I learned that all my life the Mexicans, who were in Bradford for the tomato harvest, had been told never to enter our stores, banks, or churches.

The Mexicans took the invitation to go to church, but they went to the small Catholic Church. None came to our Methodist monstrosity. The Catholics were a minority in Bradford and had a little church. I didn't know almost all Mexicans were Catholic. I expected them to come to the biggest church in town.

There was quite a bit of discussion among the student body about what the Mexicans were like. Gene Harshbarger, one of my best high school friends, and I were amazed by the dichotomy of Mexicans going to a Catholic Church, not to either of ours. Gene went to a different church yet. He went to the Pilgrim Holiness Church, but I know nothing of its doctrine. There were around 25 churches in our small town. The churches grew in response to the influx of different people through the railroad industry. Clever fellows that we were, Gene and I elected to go, for the first time in our lives, to the Catholic Church to get a glimpse of the Mexicans. When I told my mother I was going to the Catholic Church that Sunday, a look of absolute horror came over her face. She tried to joke, "I have nothing against Catholics, a few of them are my best friends," although she never referred to any of her Catholic friends by name. It was a different time then. John Kennedy was the first Catholic President of the United States.

Going to a Catholic Church was a tremendous eye-opener for me. I saw Mexicans sitting in a church! This first real experience of witnessing a mixed ethnic congregation disrupted my personal context of religiosity.

The mass was in Latin. Latin was taught at Bradford High School then, but there were only six of us in the class. It was college prep. How could the Catholic congregation understand? In my naive mind, I thought maybe all Catholics had training in Latin so that they could comprehend the message. But, the priest faced the altar, not the congregation, and his words were uttered almost in secret. Later, I learned my Catholics friends couldn't understand any Latin.

That day is when my wondering began in earnest about how each branch of Christianity seems to have a built-in ideological belief that they have "the" right way, and everyone else is wrong. My first visit to a Catholic Church had an important impact on my life. The occasion was so different that it stuck in my mind for several weeks. After all, I was only 17 growing up in a small, all-white, Mid-Western town.

Reflecting on the situation that day, I thought it was unfortunate the children of Bradford were not raised to understand the rich diversity of Christianity. I thought about persecution every Friday when fish had to be served at the school cafeteria to accommodate the Catholic belief of not eating meat on Friday. Many Protestant children referred to the Catholic children as "mackerel snappers" or "crappie crunchers." Later I grew to understand the Catholic custom of eating fish on Fridays as one of the last vestiges of fasting in the Christian community.

In 1966, there was a Vatican Council. The Vatican ordained the custom of avoiding meat on Fridays dropped. I have never been given an explanation as to why, but I assume an alleviation of Catholic persecution was part of the formula. The Vatican also switched mass to English--to modernize. And priests were directed to face the congregations.

I later, however, held one personal grudge against the Catholic Church. My grudge was the by-product of a mixed marriage. In 1965, I married a Catholic, Nancy. We had a "debate" concerning which church we would be married in since I was Protestant, and she was Catholic. According to Nancy's doctrine, she could not marry in a Protestant church without some traumatic religious problems and maybe even excommunication. Consequently, I had to go through what was known as "instructions."

The instructions were a brief introduction to the Catholic faith. I rather enjoyed the education. I was dumbfounded to learn that the Catholic Bible is different from the Protestant Bible as a result of the inclusion of additional books. Constantly, the point was brought up that the Catholic religion is the oldest branch of Christianity. I was informed the Pope is infallible. I was 19 years old, and I'd go back to my Protestant friends and say, "Hey, you guys know the Pope cannot make a mistake?" If it had not been for those instructions, I'm not sure I would have understood comedian Lenny Bruce's line, "Sell the ring." The ring, of course, is the ring which the Pope wears that is some type of symbolic connection between heaven, the Pope, and the rest of the Catholic world.

I had just graduated from high school and here was a new slant on Christianity for me. The difference between Nancy's church and mine was overwhelming. Catholics are dogmatic. They are baptized at birth by doctrine. They have a hierarchy of sins. I liked that because it reminded me of the penal code of our society.

The priest told me Catholics believed the communion wafer turned into the body of Jesus, and the wine turned into his blood--transubstantiation. Did they really believe this? Only a few Catholics with whom I've talked believe transubstantiation actually occurs. But it was certainly believed until a couple of hundred years ago.

The concept of transubstantiation intrigues me tremendously. Now, fewer Catholics believe in it. However, one Catholic was quite articulate in explaining to me that in certain cases transubstantiation might occur since man, like Jesus, is capable of experiencing miracles.

Then came the event which bothered me and was the reason for my grudge against the Catholic Church. I had to sign a contract whereby I agreed our children would be raised as Catholics. If we didn't raise them in the Catholic faith, my wife would have some type of religious problems. Well, I signed it. The entire matter was cleverly arranged by the Vatican. It put me literally between the rock and the hard place.

That act of signing over our children to the Catholic Church haunted me. I kept thinking: Isn't that a basic denial of freedom of religion? I would have preferred our children wait and go to a church when they were old enough to understand what was going on around them. I wanted them to make their own decision. But I signed them away. I was asked by my parents, at about the age of 11, if I wanted to be baptized. It was my decision, although it was influenced by my childhood context. While I was baptized, I never did sign the papers that would make me a member in a Methodist church. I appreciate that both decisions were mine to make. The Vatican Council of 1966 dropped the signing over of little spirits between mixed couples.

For the first two years we were married, I worked at General Motors' Frigidaire plant in Dayton. At that time, it was the third largest factory in the world. I met a lot of new people. I heard from a few adamant Baptists that I was going to go to hell unless I was born again. This was new to me. If I could go to a Catholic Church, I might as well go to a Baptist church and understand "being saved."

I went to see my first full-immersion baptism. The Baptist told me that I was not really baptized since I was not immersed in water but only had water patted on my head. I just thought that Bradford, Ohio, had a difference of religious opinions between Protestant and Catholic. Those Baptists talked about Catholics like they were non-Christians. They snickered that Catholics only sprinkle water for the act of baptism. I told the Baptists their baptism was still one step removed from repeating the real act. Baptism should be done in a river. Better yet, it should be done in the Jordan River. Nevertheless, through my visit to a Baptist church my education continued on the religious bigotry that exists in the name of Jesus.

GOING BACK TO THE NON-MATERIAL WORLD

Nancy and I eventually grew apart and divorced. I don't know that she was ever excommunicated, but while together, we did explore other religions. We took a trip that made a profound impact on both of our lives.

At the time, 1969, I was enrolled in a comparative religion class at the University of Missouri, Columbia. The final paper required a visit to four different churches and to do the ol' compare and contrast. I took the assignment seriously. I wanted to know more about religions. Together Nancy and I planned a trip home to Ohio for Christmas.

We stopped on a Friday afternoon in St. Louis. I can still remember looking for Skinker Boulevard. It was lined with different churches. We were looking for the Vedanta Society. The two-story building looked like a private home owned by a wealthy individual; not the type of building in which I expected to enter the world of Hinduism. Inside we were instructed to wait for the Swami. Sounds mystical, doesn't it?

We sat in a room with three rows of about ten folding chairs facing a small lectern. Incense wafted through the air. Finally, a disciple said, "This is Swami Satprakashananda." We stood. For the first time in my life, another individual bowed to me. Nancy and I both bowed back.

The Swami sat with us for about an hour. He kept asking, "From where did that tree outside the window come?"

"A seed," I would respond.

"And the seed?"

"A tree."

"From where does life come?" The Swami's face was stoic.

Swami Satprakashananda wrote the book *Methods of Knowledge*. It is a treatise on epistemology. If I hadn't been taking a philosophy of science course with John Kultgen, one of the world's experts on Alfred North Whitehead, I couldn't have even pretended to understand the Swami's book.

We left the place understanding that the Swami began meditating as a child. He had meditated over 70 years. That was my first meeting with people who believed Jesus to be an enlightened being, but not the Son of God. An eerie feeling kept floating through my head for the next couple of hours. I was not a devout Christian, but I was raised to believe that those individuals who did not believe Jesus was the Son of God would go to hell. I couldn't believe that the Swami was going to hell.

We checked into our hotel room and prepared to attend a ceremony at a Reform Jewish Synagogue that evening. The Synagogue was located next to the Vedanta Society. It was an enormous building with a dome top. (Now the building has been converted into a museum.)

The week before, we had scheduled an appointment with the Rabbi. He met with us about one hour before the service and explained how the Reform Sect had broken away from the Orthodox Sect. Up to this point in my life, I thought all Jews believed the same creed.

Near the end of the conversation with the Rabbi, his voice faded into the background, and a rush of unreconciling religious ideas blasted through my mind. That afternoon I had been with the Hindus, and now here I was with a second group that didn't believe Jesus to be the Son of God. Furthermore, I had learned that all Jews did not uphold the same doctrine. Where was all this religious diversity coming from?

Somehow, human individuality had put its stamp on religion. Everywhere I turned someone had a different explanation of "religious reality." Religious differences are real, especially when tied into race. In the ongoing process of change, reinterpretation of any religious doctrine is inevitable. That's why churches split off from one another. Of course, that difference will always be explained as a greater truth. So there I sat detached from the Rabbi, Nancy, and the synagogue, with one crushing thought: "What is the truth?"

The next day we drove to Chicago to attend a Soto Zen service. It was during that drive from St. Louis to Chicago that I really began to wonder about the relationship between materialism and spirituality. I thought back to Jesus' words that it would be easier for a camel to pass through the eye of a needle than for a rich man to enter the kingdom of heaven. Could his words have been a metaphor that if one is attached to the material world, one cannot enter into a spiritual realm while one is alive? I couldn't answer the question; I just had thoughts. And I had that one outstanding question: "What is the truth?"

In Chicago, we called to get the hours of the Sunday Zen service. The next morning, without an appointment, we arrived at a suburban-looking house. Two individuals dressed in formal black robes were sweeping the freshly fallen snow. I asked if the Swami were in. With disgruntled looks, they informed me that, "Yes, the *Master* was there." I was obviously still learning about religious diversity.

We met with the Japanese Master before the service. He had a difficult time with English. But the word "enlightenment" was there frequently in between the other words. And somehow meditation was linked to enlightenment. We were told we would sit facing a wall for only thirty minutes, and then get up, walk a bit, and then sit thirty minutes more facing the wall.

There I was in a three piece suit. I could not sit cross-legged and up straight. Someone kept coming to straighten me. Nancy, next to me, sat full lotus through the entire ceremony. Sweat was rolling off of me, and I thought my back was going to break. Afterwards, the Master didn't seem as if he wanted to talk to me, and we left.

The pain in my body dampened any immediate insights I might have had about religious diversity. I asked Nancy, "How could you sit like that?" She said she had to; it would be too distracting for others if she didn't. She laughed with her remark, "You just insulted their religion." I had to admit I never thought about discipline and religion being combined. I couldn't imagine ever going back to a Zen temple.

That evening we were back in Bradford, Ohio. The fourth and final visit would be with the Dunkards the next Sunday. The Dunkards are a type of Amish who often avoid using modern machines, such as automobiles. They still use horses and carriages--even on the highways. I've gone back to Bradford with friends from other states. Many times my friends shouted, "Hey look!" I question, "What?" For me the horses and carriages were a normal part of the landscape.

The Dunkards took most of their kids out of school at the age of 16 when the law allowed. I never saw them on Sundays since their churches were not in Bradford proper, but in the country. Because of this cultural practice I never thought of them as unique in my early religious experiences. I always viewed the Amish as just another Protestant sect.

On a cold, late Saturday afternoon, Nancy and I went driving and found a church out in the country. We drove to the closest house. It was a typical old, Mid-Western country home. But this one lacked paint and the weathered grey boards showed a somber presence. It was two stories with high windows. The windows were without curtains as the Dunkards abstain from decoration. A large front porch looked out on a spacious front yard. The gravel driveway took us around behind the house.

A low flickering light of a kerosene lantern shone through the back door. I knocked on the door. In the room, a woman was sitting in a rocking chair in front of a wood burning stove. There was nothing else in the room. She didn't even look at the door. I surveyed the room as I waited. No pictures on the wall, no knickknacks, no phone, no radio. For me, the quiet of the scene was like an Alfred Hitchcock movie. Why didn't the woman look?

I prepared to knock again when a bearded man suddenly appeared at the door. I was momentarily startled. Opening the door, he gave a quick salutation. Likewise, I quickly explained my mission. He invited me to step in. Once inside, he told me the hours of the church services. He told me I was lucky to have come that weekend since they only meet in the church every other weekend. He invited me to stay the night until the next day's service. His invitation was genuine. I wanted to stay, but had committed to many family obligations over the holidays. I explained my obligations. I assured him I'd join him in worship the next day.

Fortunately, my Uncle Cliff, in an extended conversation that night, told me about their worship. The men kiss on the lips when they meet. I didn't believe him.

Nancy needed a rest from the religious sojourn and opted not to attend the service. When I arrived, I saw that there were two separate doors on the front of the church. The men were entering through the right door and the women through the left door. I blended in with my beard and dark pin-stripe suit. As I stepped through the door, I saw the men greeting one another and sure enough.... I immediately sat down near the back.

The women sat on one side, the men on the other. One man was designated to keep the wood-burning stove going, but it wasn't big enough to fight off the freezing cold completely.

The Dunkards do not have ministers. Rather the duty of delivering the sermon circulated through the male members of the congregation. The sermon that day was different to say the least. The man in charge of this sermon repeatedly boasted in a raised voice that Jesus would return in the eastern sky. He must have said it about 30 times in the one hour he was in front of the congregation. Other than talking about the direction from which Jesus would return, he read a few passages from the Bible.

When the Dunkards prayed, they turned, got on their knees and bowed on the benches. When they sang, there were many false starts. It was obvious they didn't indulge in music outside of church. It was really hard for me to imagine living without a daily dose of good music.

The entire event lasted about two hours. The rickety benches were wearing on my rear end. I kept thinking, "God, when will this ever be over?" It finally ended, but everybody just sat there and slowly began talking with one another. I was surprised. Not one person left. I didn't want to be the first person out, but push came to shove, and I went out the door. It was an exodus. I guess the children can't leave until an adult does. As I drove away, all the children who were dressed in black were playing in the white snow.

The Dunkards with whom I had grown up, and never somehow noticed, gave me my first real taste of the non-material world. This day, I saw them within the framework of the Hindus, the Jews and the Zen. The Amish were definitely trying to minimize their involvement with the material world. Some have cars and tractors, but their basic philosophy is that the material world corrupts the soul.

But how did that reflect on their spirituality? I didn't know if they were any more spiritual than I. Then I began to consider: What is spirituality anyway? I think it is somehow a blissful state. If that is the case, the Dunkards seem to be austere; not blissful. Jesus, too, seems to me to be an austere person, and not blissful.

Why do all Dunkards dress the same? I thought about this question a lot. As a Methodist, I was raised with the custom of wearing and watching everyone in the congregation wear some new, snazzy clothes every Easter. It was a big ego competition. The Dunkards, by wearing the same clothes, avoided that ego competition. I assume the Dunkards wear the same dress for the reasons that monks of any religion do, to negate the ego over personal appearance. So, for me, the Dunkards moved Christianity one step more toward the spiritual, at least in terms of clothes.

That evening I got hold of a concordance and located the only passage linking Jesus with the east. In Matthew 24:27 Jesus said, "For as light comes from the east and shines as far as the west, so will be the coming of the Son of Man."

While in the concordance, I stumbled on a reference to clothing styles.

> Jesus was talking to people about John the Baptist. He asked, "What did you go into the wilderness to see? A reed swaying in the breeze? No? Then what did you go out to see? A man wearing fine clothes? No! Those wearing fine clothes are to be found in palaces." (Matthew 11:7-8)

GOING TO MEXICO

In 1970, I made my first journey to Mexico. What a discovery! I felt this incredible culture had been somehow hidden from me. Hollywood tried to make Mexicans all seem like thieves. My hometown treated them as such. Why had I never been taught in school about this festive, colorful culture?

To this day, I wish I could have known the migrant workers in Bradford. Maybe I could have become friends and visited with them and their families in Mexico.

During my 1970 summer stay in Mexico, I lived in the quaint village of Tula, Hidalgo. There were not many cars in the town, and most of them were 1950s model American cars that were in surprisingly good shape. There were a few 1970 model cars.

The poorer people often trekked along in bent profile with large bundles of bound, dead tree stems on their backs. The bundles were supported by a large cloth that went around their foreheads. The tree stems would be used for cooking fires.

On Sunday evenings, the town square with a beautiful gazebo and many benches was the hub of social interaction. The young girls walked in one direction and the boys in the opposite direction for almost three hours. Occasionally, a couple might stop to talk, and if the conversation warranted, they would retire to a bench.

One day driving back from Mexico City, 60 miles to the south, the concept of pilgrim and pilgrimage unfolded before my eyes. I passed lines of people walking from Queretaro to Mexico City, a distance of 100 miles. Pilgrims from Tula joined them. I had thought pilgrims walking like that only existed in the Middle Ages. Where were those pilgrims going? Why were they travelling? Would their pilgrimage be repeated? When would they be going again? What were they getting from their pilgrimage?

The facts started to unfold for me. Ninety-nine percent of the country was Catholic. Not only were they Catholic, but their Catholicism was different from what I knew in America. I never saw Americans walking on a pilgrimage. One Sunday evening, I was invited to go to church with a friend, Edith Garrido. The church was a cathedral built in the 16th century. It was a massive building. The two large outer doors stayed open letting in fresh air during mass.

Edith was stunningly beautiful and always wore the finest clothes. I had thought the entire congregation would be dressed the same. But we were in the Third World. There are the few rich and the poor masses. None of the poor masses wore ties. The majority of the men wore faded work pants. The dress of many could be best described as tattered. Some couldn't even afford closed shoes, but wore simple sandals. Those poor could not afford modern medicine. Most went on pilgrimages to petition for protection from sickness or relief from sickness. For the first time, I had actual images of groups similar to those to whom Jesus ministered.

My conversations with Edith were elevated and something I still cherish. She was one of the most socially conscious people I ever met. In those days, I was a Che Guevara fan. I believed Latin Americans needed to band together through revolution for the good of the masses. Edith thought the church should take a greater role in changing the direction of society. Then one day she told me she was going to become a nun. She did, and I never saw her again.

Tula opened my eyes to many realities. I was there to participate in an archaeological expedition. I learned an important lesson in life from living with a small group of Tula residents who faked artifacts to sell to tourists. Watching their daily rituals made me aware of a new dimension of child labor. Not only were the little kids sent to sell artifacts to the tourists, but they had to lie. They were unrelenting in their facade. More than once, my friends would send one of their children to me, just as a joke, to make the sale. I would stand there and say, "Who made this? Was it Lupe? Was it Alfonso? Was it Jorge?" (The names of the fakers.) But the answer was always, "No, I found it in the field over there." Then the father or uncle would laughingly inform the child that I knew it was fake.

There were and are many superb fakes being sold daily in Tula. There are faked stone statues that most people will never know if they were made in Tula yesterday or 1000 years ago. Many artifacts from throughout the world have been purchased for megabucks through New York auction houses after being "authenticated" by supposed experts. But later, the pieces were discovered to be fake.

I had never been around forgers before. Many evenings of that summer I sat on the large pyramids of Tula watching the sun set, and I became much more focused on how difficult it really is to determine truth. I saw tourists buying the artifacts without question. They thought they were getting something antique and valuable for just a little money. But how much does someone have to question before arriving at the truth, if ever? An artifact is tangible; but a religious belief exists only in the mind of the believer. How can we determine truth?

A MATTER OF PERSECUTION

The difference between myself and Mexicans was so mind-boggling that I had to see their roots. I decided to make a one-week trip to Spain.

That 1972 trip was made over 25 years ago, and the details have faded. But one characterization integrated into my being: Spain was so different from Mexico. The Spanish were proud, and poverty was not conspicuous. This was in part due to Spain's dictator, Franco, who at one time ordered beggars executed. The lack of poverty was also in part due to U.S. military aid and presence. That military presence was a major influx of dollars into Spain's economy. Spain was then second only to Israel in foreign aid received from the U.S. So, Spain gave the impression of being a First World country.

On the other hand, Mexico, the United State's neighbor, is part of the exploited Third World. The longest border between a rich country and a poor country is the Mexican-U.S. border. I have never determined where this fits into the Christian formula of love thy neighbor.

While traveling to Spain, I linked up with seven tourists out of Cleveland. Our new group didn't know one another well, but we somehow stayed together as a group. When the group discovered I could speak Spanish, they commandeered me whenever possible. Five of them were Jewish, and their interests determined much of our itinerary since they wanted to explore Jewish history in Spain. Through their eyes, I continued amending my picture of Judaism.

We visited an old abandoned synagogue that had a plaque explaining the persecution and expulsion of the Jews. It was a small, plain stone building. Until that trip, I naively thought Jews resided only in the United States, Germany, Israel, and Russia.

My traveling companions taught me about something called the Diaspora. Sometime about 500 B.C. the kingdom of Israel was conquered by

Babylon, and many of the Jews were taken as slaves to Babylon--more than 500 miles to the east. Later, Jews were taken as slaves to Rome. That journey was close to 2000 miles away, a distance the Roman army could travel in a month. Many of these Jews became members of other cultures and even lost their language. The Diaspora is the scattering of Jews out from Israel.

My traveling group introduced me to their Jewish contacts. The contacts only spoke Spanish. I was amazed. They didn't even speak Yiddish. They informed me that we were in luck since there was a Bar Mitzvah one night during our stay. I would see the rite of passage for Jewish males going from boyhood to manhood. We were treated as if we had lived with them our entire lives. Since I didn't understand much of the religious symbolism, the Bar Mitzvah was more like a big party. But at one point I became detached from the scene and realized I was at a rite of passage older than Christianity.

RELIGION AND THE LAW

In 1974, I read in a Chicago newspaper that Pancho Villa's widow was still alive and running a Pancho Villa Museum in Chihuahua, Mexico. I couldn't miss it. I had always wanted to explore northern Mexico, and this presented the opportunity.

When I told people I was going to meet Pancho Villa's widow, some asked, "Which one?" It turns out that during the Mexican Revolution in 1910, Pancho was out terrorizing northern Mexico, and apparently he was in the habit of marrying women along the way. But I have never had this verified as historical fact. Pancho didn't have much respect for the Catholic Church since that was one of the institutions against which the Mexican revolution was aimed. In fact, after the revolution, nuns were forbidden to appear in their habits in public.

I crossed the border in El Paso and bought a ticket to Chihuahua. I found the museum, and there was the widow in a wheelchair. She had plenty of energy. When we finally got the chance to speak she asked, "*Donde vienes?*" Where do you come from?

I replied, "*Yo vine de Chicago.*" I came from Chicago.

In adequate English she said, "Oh, I'm very sorry. It is so far."

She autographed three post cards for me. As for the answer to which of Pancho's widows she was, she had the bullet-riddled car in which Pancho was killed. It was a big convertible-type car I had never even seen before, but then the Mexican revolution was in 1910. I let my right index finger explore one of the bullet holes. The jaggedness of the hole sparked a thought. He was a true life revolutionary. I guessed this was the closest I had ever been to one. Conflicting realities bolted through my mind. Wait, George Washington was a revolutionary. A lonely conclusion slowly eked through me: I guess how a revolutionary is remembered is by how successful his or her revolution is.

As revolutionaries, Pancho Villa and Jesus both had a commonality: they were killed.

Leaving Chihuahua, I was more exposed to the world. My bus ticket was punched through to Mexico City. Relaxed in my seat, I was ready to enjoy images of Pancho Villa and his hordes sweeping through the deserts of northern Mexico. But a tall, blue-eyed German fellow sat beside me and began a conversation in rather good, but broken English.

Henri was a Mennonite, a sect of the Amish. I had heard there were large colonies of Mennonites in northern Mexico, but I never understood the connection of coming from Germany to northern Mexico. Henri told me his people had left Germany almost 250 years ago and settled in Canada. But as the education laws grew tougher, the Amish were required to send their children to school, causing some to move continually south. In Mexico, they paid the famed *mordita* ("the bite"--a bribe) to assure that their kids never had to go to school. His family had been on the same land for 200 years.

Henri had gone to the United States as a legal migrant worker and had done rather well for himself. He went back home once with a travel trailer to go to Guatemala. His parents were disturbed he had bought into the material world. But they were hoping he would return home one day. This was his day. He was going home to find a wife. He felt he had to marry a Mennonite. He invited me to stay with his family. Since the ticket to Mexico City was only $10, I gladly accepted, excited to learn more about the Mennonites in Mexico.

Entering Henri's town, my head involuntarily nodded at the novelty. The houses were not the flat Mexican type, but the gabled roof of European style. The place was populated with similarly bearded Mennonites. Each was almost a carbon-copy of the other with wide-brimmed straw hats and pale blue shirts framed by suspenders. Henri's father was there to meet him. I conversed with the father in Spanish as we made the truck passage to his house. The father, like Henri, was born in the house where we were going.

Inside the house, the women in their long dresses were churning butter. Henri spoke to his sister in German. That woman was too pretty for words; blond hair, blue eyes, milk complexion right there in northern Mexico. I was dumbfounded to know such a young, beautiful German woman was born and raised in northern Mexico. I stared too much. So Henri, in broken English, came to my aid, "Terry, this my sister, but she understand no English or Spanish." The stunned look on my face betrayed me. The realization slowly sank in that none of the women ever went out into the community. They were cloistered. The only literature to which they were exposed was the Bible. It was religion and the law.

We had dinner of roast beef, mashed potatoes and gravy, fresh green beans, fresh baked bread and butter. I never thought of eating that type of food in Mexico and have the conversation around me be in German.

They had a guest room in one of the small barns. It was a little room with a bed, a chair, and a small table. On the table was a kerosene lantern. Henri told me how to turn the wick in to extinguish the flame, and he bade me good night. Lying in the dark, I thought back seven years, when I was invited to stay with the Amish in Ohio. There was too much to think about. The quiet was refreshing.

NO ANSWERS

All my traveling and all my looking were only giving me a cross-cultural understanding of religion. That knowledge didn't give me any basis for understanding or directly experiencing spirituality. I was perplexed by the difference between the Amish and the Methodists. Who was more spiritual?

I still didn't have an understanding of what spirituality really was. Sure, I could go to the dictionary and see that spirituality was a concern with the spiritual world and not the material world.

Is being spiritual and being religious the same? I began to think not. Somehow neither the Amish, nor the Methodists, nor the Catholics, as religious people, seemed particularly spiritual to me; but some of the practitioners of all three did seem to be religious. That is, they live by certain creeds devoted to doing good in this world and obtaining a place in an afterlife.

To understand spirituality, I felt I needed firsthand experiences, but I wasn't sure how I was going to get them.

3

FIRST FAST

In 1975, I was finishing my doctoral work at the University of Illinois. I was awarded the Ogden-Mills Fellowship at the American Museum of Natural History for 1975-1976. My proposed research for the fellowship year was to develop a computer database for cataloguing clay figurines. Figurines are human images made of clay or stone, varying in size, made by many groups throughout history. I wanted to use figurines as a way to track the interactions of religious ideas between different groups.

At the American Museum of Natural History, my office was a large round room with continuing windows to the north, west, and south. I shared the top floor of the southwest tower with Rhoda Meatraux and Margaret Mead. At first, I wasn't really sure what to make of Margaret since we only passed in the halls and never really conversed. One day she invited me to lunch, and for one hour she mesmerized me with her ongoing personal experiences of living in different cultures. As she talked, I realized she was referring to a time long gone by. I thought of the Mexico I saw in 1970 and the vast changes that occured in the name of globalization. But, Mead was a witness to worlds that had vanished before I was born. That one-hour lunch was a catalyst for me. I desired to seek experiences and get out of the book-learning mode.

I had lunch with her one more time. I have never been in the presence of a person who had such a tremendous sense of self-destiny. She detailed some of her unique childhood experiences for me. I was particularly fascinated by one story of how she was introduced to evolution. Her parents entertained faculty members from the University of Pennsylvania each Sunday. Her father taught finance and commerce. One Sunday, she was given a string of strange animals that had been put together as a joke regarding some professor's lectures on evolution. As she relayed the details, I thought: How wonderful an experience! How many children of that time period, or any time period, would be privileged to such advanced learning? (This story appears in her autobiography, *Blackberry Winter*.)

Our second meeting codified my motivation to gain experience through doing. My religious experiences to date had only been observations of others. I vividly remember that evening walking home from the museum. I decided to save my money and take a year or two off and travel. (Margaret died the next year, and I never got to tell her what those meetings did for my life.)

I was not able to develop the computerized figurine database at that year for many reasons. The biggest problem was that many museum materials were not excavated by archaeologists. Thus, there was no way to be sure where the figurines came from. Most people are not aware that many large collections in museums are donated from the estates of people who traveled extensively and purchased the pieces. Giving such pieces to a museum is a means of obtaining a tax deduction. In many cases, the pieces are not authentic antiquities, but convincing fakes, like those I had seen made in Tula to fool tourists. As a young archaeologist, I was unaware of how much material in museums is not the product of archaeology.

But I learned to analyze figurines in detail. Like little cosmoses of clay, frozen in time, they would look at me. I asked, Who are you? What did your maker believe? Many of the figurines I befriended were produced by the Aztecs. I especially began to wonder who the Aztecs were as spiritual beings. They were animists who believed everything, including rocks and stars, have spirits. According to Aztec religion, one must interact with and show great respect for all the other spirits of the universe to achieve one's greatest potential on earth. However, for the Aztecs, that respect also necessitated sacrificing humans to the gods.

I was studying the Aztec culture in intense detail. The Aztecs had the longest institutionalized fasts in the world, 80 days. I began to think maybe fasting was the experience I needed to understand spirituality. What a paradox that I learned to fast in Manhattan. Go to the Big Apple and learn to abstain from food? Sometimes the paradoxes of life are bizarre. Maybe when I get old, I'll devote a couple of years to studying paradoxes.

In New York City, I came to realize that we are a society of excessive consumers. A 40-day fast contrasted with everything around me. Sometimes I walked down Fifth Avenue and simply watched people go into shops to satisfy their need for consumption. I became mesmerized by the material world. I asked: Why are we buying so much? Is it addiction? Or are we trying to fill something inside us that can never be filled?

In October of 1975, I did my first three-day fast. It was rough! The first day I survived on the novelty of the event. The second day, I wanted to eat everything in sight. I still remember a sudden insight: I was *so* conditioned to eating at regular intervals. Why? What cultural dictate ever created that behavior? My society wanted me to consume, consume, consume three times a day and in between those times if possible. I was not from a society that ever pretended to promote abstinence.

The third day was bizarre. I awoke that morning thinking, "Wow, I made it." I knew I could make it to sundown, no problem. Then about noon, the weirdest sensation began to creep into my lower legs and the feeling mounted by the hour. It was as if my legs were filling up with lead. By five o'clock, when I got back to my apartment, I felt I was walking with weights around my ankles. I've been told the feeling was 29 years of accumulated waste in my body finally breaking loose. According to one theory, fasting utilizes waste the body doesn't ordinarily get rid of. That night I broke my fast with hot dogs. Later a friend, Steve Armsey, and I went to an Indian restaurant to get the flavor of the movie we were about to see, *Distant Thunder* by Satyajit Ray. The theme of the movie is about the human-induced famine in Bengal in 1942. The food, mainly rice, was diverted for military use and millions starved to death. It was the largest human-induced famine in history.

After the 3-day fast, I wanted more of an escape from the everyday world I was indoctrinated into. After I visited the Zen center in Chicago in the late 60s, I thought I would never wander back into a Zen center again. However, in the intervening eight years, I had read Hermann Hesse's *Siddartha* and Eugen Herrigel's *Zen in the Art of Archery*. I reassessed another go at Zen. I also wanted the physical discipline, and withdrawing from the Big Apple for a couple of hours a day seemed like a reasonable plan. That autumn of 1975, I joined a group of Soto Zen Buddhists.

Unlike Christians, Buddhists believe that salvation must come from within each individual. Believing in someone else will not achieve salvation for Buddhists. Meditation helps negate the ego. With negation of the ego, tranquility swells. Eventually there is enlightenment. The point of meditation is to think about nothing, to empty the mind. The Master Kando Nakagima would ask us, "What is the sound of one hand clapping?" Silence.

For me, being a Zen Buddhist meant trying to meditate on a daily basis. I came to like meditation. It is a pleasure not to have constant thoughts of daily life. I didn't have to shave my head, but I did wear a robe while meditating. It made crossing my legs easier. I usually sat daily from 7 to 9 p.m. Sometimes I meditated eight hours on both Saturday and Sunday.

Master Kando Nakagima frequently told us if we began each day with a meditation period of only 20 minutes, our lives would be much different.

At first, the meditation was a bit difficult. But after the first two weeks, I was able to sit without discomfort. If I had any discomfort, I would simply stretch forward a bit and return to an upright position.

Once a year, the Zen group I was in did an eight-day meditation which is called *sesshin*. In 1976, sesshin started on August 15th. The ending date of August 22nd was also my birthday. I would turn 30, a traumatic birthday for some. I began to fast on August 9th, seven days before sesshin started.

The meditation site was in a large house in Bronxville, N.Y. As I understood it, a wealthy Japanese lawyer owned the house, and he let the Manhattan group use it for sesshin. There were about 20 of us. Some of the members had completed a sesshin two or three times before.

Sesshin went something like this. A bell rang at 5 A.M. We went downstairs to the zendo, the meditation hall. The one long room in the house easily accommodated all of us. We sat along the wall since we meditated facing a wall. However, first thing in the morning we sat facing the room, and hot barley tea was brought to us by designated members. After drinking it, the Master rang a small bell, and we turned and faced the wall. We meditated for 40 minutes. At the next ringing of the bell, we walked for a short time. Then we sat and meditated for an additional 40 minutes. Finally, there were some reasonably short chants which we did with our hands in prayer position in front of our face.

After the initial two hours of meditation, we ate breakfast. The Zen don't fast. They simply eat sparingly. I sat at the table and only drank juice.

Each day certain members were responsible for preparing the tea, the meals, and cleaning of the dishes. I helped with the cooking of the food and cleaning the dishes, but I continued to fast.

Next there was a work period to clean the grounds. Then two more hours of meditation, then lunch. Following lunch was a free period. Next, another two hours of meditation followed by dinner. Finally, there was an evening meditation for two hours.

Sesshin can be many experiences to many people. That specific sesshin had special circumstances for me. I had just finished a unique year in New York, and I had no job for the fall; nor did I want a job. I had enough money to see me through for six months, if not another year. So, there were no preoccupations for me. I would be, if for only a short time, free from the responsibility of going to work. This preconditioned what I would experience during sesshin--I could relax.

That first day of meditation was wonderful. A serene tranquility slipped in and out of my mind while meditating. Too often, however, I thought petty thoughts of myself in competition with other individuals.

- The second day the petty thoughts began to diminish. I knew I was on my way. I still had six more days.

On the third day, the Master Kando Nakagima told us that if we could, we should not sleep but meditate through the night. It is my understanding that Zen masters go for long periods without sleep. I meditated a couple of more hours that night, but then went to sleep.

On day four, my mind began to enter the ecstatic. It was my first real spiritual experience. When I narrowed my eyes for the beginning of morning meditation, the material world was almost gone. Occasionally, there was a fleeting petty thought.

That day during the free period I reflected on what it must be like to live in a monastery. It certainly would have its spiritual benefits.

Days five, six, seven, and eight were euphoric. Each night I meditated a bit longer, but I never did meditate through the night. Each day my mind entered a deeper tranquility. I wondered if there must be a limit to it. Or is tranquility infinite? I have come to think the latter.

The last night of sesshin was surreal. We were allowed to sit one on one with the Master Kando Nakagima and ask him questions. I still couldn't understand the meaning of shutting out pain, the Zen concept that the outer world doesn't exist. I was concerned that my knees ached tremendously after eight days, and sometimes it would interrupt my meditating. Kando asked me, "For you, which is greater, pain or hunger?" I simply nodded.

Just as we were about to embark on our last two hours of meditation, from 9-11 P.M., a house across the street began to party. It was Saturday night, August 21st. The music was blasting. It disturbed some of the members, and they asked the Master permission to tell the neighbors to turn down the sound. But Kando said, "Shut it out; it doesn't exist." As the neighbors boosted the volume, the first words to infiltrate the meditation hall were from the Eagles, "Don't let the sound of your own wheels drive you crazy." I've always wondered if the neighbors played that song on purpose. Maybe they said, "Hey, let's give them something to think about." I hope I run across those people someday, and they can answer my question.

The next day, after morning meditation, I walked away at the age of 30. I caught the mass transit into the Big Apple. I said good-bye to a few good friends. About four o'clock, I went to the George Washington Bridge, stuck out my thumb and began to hitch through the night to Bradford, Ohio. The fasting and the meditation had given me a new dimension of tranquility; I didn't care if I got a ride. It was a cool, cloudless evening, and I enjoyed watching the stars. It was a cosmic trip throughout the night. I never stood anyplace more than ten minutes. I was in Bradford at 8 A.M. the next day.

There is an epilogue to that sesshin. For that one year in New York, I had been fighting the habit of smoking cigarettes. I would smoke for a month and then go off for two. I had only smoked for about three years. The first year my smoking was casual. The second year I smoked a pack of Lucky Strikes a day. The third year, that year in New York City, I was trying to quit. I can still remember slowly grinding a cigarette butt with my right foot as the subway train pulled into the station to take me to Bronxville. During the sesshin, I had no conscious thought, ever, of wanting to stop smoking. Nevertheless, I did not smoke for another year. In the 20 intervening years, I have probably smoked about one pack of cigarettes in total. Something powerful happened for me during that sesshin.

I fasted five more days. That 20-day fast was easy. I broke the fast with an orange. I held the first section in my mouth for a good five minutes before the refreshing juices glided down my throat. I savored each section.

The day I broke that 20-day fast, I concluded then I must constantly try to balance materialism and spirituality. I began to think of doing a 40-day fast. It wasn't just a passing idea; it was something tangible inside my body. I thought about doing it that fall, which would have been the age when Jesus did his. However, I wanted to fast in the deserts of Jordan where Jesus did his. But that was going to take some preparation since I knew nothing about Jordan. Not being very rigorous or dedicated about accomplishing goals in those days, my sights were set on the age of 40. That would give me ten years to prepare. I felt I needed to explore my own spirituality more to make the most of a 40-day fast. Fasting from food is one aspect of abstinence, but going alone to avoid speech is yet another. An exploration of the dimensions of silence was next in order.

FIRST QUEST

There is an aspect of compulsion in my personality. For the next couple of weeks, I toyed seriously with the idea of doing a 40-day fast immediately instead of waiting an entire decade. I couldn't afford financially to do it in Jordan, but I knew many other tranquil spots.

Yet, contemplating that much isolation, I figured I better work up to 40 days. I rationalized: What if my first fast back in Manhattan had been 20 days and not three? I decided to do a Native American vision quest.

During a vision quest, one must sit and abstain from food, water, and speech for four days. The absence of food is one challenge; the absence of water is quite another. As for the absence of speech, from the day we are born, our consciousness is assaulted with speech. The absence of speech permits our mind to experience another reality.

I had no living teachers, only the literature I read. And most of that was on the Omaha Indians. I was supposed to do the vision quest with only the clothes on my back. In the Omaha philosophy, one should never reveal the details of what one saw during the quest to anyone for the remainder of one's life.

Somewhere in the beginning of October, 1976, I hitchhiked to the mountains of Pennsylvania. I was not prepared for the cold temperatures. The first night I was so cold that even if I had a vision it only would have been a blur because I was shaking so much. The second night I built a fire.

The morning of my third day I abandoned the effort. I did not have the patience required for a vision quest. Although my attempt was a failure, I knew the second try might be a success--I would do it when it was warmer.

A week later, I moved to Iowa for a two-month archaeological stint. During the initial time in Iowa City, I explored Tibetan Buddhism with a group at the university. The message was the same as that of the Zen: Empty the mind. However, I found it strange to meditate with my eyes open. I stopped attending the meetings, but continued meditating on my own.

IT IS MORE BLESSED TO GIVE THAN TO RECEIVE

In January of 1977, Mike Muse and I were exploring the prehistoric effigy mounds north of Dubuque, Iowa. We were headed back home to Iowa City, but as evening set in, so did a major snow storm. The radio warned of a blinding blizzard. I had heard about a Trappist monastery near Dubuque. I didn't know much about the Trappists, except that they abstained from speech. This was my chance to explore that aspect of silence during a fast.

We followed the signs through the rolling crests of the Iowa landscape. Suddenly atop the highest spot, mammoth gothic buildings reached out to the night sky. What a movie setting this would be. I hadn't known there were such places in the United States. For some reason, I was expecting rickety, two-story, wooden buildings.

Mike and I walked to the dimly lit, large wooden doors. Inside a robed monk walked toward us. He hadn't shaved in a couple of days. He smiled and nodded in the form of an abbreviated bow. We returned the gesture. "Welcome," he whispered. We exchanged greetings. I told him we would like to know more about the Trappists.

The monk invited us to follow him into an office. He seated himself behind a desk and motioned for us to sit in comfortable chairs in front of the desk. His clear blue eyes were focused. In a continued low voice, he asked our religious affiliations. Mike said, "None." I replied, "Zen." He turned around to the bookshelves behind him and plucked out *Zen and the Birds of Appetite* by Thomas Merton. "Maybe you have heard of this. One of our monks was interested in the similarities between Zen and Christianity."

Outside of greeting people coming for retreats and repeating Gregorian chants seven times a day, the Trappists take a vow of silence for life. There are two sects originating out of Europe. The Iowa Trappists came from Ireland, and those in Kentucky came from France. Also near Dubuque are the Trappistines, the female counterparts. The Iowa Trappists are busy tending to their extensive farmland. All the produce goes to feed the monks and the people who retreat there.

I asked the monk about abstaining from speech. He quietly stated,

"There is a tremendous power in silence. It is difficult to explain in words, but rather it is something you might experience."

He informed us that the evening meal would soon be served. While they are vegetarians, they serve meat to their pilgrims. Humble business, I thought. There was no cost. And there was always a large urn of coffee and cookies near the kitchen. He told us the time for the next chanting and gave us our assigned room numbers.

Because of the blizzard, we were the only outsiders. We walked alone down the long, dimly lit corridors. The rooms were simple, but comfortable. Of course, there was a Bible. I flipped it open and was reading Jesus' words.

Luke 14:

8   "When you are invited by someone to a wedding banquet, do not sit in the most preferable place; for one more highly esteemed by your host than yourself may have been invited by him.

9   "And as your mutual host arrives, he may say to you, 'Make room for him,' and then feeling deeply embarrassed, you proceed to take the lowest place.

10   "Rather, when you are invited, go and sit in the lowest place so that, when your host arrives, he may say to you, 'Friend, move up higher.' You will then enjoy honor before all your fellow guests.

11   "For whoever makes himself prominent will be humbled, and whoever humbles himself will be set high.

12   "Also, when you give a dinner, do not invite friends, relatives, or well-to-do neighbors; for they may invite you in order to repay you.

13   "Instead, invite the poor, the maimed, the lame, and the blind.

14   "Then, blessings will be yours, for they have nothing to repay you, but you will be repaid at the resurrection of the just."

I sat there thinking in the slang of my day, "That is really hard core!" Imagine not inviting your friends or neighbors to a party. I wondered if one day I would do that.

Mike and I met for dinner. It was a smorgasbord arrangement. The food was good.

Afterwards we wound our way through the long corridors to the chapel for vespers. The chapel was long but narrow so that the 20 or so monks faced each other at about ten feet apart as they melodically did the Gregorian chants.

The interior walls reached high to a vaulted apex in the same grey as the outside stones. The stone wall configuration made excellent acoustics for embellishing the sounds. The chants were inspiring.

Until that evening I was angry about signing my son's religious freedom away because of a Catholic mandate. But later in the solitude of my room, my anger stopped. The signing was something that had happened, and it was over.

It was the Trappists who made me believe that, "It is far more blessed to give than to receive." For just a brief second I thought I'd be angry with my Protestant upbringing for not letting me know about the Trappists. But how banal to replace one petty anger with another. It must be something in my personality. I'm one of the fortunate individuals with a Protestant background to have known the Trappists.

The next week in Iowa City I located *Zen and the Birds of Appetite*. Merton's message gave me a new conceptualization of Zen and Christianity. With meditation and seeking one can break through the limits of cultural and structural religion and arrive in a simple void where all is liberty, or in the Christian concept, "birth in the spirit." In the case of Buddha and Jesus, there was an emptying of the mind. If one can truly empty the mind, one can experience a psychic limitlessness. I had begun to experience the first stages of this with sesshin.

Merton had written many books. I don't see how he had time to pray with all the books he wrote. He had lived with the French order Trappists in Gethsemane, Kentucky. I vowed I would make it there one day.

I made one quick trip to Gethsemane that year. Unlike the Iowa Trappists, those in Kentucky were poor. They could not afford to feed anyone. Their lack of wealth was reflected in their small-scale architecture. To make ends meet, they made and sold fruit cakes.

On a subsequent trip a few years later, I asked if I could see the grave of Merton. The monk on duty simply nodded and pointed the direction. I walked into the graveyard full of small white crosses and looked for a monument to Merton. I walked and looked and I looked and walked. Finally I realized, he was only bigger than life in my world. His simple, white cross, like all the others in that graveyard, dignified his humanity.

WITHOUT MONEY

Crossing paths with the Trappists had a profound effect on my life. I thought about monastic life frequently after being with them just that one day. I was most intrigued that they didn't have a daily concern with the physical aspects of money.

I wanted to see what it would be like not to think about money. Not to have it on my body. Not to reach in my pocket and feel a coin. From April to September of 1977, I went without money.

I paid my Iowa City rent in advance, and I lived only on rice and water. From time to time, people gave me vegetables from their gardens. I had a routine. I would meditate about two hours in the morning. Afterwards,

I would read the *Shobogenzo*, the basic philosophy of Soto Zen written by Dogen Zenji. (In September, I sent the book to a friend, John Workman.) Then, I would go see my friend Charlie Vinton and have a cup of coffee and listen to jazz with him. Home again, I'd have a light lunch of rice. I would draw for a couple of hours, nap, then continue my drawing. In the evening, I returned to Vinton's for a cup of coffee and listened to some more jazz. If it were not raining, I would go to the Iowa River and watch the sunset. I passed the evenings in the quiet of my apartment. I ate one last bowl of rice before going to sleep.

Throughout the first week, there was an involuntary reaction of reaching into my pocket just to jiggle coins. But there were no coins, and my conscious and sub-conscious found themselves confronted. Eventually, the physical aspect of money faded into the background. I was free of it, if only for a short while.

That experience convinced me that I would really not be cut out for monastic life. It was simply too redundant for me. But I was still on a journey for something blindingly spiritual. I decided to try another vision quest.

SECOND QUEST

It was time to make a second attempt at a vision quest. In October of 1977, I went to Kentucky. My father lived in Bowling Green then. He had some very secluded land thickly covered with pine trees. That is where I went. I took a tent to avoid mosquitoes at night.

My father dropped me off. The first day I fidgeted around. It was a day of lingering thoughts about the world I had left behind. But the lack of water quickly erased ties to the work-a-day world. My body wanted water.

The second day my mind became preoccupied with water, but about mid-day a tremendous relaxation floated through my being. My spot was at the base of a large tree. I leaned against it. It was there that I became immobile.

I never knew whippoorwills were nocturnal. They are a beautiful clockwork signaling the setting sun.

The third day I began to think that the next day I might have a vision, if such things do occur. All the sounds of the forest became amazingly acute in my mind. That afternoon I was on my spot, and I saw a rodent, I guess, coming from a distance. I watched it. What an existence. Its eyes constantly casting to and fro for food, for enemies, to see its path. It ambled.

I knew my "civilized" human scent was gone. My body no longer gave off the odor of freshly-eaten foods. Thus the rodent didn't smell me as a "normal" human. It was approaching so that it would pass about ten feet in front of me. When it was almost straight in front of me, it looked at me as it continued in its normal manner and then the proverbial second take. Its head quickly snapped, and we looked eye to eye. I could see the thought process, "Why am I seeing a human and not smelling it?" Then with everything genetically programmed for survival, it bolted from my sight.

I felt bad the animal feared me. I wanted to exist with the animal without this sense of fear.

The fourth day I was on my spot. More than once the sensation of thirst reminded me of who I was--a thirsty man. I was amazed that my body continued to urinate even though I had no liquid intake.

That night the vision came. It was brief. I remembered directions from my readings: close your eyes and then open them. If the image is still there, it is a vision and not a dream. I did and it was. It was real.

My vision was mine alone. It has never been shared.

The next day my father picked me up. I tried to speak, but my vocal cords had relaxed, and my voice only squeaked. At home, I thought I would drink an entire ocean, but I drank only a half a glass of water.

That evening I drank maybe two quarts of water, ate a couple of hot dogs with mustard, and some corn. I quickly recovered, and the next day I was back to the material world. But I saw materialism differently, and I always will. My vision was on constant recall. I thought about it almost every half-an-hour for the next several months.

My vision had to do with my future, and the events eventually happened. The not-mystically oriented may explain the vision as aberrant synapses, but that explanation doesn't make my vision any less real. Two decades later, I still think about the vision every couple of days. It still has much power in my life.

People harass me for the details of the vision. "Hey, did you really see something?" Others like my wife, Michelle, admonish, "Come on, you can tell me the details. I won't tell anybody. Why don't you want to tell? Don't you want to share it with someone?"

I'm not really sure what would happen if I were to reveal the details of my vision. I feel in my heart that the spirits of the universe would feel betrayed, and they would not treat me kindly. I keep my silence.

In October of 1977, I thought about doing a 40-day fast. If not then, when? A good ten-month job offer came in November of 1977, and I took it. It was time for archaeology again.

THE ONE CHANCE?

In August of 1978, I reevaluated my idea of waiting until I was 40 to do a 40-day fast. I had the time in the fall of 1978. It was truly a tough decision, but in the fall of 1978 I went around the world, drank fine wines, ate fine food, and went to 120 museums in 30 countries. But the trip was not all hedonistic. I had several religious pilgrimages on my agenda.

Walking onto Stonehenge on the evening of a full moon, I imagined ancient Druidic rites. The extreme quiet of that evening still sticks in my head. The next night I slept on the even older megalithic site of Avebury Circle. That site attracted me like no other. It is the only site I have visited in some 50-odd countries that still beckons me.

I visited the Vatican. I saw Pope John Paul II give his second address. I went to St. Peter's Square early that morning and sat by the middle monument reading the *I Ching*. I lost track of time and my surroundings. When the announcement came that the Pope was in his second story window, I stood. I was stunned because the entire square was filled with people. I couldn't believe I had been so absorbed in reading that I didn't notice this crowd, but it was a sedate gathering. After all it wasn't a rock concert. They had come to see the Pope, and the decorum was that of a church.

And there he was, as I had seen so many times in pictures, part person, part icon. But today the person part was bigger than life. I wasn't Catholic; I wasn't even Christian, but the Pope was bigger than life. I find it strange that I often go out of my way to tell people I saw the Pope.

After the Pope's address, most of the crowd dissipated. But many remained to have an afternoon picnic with packaged tour food. I watched the crowd and tried to imagine what it would have been like when the first Pope made an address.

As the people left, leaving their garbage behind, the homeless came to scavenge for remaining morsels. One man with long grey, matted, dirty hair and a three feet long matted and dirty beard had a unique scavenging technique. He gathered some boxes into a pile. Then he would march up and down sections, gather boxes and bring them back to his pile. He established a mound about three feet by three feet of around 20 cardboard lunch boxes. Finally, he sat down and slowly went through each box. I watched him eat. Again I evaluated the matter of materialism and spirituality. I could only conclude that poverty isn't ipso facto intense spirituality. So, I was left wondering: How does one break into that spiritual realm that Jesus was in?

I flew from Rome to Istanbul where I sat in the Blue Mosque. It is a beautiful building. The language barrier was too difficult, and I couldn't really make an entrance into the world of Islam. Istanbul has its heavy-duty night life, and I was not sure where the abstinence from alcohol prevailed in the Islamic world. I assumed that it was like the Christian world: There are extremes of following or not following the scriptures.

My assumption became an obvious reality when I went to Iran and witnessed the last days of the Shah. Many Americans don't understand what happened when the Shah was deposed. The orthodox Muslims saw the American Christian society as the evil corruptor of their religion and society. When the revolution began, the first places destroyed were liquor stores. Islamic religion strictly forbids alcohol. Just before the Shah was deposed, women marched in protest of having to return to wearing traditional clothing, especially the veil. As a result, many women reputedly had their faces slashed with razors: religion and the law.

I went to Shiraz to see the great archaeological site of Persepolis. I was told not to go that day since it was a Muslim holy day and Americans would not be welcomed. But I didn't know if I would ever make it back to Persepolis, so I went. I was the only white person. In the town, some children threw rocks at me, but I turned and stared at them with a sincere countenance. They quietly withdrew. At the site, a couple of people tried to intimidate me by asking me in broken English why I had long hair, and then touching my ponytail. I smiled and said, "Because I like it." It passed as a minor event. If only they had known that my ponytail was doubled up.

A few days later, I landed in Delhi, India. One of my goals was to stay with the holy Hindus in the jungles of Rishikesh. Since India had been part of the British Empire, many people spoke English, and the language barrier was not that difficult.

In Delhi, I took a morning train for Rishikesh. On the train a man of my same age befriended me. He was going home after a trip abroad. He offered me the opportunity to stay with his family. I accepted.

Talking to those Hindus in their home was a good experience. The home was a typical, modern western-style building; although, it was small. The mother was a political science professor at a nearby university. The father was a businessman. They explained the entire matter of reincarnation to me. It was the brief encyclopedia synopsis that I had learned in comparative religion classes, but here it was from the mouths of "ordinary" people like my mother and father.

What I was never taught in my synopsis of college Hinduism is that the Hindus in Rishikesh were vegetarians to the extreme that they would not eat eggs for fear they were fertilized. Not just that household, but the entire town. As a result, the women explained to me that they were extremely artful at cooking with spices. It is the only time in my life I actually felt the energy of the food go through my body as I ate. When I relayed this incident to friends upon return, many said, "It was a religious experience, huh?" No, it was a culinary experience, and one I never expected.

The next day, I bid them good-bye and headed through town to the Ganges River. I passed by small ancient temples that had fallen into ruins and I observed the trees and other vegetation breaking them apart. I had a better appreciation of how entire cities one day lie beneath the surface of the earth as archaeological sites.

I was blessed this day to witness the celebration of the recent death of a large brahma cow. It lay in the middle of a narrow street. Beautiful multicolor arrangements of flowers were leaned against its body; completely surrounding it. In the west we hear that the cow is holy to the Hindu, but it never meant anything to me until that day. I didn't have my wits about me to ask what the ultimate act for the cow would be. I assume it would be cremated. One day I hope to return and ask many questions.

Arriving at the Ganges, I was smiling. I saw what I had envisioned at many archaeological sites around the world, especially the Midwestern United States and Mexico. The populace centered many of their daily activities along the river--from funeral rites to bathing. The quick flowing waters were constantly refreshed. At places along the shore were concrete steps going down into the river. There people stepped into the river to bathe. The water was gushing as this is where the Ganges flows out of the Himalayas.

I watched the people for almost an hour. Some were throwing grain into the water. Subsequently, there was a turmoil on the surface of the water. Many people were being taken back and forth to the other shore by small boats. Among the passengers were the orange robed, long haired, bearded holy men.

I decided to remove my shoes, pull up my pant legs and step into the river. As I stood there massaging my calves, a rather large fish, a foot or two in length, nudged my legs. I was startled and pushed it away. A man saw me and said, "They only want to be petted. The fish here have never been taken for food. They know no fear of humans. They are part of our spirit." I nodded in respect and petted the fish.

Sitting back from the river on a sand bar, I wondered how I would negotiate going to the other side. I fell asleep with my small backpack as a pillow. Maybe an hour into my sleep, I heard a fast sounding swish culminating in a thud. I barely opened my eyes to see one of the orange robed holy men standing there. I was extremely exhausted and fell back asleep. When I awoke, the man was sitting about three feet from my legs.

He was young. I can't offer an estimation of his age because I'm a total failure at that sort of thing. He nodded to me. As he gestured by pointing behind me, he said, "Ashram, money." Then pointing across the river, "Jungle, no money. Jungle good. Jungle go?"

I pointed to him and then to myself. He nodded and off we went. We were ferried across by one of the small boats that held about 20 people.

The sound that I had heard while I slept was his silver-colored trident. He had thrown it into the sandbar. He walked with it over his shoulder as it was the holder for a silver-colored pot which contained some type of belongings.

We wandered the narrow trails for about eight hours. Occasionally we passed other orange robed yogis, and once in a while we stopped to pick and eat berries. Toward evening we arrived at an open-aired shelter about 40 feet by 40 feet.

With my pack under my head, I nodded off. When I awoke, he had cooked rice in his pot over an open fire. He put rice on a leaf and offered it to me.

We both meditated that evening.

The next day we continued our wanderings, and in the early afternoon we arrived at a fairly large temple complex. The temples were made of white washed concrete. I was shown a small room with no windows and two wooden doors that did not match precisely when closed. The yogi bid me sit, and he left.

I meditated and slept. The next day I wandered about the temple complex and outside it. I bought some bananas from a vendor. I went back to my room and sat with the door open. The yogi had not returned by evening so I repeated meditating and sleeping.

The next morning the yogi came by and beckoned that we should depart. Outside of the temple compound he began madly motioning with his hands flailing to the side of his head and speaking in a very raised voice. I hit my front pocket gesturing money, and he nodded. I pulled out some money and held it out. He grabbed some of it and ran back to the temple. I wondered what happened to the earlier philosophy, "Jungle good. No money."

Within a couple of hours we were back at the Ganges. He motioned that he was staying. Again there was some animation about money, but much more subdued. Again I held out some money, and again he took some. I crossed the Ganges and returned to Delhi.

From Delhi I flew into Hong Kong. It was a two-day party. And then onto fast-paced Tokyo. In Tokyo, I was introduced to incredible jazz clubs and all night partying. After a couple of days, I hitchhiked to the ultimate Soto Zen Temple in Eiheiji, Japan.

I arrived at night. It was snowing. All I could see were a few little gift shops, I didn't see the temple. I insisted to the driver that this could not be Eiheiji, "Not Eiheiji!" But he gestured that I need only walk up the only street leading from the road we were on. We bowed, and I departed.

I arrived at a large, but impressive, wooden gate. I wondered what the protocol was for entering. My thought was answered by a monk coming from around the corner. He was wearing sandals without socks. The snow was quite deep. I was impressed. He said something to me in Japanese. I grimaced and shrugged to show that I had no comprehension of Japanese. He grabbed me by my right bicep and began escorting me, with some force, through the gate. He led me to a rather large temple. Inside the temple he showed me to a back room where there were sleeping mats. He pointed to them and then waved at me to follow him to a room where he pointed to the traditional Asian floor toilets. With one hand on my left arm and the other on my back, we returned to the sleeping mats. He turned and bowed, I reciprocated, and he left. For five days, I had the temple to myself.

The next morning I walked out of the gate thinking that the temple was not that impressive, at least in terms of size. I walked up into the mountains and spotted my first persimmon trees. There was still abundant fruit. I picked a few and continued climbing and eating.

Returning to the temple, I meditated for a couple of days. The fourth day I went out and walked around the corner where the monk had come from. I eventually wound my way to the main entrance. I stood in awe. I had no idea. The main entrance is maybe about 20 feet wide. Upon entering I was looking at four large statues, two on the left and two on the right, all facing me. Each stood about 20 feet high, each was painted in living colors, and each was in full motion. The motions were those of the martial arts. These, the guardians of the Dharma (the teachings of Buddha), were trampling under their feet the demons of perversity. Mesmerized, I stood studying those multi-colored, life-like statues for about an hour.

Inside the complex, I wandered around for a couple of hours. Several of the large buildings serve as a retreat, and there were many lay persons there to meditate.

I left and went into the mountains to eat and gather persimmons. Then I remained in my own building for a couple more days. On more than one occasion, I thought of Merton's comparisons between the Zen and the Christians and I thought about my unique experiences with the Trappists and the Zen. Because I visited during the winter, I had everything to myself--solitude and space.

Back in Tokyo, it was jazz clubs, sake and all night partying. I was something like Hermann Hesse's Siddartha flip-flopping between two worlds.

One question I had asked earlier in my life came back during that trip: Where is all the religious diversity blanketing the face of the planet coming from?

A DECADE AWAY

In 1979, I took a job as a field director of an archaeological project in Peru. That project lasted until 1982. Put as bluntly as possible, Peru is a country which likes to party. Those three years pretty much set the tone for the next seven years.

From 1982 to 1992, I did little spiritual questing. I quit fasting. Those years were spent going from mild to dedicated hedonism. My 40 year marker came and went. Sometimes I ask myself why. I can only answer with John Steinbeck's statement in *Travels with Charlie*, "We find after years of struggle that we do not take a trip; a trip takes us." But I never set out to be a monk, I was only exploring spirituality.

During that period, I obtained small grants to travel to Mexico for a couple of months at a time to study specific anthropological problems. I was mostly interested in the economics of pilgrimage centers.

Two of the centers were devoted to the Virgin de los Remedios (curing). Without doubt these Catholic centers were making money. What I found of most interest is that they were Aztec pilgrimage centers, and the Catholics said, "Hey, if it works for you, it works for us." So, I was faced with the question, is the power in the place, or is the power in the deities, or is the power only in the minds of the believers? All things considered, it has to be the latter.

I talked to many of the pilgrims. Some left *retablos*, a painted picture made by themselves of the sickness and the healing. The sicknesses ranged from chronic headaches to paralysis.

All pilgrimage centers have a yearly festival, and it is during that time that many of the healings take place. I wanted badly to participate in one of the festivals. But my schedule never coincided.

In 1982, I began freelance writing for magazines. I liked getting paid for my writing, unlike writing for academic journals. The more I was paid, the more I wanted to get paid. What I liked most was that I could use colored photos in *Invention and Technology* rather than the simple black and white illustrations of something like *American Antiquity*.

My writings branched out to music and the origins of holidays. I also wrote about cuisine. One article was on why Americans feature the turkey at Thanksgiving. As a consequence, I slowly emerged as a gourmet cook and published my own recipes. I also covered topics like artificial intelligence which gave me a penchant for futuristic studies.

In 1989, I received support from the Foundation for Ancient Research and Mormon Studies in Provo, Utah, to continue with a centralization of New World figurines. I took one month to go from Pensacola, Florida, to Provo, and having little money, I began fasting again. The solitude of the drive gave me time to reflect. My intellectual focus began shifting back to the spiritual aspects of life.

I liked living in Provo. It has beautiful high mountains to the immediate east, and on the west is a pleasant lake where I spent many weekends. The social atmosphere of Provo was also relaxing. Crime is very low because of the Mormon population.

Brigham Young University provided an intellectual milieu that in one way or another permeated pretty much the entire populace. Unlike most college campuses, dedicated to wild behaviors, BYU was devoted to moral behavior. Smoking, coffee, and alcohol are forbidden on campus.

Living in Provo was my first time in a Mormon community. Mormons certainly pray more than any other group I had ever been around. They are very moral people, but I didn't see them as any more spiritual than Methodists or Catholics or Amish.

One day after hearing Annie Dillard give an inspiring reading from her book *Pilgrim at Tinkers Creek*, I again contemplated doing my 40-day fast. I read her book in the following week, and every moment as I read, I wanted to go into 40 days of isolation. One line I often recite to people is, "We have not yet encountered any god who is as merciful as a man who flicks a beetle over on its feet."

In the fall of 1989, I returned to Pensacola to be with my family. During that sojourn, I met my wife Michelle. We began writing together. We did some academic writing and then we gravitated into freelance.

I spent the next couple of years between Provo and Pensacola. During that time, I finished *The New World Figurine Project, Volume 1* (1991).

THE MOON AND A DROP OF DEW

March of 1992, I accepted a job working on an archaeological project from the Bishop Museum in Honolulu, Hawaii. It was a wonderful opportunity to learn about ancient Hawaiian religion. They were not unlike the Aztecs with their human sacrifice.

Hawaii is a rather hedonistic place, but because of the Asian population, I had ample opportunity to continue learning about Buddhism. Not far up in Kalihi Valley where I lived, there was a Rinzai Zen temple. I always remember Kando Nakagima telling me that the Rinzai were very strict. He told me once he was traveling in Japan, and he was staying in a Rinzai temple. He said he felt very ill, and he laid down. The temple master came and kicked him and told him to get out of the temple because "...pain does not exist." Kando said it was the first time that he had to sit in the snow.

With Kando's story in mind, I ventured up into the valley. I was welcomed as a once-practicing member of the Soto sect. I received my instructions. They meditate with their eyes open. The Rinzai place their right hand in their left, the opposite of the Soto. They face sitting away from the wall, not toward it. We meditated for an hour, and then I was informed that we would move to another building for the exercises. I couldn't believe it, they were Samurai. The next thing I knew I was watching sword fights. I continued to go for a couple of weeks, but the martial arts aspect didn't appeal to me so I stopped going.

But the Rinzai master did give me many meaningful stories to think about. One was about a Zen master contemplating a drop of dew containing the entire moon in its reflection. Afterwards, I too observed the moon's reflection in a drop of dew. It was bright and quite complete. It felt so different to look down on the moon and not up.

There's a transporting quality in reflections. One day I stopped to reflect on my religious experiences. I wondered if I had a greater variety than anyone else. Not that it mattered, but I wondered. Then I realized, my religious experiences were diverse, but weren't they somehow superficial? The vision quest was intense, but it was an isolated experience that didn't change my lifestyle. Were my experiences spiritual, or was I nothing more than a detached social scientist sampling a buffet of religious events?

Something inside me was lacking. I lacked questions I didn't know how to ask. Where to begin? What does it mean for someone to start an entirely new religious movement? Who were Buddha, Jesus, and Mohammed? I didn't have the cultural background to know about the first and third, but maybe I could delve into Jesus--the man, the man who after his 40-day fast changed the course of Western Civilization. I wanted to do a 40-day fast, but when?

THE ANNOUNCEMENT

By August of 1993, whatever I had for anticipation was enough. Both Michelle's and my birthdays are in August. We always try to do something unique for our birthdays. Our first celebration was a first time ever sky diving trip. In August of 1993, I somewhat selfishly decided to dedicate myself to accomplishing a 40-day fast. Everything just seemed right, and we had adequate finances, so I left the Bishop Museum.

We had a beautiful living situation in Kalihi. Our two-room bungalow was surrounded by assorted tropical vegetation delicately planted over a fifty-year period by Mrs. Char, our landlady, and her deceased husband. We shared the backyard with Mrs. Char, a Seventh-Day Adventist, and a retired couple, Mr. and Mrs. Sakai, Buddhists. All three were of Japanese descent. It was humorous when Jehovah Witnesses or Mormons came to the house because the Sakais were mildly frightened by the encounters.

Our backyard was an image of paradise--beautiful palm trees, wide Plumeria trees, pots and boxes of vegetables and orchids, greenery in every corner. The backyard went down three terraces and stopped at a stream. The top and middle terraces were lined with royal ilima bushes and various shrubs. On the bottom terrace, I planted vegetables and herbs. Our basil crop produced the best pesto on earth.

I announced to Michelle my decision to orient myself toward a 40-day fast. The roof caved in. She was convinced she should come to monitor my health once a week for the first two weeks and every other day after that. Then she'd throw in, "What if they exaggerated Jesus' fast and it was really only four days? It is an old story. Or what if fast meant something different then, like you have to eat once a day? You wouldn't be doing it like Jesus."

Michelle is not a Christian, although she was taken to a Baptist Sunday school occasionally. She wasn't too concerned with the religious aspects of the fast, but she was curious about the scientific aspects: pulse rate change, hormone balance, etc. I knew her comments originated from love and a desire to have a handle on everything, but I couldn't help feeling she was distracting me from fulfilling this endeavor. Telling her about fasting, Jesus, and the Bible was energy demanding. I knew it was going to be a challenging endeavor. Every now and then I'd find myself asking in half jest: Why me, God?

BACK TO THE BOOKS

In the process of browsing biblical scriptures for information on fasting to broaden my knowledge and help Michelle understand what I was doing, I suddenly found myself deep in biblical studies. What do we really know about Jesus? We only have four individuals, Matthew, Mark, Luke, and John, giving us "first-hand" accounts about Jesus. I began to scrutinize the first-hand accounts, and I discussed the Bible with anyone who would talk to me in a rational manner.

I was finding some pretty major contradictions. Matthew writes Jesus screamed out his last words; whereas, John says Jesus' last words on the cross were spoken quietly. That's quite a difference, especially from two of the twelve disciples. Furthermore the last words are different. Matthew has Jesus screaming, "My God, my God, why hast thou forsaken me?" Mark also has the same characterization. Luke has Jesus crying aloud, "Father, into thy hands I commend my spirit." John has Jesus quietly saying, "It is over." How do we make decisions as to which version to believe?

The last I had ever discussed the Bible "in-depth" was in the late 60s, and I was still of the opinion that everyone believed that the Bible was divinely inspired through the pens of Matthew, Mark, Luke, and John. Almost 25 years later, my eyes were opened to new views of the New Testament.

I consulted a New Testament scholar at the University of Hawaii, Manoa. The scholar, Fritz Seifert, suggested a book by Howard Clark Kee, *Jesus in History*.

Relaxed and articulate, Fritz explained a small part of what I would discover in Kee's book. "You know that all of Mark is in Matthew and Luke. There are also similar additional materials in the latter two books. There is the supposition that the additional materials were obtained from a manuscript not yet found which has been labeled Q. Q is short for *Quelle*, which means 'source' in German. This is very serious scholarship; not slipshod." In brief, of Mark's 661 verses, 606 are found in a similar form in either Luke or

Matthew. That is why Matthew, Mark, and Luke are called the "synoptic Gospels". They are the similar or synonymous.

For example, the healing of the leper described in Matthew, Mark and Luke have almost identical words of Jesus.

Matthew 8:

2   And, behold, there came a leper and worshipped him, saying, "Lord, if thou wilt, thou can make me clean."

3   And Jesus put forth his hand, and touched him, saying, "I will; be thou clean." And immediately his leprosy was cleansed.

4   And Jesus saith unto him, "See thou tell no man; but go thy way, shew thyself to the priest, and offer the gift that Moses commanded for a testimony unto them."

Mark 1:

40   And there came a leper to him, beseeching him, and kneeling down to him, and saying unto him, "If thou wilt, thou can make me clean."

41   And Jesus, moved with compassion, put forth his hand, and touched him, and saith unto him, "I will; be thou clean."

42   And as soon as he had spoken, immediately the leprosy departed from him, and he was cleansed.

43   And he straightly charged him, and forthwith sent him away;

44   And saith unto him, "See thou say nothing to any man, but go thy way, shew thyself to the priest, and offer for thy cleansing those things which Moses commanded, for a testimony unto them."

Luke 5:

12   And it came to pass, when he was in a certain city, behold a man full of leprosy; who seeing Jesus fell on his face, and besought him, saying, "Lord, if thou wilt, thou can make me clean."

13   And he put forth his hand, and touched him, saying, "I will; be thou clean." And immediately the leprosy departed from him.

14   And he charged him to tell no man; but to go, and "shew thyself to the priest, and offer for thy cleansing, according as Moses commanded, for a testimony unto them."

However, there are 200 verses which are common to both Matthew and Luke, but not found in Mark. Where did they come from? Some biblical scholars say they came from "Q."

Not all scholars accept the "Q" theory. I wasn't sure what to make of it. The commonalities are interesting, but I find the explanation of copying somewhat strange. No matter who is copying from whom, why are there existing variances? Shouldn't it be either word for word or a close approximation?

And if there is the copying from two sources, why in the synoptic Gospels are there two different versions of Jesus' last words on the cross? The "Q" theory didn't give me any answers.

As for the Bible being divinely inspired, I don't believe God would make such confusing contradictions.

At first, the contradictions I found made me believe the Gospels were written by three or fewer people. Reading in detail, I began to have suspicions that Matthew, Mark, Luke, and John were written by one person, and the contradictions were planted to make us believe there were four individuals. Of course, in the end, this is something I may never prove.

Michelle argued, "That doesn't make sense. Why would anyone want you to think there are four people writing?" My reply: If all we know about any individual comes from four people, we might be more inclined to believe the information than if it came from just one person. Proverbially, "There is safety in numbers."

I stand by the fact that to have Jesus' last words not only being different, but being screamed out according to one disciple and whispered by another disciple, is greatly suspicious. This is not something someone would have been wrong about unless there was an underlying motive.

As I searched for motives, I found the character of Jesus changing through the four Gospels. At the time I was working on this problem, I was using the *Good News Bible* printed by the American Bible Society, N.Y. Each Gospel has a brief preface. In Matthew, Jesus is the great teacher. In Mark, Jesus is a man of action. In Luke, Jesus is the savior of all mankind. In John, he is the eternal word of God. I wasn't sure, but these characterizations seemed oddly unique. I suspected these different characterizations were a purposeful endeavor to give the fullest presentation of Jesus while covering the same stories. If there were four different authors writing in different times and places and copying from one another, I would think that there would have been much more overlap. With Jesus' last words alone, there is a toning down that follows the characterizations. In the beginning, the revolutionary teacher screams out his last words of vengeance, and in the end, the eternal word whispers his last words of reconciliation.

Michelle was convinced I was beginning to have delusions about one writer trying to fool biblical readers. Suddenly we were having heated discussions over the Gospels. I told her my mission was not to prove one person wrote the Gospels. All I really wanted to do was fast 40 days and see if it helped me with my own quest for understanding the balance between materialism and spirituality.

Michelle came up with an idea which works for the writing of the Gospels. Perhaps they were written by a team of four, who coordinated their efforts or farmed out different assignments to one another.

I could accept that. The contradictions didn't make sense except as an attempt to make me believe four different people were writing four different characterizations of Jesus. Quickly Michelle would jump in, "Perhaps it's all wrong and Jesus never existed anyway." I would counter, "The contradictions don't make the story any less true. It just means we have to work harder at reconstructing the identity of Jesus."

Where to next? It was the crucifixion, the vinegar story as I call it, that roused my suspicions that perhaps the Gospels were written by one person. I had to analyze the story in detail.

4

WHO SUPPLIED THE SPONGE?

Many people grimace when they hear Jesus was served a sponge full of vinegar as he hung on the cross. Their grimaces might turn to smiles if they were to go a day without water and then take a sip of vinegar. Christianity might be a more wholesome religion if its adherents tried to experience similar actions and events to those they read about.

Similarly, I obviously had to be more rigorous in my reading of the scriptures if I were going to in any way discuss the idea that one person wrote Matthew, Mark, Luke, and John.

Many statements in the Bible are open to a wide-range of interpretations, especially 2000 years after the event. In fact, the vinegar story, as I call it, is about as confusing and contradictory as we have. There are three different accounts of Jesus on the cross. There are also confusing differences about what Jesus was offered *before* his crucifixion.

Matthew tells us Jesus was offered wine with gall. Jesus tasted the mix, but would not drink it.

Mark says Jesus was offered wine with myrrh, but refused it.

Luke and **John** don't tell us of any liquid offering to Jesus before his crucifixion. There is no reason why they should tell us since we have been told twice.

I then looked at a few differences and similarities in the story of when Jesus was offered vinegar *while on the cross.*

Matthew writes as Jesus hung on the cross, "...one of them ran, and took a sponge, and filled it with vinegar, and put it on a reed, and gave him to drink."

Mark's writing is almost identical to Matthew's. As Jesus hung on the cross, "...one ran and filled a sponge full of vinegar, and put it on a reed and gave him to drink."

In **Luke's** version, "The soldiers mocked Jesus, coming to him and offering him vinegar."

John said while Jesus was on the cross "...knowing that all things were now accomplished, that the scriptures might be fulfilled, he said, 'I thirst.'" A vessel full of vinegar was brought to the cross. A sponge was filled with vinegar, put on a hyssop (a type of plant) and put to Jesus' mouth.

SOME INTERPRETATIONS

During high altitude hikes, I use vinegar to relieve my desiccated mouth. This allows me to conserve water. Vinegar won't replace the vital liquids, but the relief it brings to a totally parched mouth is divine. Funny how that word is thrown around. But, more importantly, the vinegar which we use for pickling today is not what Jesus tasted. Wine vinegar or sour wine was a common drink among the poorer classes in those days. I'm sure it was refreshing for one being crucified.

Knowing he was going to die, Jesus wouldn't have necessarily asked that his thirst be abated. Perhaps he asked for the vinegar so his last words would be audible to someone other than himself.

As for the offering of liquid before crucifixion, **Matthew** has an offering of wine with gall. Gall is animal bile. This sick version is not again repeated. It doesn't have to be. The effect of dramatic tension between good and evil is where one would want it, once and right in the beginning, in Matthew. In some dictionaries, gall is said to be a metaphor for bitter punishment for evil or deep resentment. Writing in biblical times was highly metaphorical; thus, animal bile offered to Jesus is the juxtaposition of good and evil presented right in the beginning of the New Testament. And it is in Matthew that Jesus is juxtaposed to the world as the great new teacher.

Mark's version is more palatable. But as a child, I didn't understand. I only had wine at communion and I never even saw myrrh until I went to the Middle East as an adult. By then I had drunk ouzo in Greece. So, what would wine taste like if we put myrrh in it? Was Mark balancing out what Matthew overdid?

Luke and **John** don't mention Jesus being offered anything before his crucifixion.

Viewing the liquid before crucifixion in terms of characterizations, I saw Jesus as: a teacher/revolutionary in Matthew, a man of action in Mark, a savior in Luke, and the eternal word in John. Thus the tainted mixtures are found only in the first two Gospels which portray Jesus' more human qualities, and not the last two which portray him as more divine.

While Jesus was on the cross, Matthew and Mark both write of someone running to get Jesus a sponge of vinegar. Someone running indicates there was a quick need for the vinegar. Did Jesus ask for it, or did the people around him know he needed it? In Mark and Matthew, Jesus is portrayed as a man, so we have human qualities, such as running. In Luke and John, there are no people running.

Luke associates vinegar with the verb to mock, and the mocking was done by soldiers. Readers of the scriptures should not think that the soldiers' mockery of Jesus was an isolated incident. Historical documents indicate that the entire process of crucifixion was one of mockery, especially by the individuals driving the nails.

All this considered, the Luke passage becomes difficult to interpret. If the soldiers are mocking Jesus, why are they offering him vinegar? Or are they holding the sponge near his mouth such that he might only smell the vinegar? I would assume the latter. However, it is possible by the time Jesus was dying, a soldier had some compassion and served him vinegar. Vinegar would have relieved his dry mouth. Luke didn't say Jesus asked for vinegar, nor was his thirst mentioned. Did the Romans give everyone who was crucified some vinegar right before death, much like the last meal granted to those about to be executed?

In **John**, Jesus said he had thirst, and he was given vinegar. Now, as far as I know, the only people who could permit the vinegar to be given to Jesus were the soldiers. But if they were as cruel as is written, they wouldn't have permitted Jesus to receive vinegar.

Again the contradictions began to look like the writing job by one person or a coordinated team; and not four different individuals in different places and times possibly copying from one another. Reading the New Testament page-for-page like we most often read books, we would become disgusted with the soldiers after Matthew, Mark, and Luke. By the time we get to John, there's no need to mention the soldiers.

However, people don't read the Bible page-for-page. People skip around. The Bible is a reference book that is used for emotional uplifting. Thus the likelihood of its composition coming into question would be minimal. After all, look how long it took for the "Q" theory to be proposed--almost two millennia.

If you think I'm reading too much into the vinegar story, look at Jesus' last moments.

Matthew writes of Jesus dying in the ninth hour. Jesus cries out in a loud voice, *Eli eli lama sach tha ni?* "My God, my God, why hast thou forsaken me?" Those standing at the bottom of the cross thought he was calling Elias. Then someone ran for vinegar to serve Jesus. Immediately after the vinegar, "Jesus, when he had cried again with a loud voice, yielded up the ghost."

Mark says almost the same thing as Matthew. In the ninth hour, Jesus cries out in a loud voice, *Eli eli lama sach tha ni*. At that point, those standing around at the bottom of the cross thought he called Elias. Then someone ran for vinegar which was served to Jesus. Immediately after, "Jesus, when he had cried again with a loud voice, yielded up the ghost."

Luke writes of Jesus dying in the ninth hour as well. Jesus cries out in a loud voice, "Father, into thy hands I commend my spirit." Having said that "...he gave up the ghost."

John doesn't write the time. Why should he? We've been told three times. However, Jesus receives vinegar, and quietly says, "It is finished." He bows his head and gives up the ghost.

There is a constant toning down of the crucifixion scene to meet the needs of the methodically changing image of Jesus. It would be unsavory to have Jesus the eternal word, as portrayed in John, screaming out about being forsaken. We are being led by the hand through a purposefully constructed writing effort called the four Gospels.

A POSSIBLE SCENARIO

These stories have the ear markings of someone writing out a scroll and giving it the name **Matthew.** The someone lets his friend read the scroll and the friend says, "Maybe you ought to tone it down. That vinegar and gall made me sick."

So, the writer goes back and rewrites it and calls his new writing **Mark**. He changes the vinegar to wine and the gall to myrrh. His friend says, "Well I don't think you should deviate from the facts. Also, when Jesus yells 'My God, my God, why hast though forsaken me?' that might be overdoing it. I think you're hostile." The friend continues, "You're also hostile toward the soldiers. You write of them mixing disgusting things in Jesus' drink. You're angry at God for taking Jesus so you write Jesus' last words almost condemning God. I really think you need to rewrite this again."

As I discussed this possible scenario with friends, some offered that my idea doesn't make sense because surely the writers would have wanted to tell the truth, and my scenario makes the writers of the Gospels look like novelists. This is precisely the point I'm after. What is the truth? What were Jesus' last words? Were they screamed or whispered?

The writer's next version entitled **Luke** is subdued. He's still angry with the soldiers so he doesn't yet want Jesus to have his refreshing moment before death. Rather he has the mocking soldiers bring the vinegar. Jesus gives God his due with "Father, into thy hands I commend my spirit." Finally, thinking it is adequate, the writer takes it to his friend.

The friend reports, "I like this better, but you know someone gave Jesus vinegar. If the soldiers didn't do this, they presumably allowed it to be done. Otherwise Jesus would never have been able to speak. There will be people who know his mouth would have been totally parched after hanging on the cross an entire day in the sun. He could not have spoken without having some moisture. I know you hate the soldiers for gambling for Jesus' clothes, but Jesus was about forgiveness."

Finally our writer succumbs. But like many a social scientist, the best way to lie, is not to lie, but not to tell the truth. So, he puts the vinegar in the story, but the soldiers aren't given credit for permitting it to be served. The writer's hostility has abated enough that Jesus says what the writer must have felt in his own head, "It is finished."

Is this a possible scenario? Is there any real evidence that one person wrote all four books? Why would one person write all four books under different names?

After many readings, I found the first four books of the New Testament *so highly* orchestrated that I could not believe, as many biblical scholars and theologians assert, that Matthew, Mark, Luke, and John were each written separately in different times and places. On the other hand, if they were copied, there should be many more similarities than there are and the differences would not be so profound. I offer that either one person wrote all four, or there were four writers working as a team. Whether it was one person or a team, the Gospels were planned and prepared so the character of Jesus changes from one of a dramatic revolutionary beginning with Matthew, to one of quiet, spiritual introspection as the eternal word by John.

As I worked through my idea, I kept asking myself, "Who was Jesus really? What were his thoughts, drives and actions?" The differences in the four accounts of the vinegar story in Matthew, Mark, Luke, and John aroused my suspicions of how accurate a depiction of Jesus I could get. Why were there differences?

Beyond these problems, I have other questions just to understand the times in which Jesus existed. Were sponges common items in Jesus' day? What was the monetary value of a sponge? What was the vinegar made of? What did the vinegar taste like? I am after knowledge and truth of Jesus and what surrounded him. I ask all of these questions to understand the world around Jesus. But at present, I find few answers.

A DREAM OF A TRIAL

Because of the criticism I received by saying the Gospels were written by one person, I began to dream of myself on a witness stand having to testify before a jury of biblical readers. I was on trial for heresy.

In one dream, the prosecutor puts a New Testament expert on the stand. I sit awaiting his words in the colorful surrealism of my dream.

"Mr. Expert, how many books are there in the New Testament?"

"Ma'am, there are twenty-seven."

The examiner walked toward the jury and planted her second inquiry, "And are there twenty-seven authors?"

"No, there may be nine. If Paul wrote Hebrews, there would only be eight. But maybe James wrote Hebrews."

"And the four Gospels, they were written by the individuals for whom they are named?" She spins and eyes Mr. Expert.

"As near as we can determine, yes."

"Mr. Expert, please be more precise for our jury. Can you or can you not determine if the first four books of the New Testament were written by different individuals?"

Mr. Expert takes a deep breath as he adjusts his body in the booth and crosses his legs, left over right, "Well, for example, the name Matthew does appear twice in the book we call Matthew. But not in the first person as an author. It was the early writers of the Church who credited it to Matthew. Matthew was one of the more obscure disciples and he was a tax collector or publican. As such, he would have been accustomed to taking notes."

"Could the book have been written by someone else?"

"Well, there is really no reason to make Matthew the author of a book he didn't write since he was a rather obscure Apostle. I think any forger would have thought to name it for one of the more renowned Apostles."

"And as for Mark?"

"The book Mark does not anywhere contain the name Mark. Tradition identifies him as John Mark. He was the scion of a Christian family in Jerusalem."

"And is there any mention of authorship in Luke or John?"

"None."

The lady sits in her chair, almost disgruntled, and propping both elbows on the desk, "And so the assignment of those names, Matthew, Mark, Luke, John, was all done later by someone else?"

"That's correct."

"And you feel the Gospels were written at different times and in different places by different authors for different audiences?"

"I do."

The examiner slowly shakes her head and, while looking out the corner of her eyes at the jury, says, "No more questions."

I am put on the stand. "Dr. Stocker, you've heard Mr. Expert say if someone were to forge the book of Matthew he would have done it under the name of a more famous disciple. What do you say to this?"

"I have never said that it was forgery. My belief is that the Gospels were written as biographies. The overall validity of the piece, the existence of Jesus, is not in question. However, the exact details are in question. Look at any biography, and you'll see it has to be enhanced with stylistic embellishments of characterization. Otherwise it would be rather dry ethnography. I find it strange that Matthew would refer to himself twice in the third person. But let's concern ourselves with Mr. Expert's statement that Matthew was a publican or a tax collector and accustomed to taking notes, true?"

"Dr. Stocker, I'm not the one on trial; please don't refer questions to me," she says sarcastically. Then with eyebrows folded in, she adds, "But yes, as I understand it."

"Well, then doesn't it seem odd to you that a publican accustomed to dealing with public documents would not identify himself?"

The examiner stands with both fists clinched and stares at me, but talks to the judge, "Your honor, would you please advise the defendant to stop couching his answers in the form of questions?"

The judge's voice booms, "Dr. Stocker, please refrain from couching your answers in the form of questions."

My eyes were still locked on the examiner's, "Yes, your magistrate."

"Dr. Stocker, you have heard the testimony that none of the books contains a statement of authorship. So, it would not be odd that Matthew did not sign his name on the document. Do you accept the fact that in the day and age when the New Testament was written most pieces were anonymous? Furthermore, the Christians were persecuted and possibly for this reason none would put his name on such documents. You do accept this?"

"Yes, and furthermore, when people write histories or biographies they usually don't name themselves. Yet, I keep thinking that one of the two Apostles supposedly writing two of the four Gospels, Matthew or John, might have used the first person at least once. Actually, the book of Luke opens with the statement, 'I investigated everything accurately,'" I made a gesture of quotation marks.

I continued, "Yet this person doesn't identify himself. Furthermore, the Gospels are dealing with the life of someone quite special. So, I would expect some kind of first person verification on his acts. You know, something like, 'I, Matthew, saw him walk on water.' But here is something that bothers me: Ask yourself, why are there four Gospels?"

The judge hits his gavel and commands, "One more question, Dr. Stocker, and I will cite you for contempt of court."

"Sorry, your magistrate."

The examiner continues, "Dr. Stocker, please state for the court why you believe there was only one writer of the Gospels."

"About A.D. 180, the Bishop of Lyons and Vienna put in writing a theory about why he thought there were four Gospels. Even in those days,

1800 years ago, the number of Gospels was being debated." Rather than ask the question, I stop and let her ask it.

"And this bishop said there was only one author?"

"No, he said there could be no less than four Gospels or no more than four Gospels because four represented the four zones and directions of the world. And four also represented the four principal winds. You have to remember that in those days the world was flat. Well, believed to be flat."

"But that makes it seem like the assignment of four is simply arbitrary."

"Not arbitrary, but symbolic."

"So, you believe there were four writers?" Her face was contorted with confusion.

"No, what I believe is that my one writer adhered to a metaphorical style of writing that existed 2000 years ago. He had to have four different versions. Four is a very symbolic number. Many numbers had and have symbolic power, such as 13. That is why Jesus did a 40-day fast and not 39 or 41, but 40. A building has to have a four-corner foundation, and that is why one person wrote the four Gospels. People thought this way in those days and yet none of the modern experts," and I glance over at Mr. Expert, "want to take this into consideration. There are many theories of the similarities and differences of the four Gospels. But none of the theories explain everything. My theory of one writer does. Take the 'Q' theory that Luke and Matthew copied from Q. Any expert has to face the music that if Luke or Matthew did copy from the same unknown source, one of them sure as hell took liberties with it."

"Your honor!" She almost screams.

"Dr. Stocker, please refrain from obscenities."

"Yes, your magistrate. But I simply wanted to amplify the point that if two individuals are copying," and I make the gesture for quotation marks while smiling at Mr. Expert, "there would be a much greater similarity than is found in Luke and Matthew."

"Now, Dr. Stocker, why would any one writer want us to think there are four writers?"

"If truth is the outcome of a vote, which it shouldn't be, but sometimes is, there is safety in numbers. So, by having four testimonies to the life of Jesus rather than one, well, we might get more people to believe in the message."

"Yet, Dr. Stocker," she waves her right index finger toward the ceiling, "isn't it true that the styles of each of the Gospels is different and that would be difficult to accomplish by any one person?"

"True, the styles are somewhat different, especially between John and the other three, but there's no reason why one person couldn't accomplish those changes in style."

"And what for you is the most compelling piece of evidence that there is one writer?"

"Matthew and John were both disciples. Now, if there is one thing I would think they'd remember, it is Jesus' last words. But Matthew says Jesus yelled out, 'My God, my god, why hast thou forsaken me. And John says, Jesus quietly said, 'It is finished.'"

The examiner blurts as though she might end the matter, "This just as well suggests they were written by different people who heard different accounts."

"That is a possibility. However, if that is the case, they are not the Gospels written by the Apostles who were at the crucifixion. We keep coming back to one point: Matthew says Jesus yelled out, 'My God, my god, why hast thou forsaken me.' And John says, Jesus quietly said, 'It is finished,'" and with those words, I slowly stand up, stare at Ms. Examiner and ask, "And which words are you going to believe?"

At that point, I wake up.

All day long, I couldn't help but regret that I didn't ask her, "And *why* do you believe the words you believe?"

THE GENEALOGIES

I posed a question to my wife, "Would you expect a genealogy of Jesus to be in the New Testament?"

"Sure," she replied.

I quickly fired, "Why?"

"For historical purposes, if nothing else," she offered.

"Exactly. Then if there are different writers, possibly copying from one another, wouldn't you expect each one to present a genealogy?"

"More than likely."

"But there are only two genealogies."

Michelle questioned, "Why then would your one writer have two genealogies? Why not just one?"

"Each of the two genealogies had a different purpose," I stated softly.

The differences between the genealogies in Matthew and Luke are revealing. Matthew's genealogy of Jesus only goes back to Abraham, and reads as a political statement linking Jesus to the power lines of Israel. Furthermore, Matthew puts Jesus' genealogy at the beginning of his writings--where one might expect it. Isn't it very, very convenient that we have a genealogy of Jesus right in the initial pages of the New Testament?

Luke draws Jesus' genealogy all the way back to Adam. In Luke, it was necessary to give connections from Jesus to Adam to show a clear connection of Jesus to God, for those who might not believe that Jesus was divine. Always keep in mind it is in Luke, where Jesus is portrayed as a savior, we have many important prophecies. So it is important to make the link between Jesus and God; otherwise, people might doubt the prophecies.

If you think I am reading too much into this, ask where in Luke is the genealogy that links Jesus to Adam? Not in the beginning like Matthew's. The genealogy in Luke serves a different function. Luke's genealogy is right after the baptism of Jesus by John the Baptist.

Is there only one writer? Does this writer use two different genealogies to establish different qualities of Jesus' life? Only Matthew and Luke include genealogies in their writings. Mark and John write nothing of Jesus' lineage. As important as it is to make sure the stories and life of Jesus are seen as authentic, why don't Mark and John include genealogies in their accounts? If the Gospels were really written in different times and places, it might be expected, at least I'd expect, to have a genealogy in the beginning of another one of the Gospels. If there was only one writer, then there was no need to include a genealogy in all four. He himself knew they were included in the other books.

In John there is no genealogy. Nor is there a 40-day fast, or temptations by the devil. My one writer has provided sufficient backgrounds in the first three books. In John, he is going to focus on the spiritual aspects of Jesus as the eternal word. After John, Jesus is no longer seen as a man in the Bible. Rather, Jesus departs earth, requiring the necessity for him to be portrayed as more divinely spiritual than in the first three books.

If the four Gospels were written in different times and places, then it should not matter which of the four books appears first. What if the Bible opened with Luke?

Luke 1:

1   Now that many have put their hands to the composition of the events that have taken place among us,
2   relayed to us by the first eyewitnesses and ministers of the Word,
3   it seems fitting for me also to write since I investigated everything from the beginning, most excellent Theophilus.

Luke obtained his accounts from "eyewitnesses." Thus, it would be ridiculous to begin the New Testament with a second hand account. I think Luke's letter opening is a device to make us believe that there were four writers. Otherwise why not start Matthew using a letter explaining why the Gospel is being written? But the one writer can't do this. He needs to begin the New Testament with a genealogy. The placement of a letter in the beginning works best in Luke.

Why did the person writing Luke and using the first person "I" never identify himself? Maybe he died before it was done. Certainly, in terms of the synoptic Gospels, it would lend a bit more credence of different authors to have an "I" in at least one book, and the placement in the last synoptic is good. It is where, if you were reading from beginning to end, one could use a bit of reinforcement of validity.

What if we put John first? We would go from Jesus' last words being whispered in the beginning to being screamed at the end. It would not work as a literary device of transition to Acts. The order of the Gospels functions to give us the best possible flow and characterization of Jesus.

FAMED LINES

To understand how our perceptions of the Bible, and images of Jesus, are skewed, I developed the idea of **famed lines** and **fragmented remembrances**. If I ask people what Jesus' last words were, most say, "My God, my God, why hast thou forsaken me?" We know those words come from Matthew and Mark. Why are those words chosen to represent Jesus' last words?

A more accurate answer regarding Jesus' last words is, "We really don't know what Jesus' last words were since there are three different and conflicting accounts."

Imagine, aliens land here tomorrow, and they pick you, the reader, to represent your culture to their planet. The aliens want a verbal image of Jesus. What will you pick for his last words? Some people might say, "Well, aliens, you have to understand that there are three different accounts." And the aliens reply, "We understand that very well, but our civilization cannot permit them all. We chose you to pick Jesus' last statement that we will present to our planet. Which of the different accounts do you prefer?"

Again the matter of truth rears its ugly head, or its beautiful head, depending on one's perspective. We as a civilization seem to overlook some profound contradictions in the New Testament, particularly the last words of Jesus. Why? What is the truth in the New Testament? I reason that we have overlooked or ignored the details of contradictions because the main message of the New Testament is Jesus' model of salvation. If one lives according to his model, one achieves everlasting life. His last words have nothing to do with his model of a moral life. At the time the New Testament was written, Christians were greatly anguished over having their savior/leader taken from them. Thus, different, but contradictory, versions of Jesus' last moments address all those anguishes.

But for the matter of ultimate truth, we cannot have it two or three ways. I should think that if there were anything definite about Jesus that Matthew and John would have known when they were penning their supposed Gospels, it would be Jesus' last words. There aren't different accounts of his birth, and yet, the Apostles didn't even know about Jesus at that time.

My one writer didn't sign different names to the books. All the books are anonymous. He had to have four different images so Jesus can be seen as a changing individual. If four individuals were writing at different times and places, it would be miraculous to have four different images accomplishing everything needed for a changing portrayal of Jesus.

If there were four different writers from different times and places, I would expect maybe two of the images to be quite similar. As it is, the Gospels are just too perfect in terms of changing characterizations to have happened randomly from the pens of four different scribes. Some people say the perfect changing characterizations are divinely inspired. That would be an odd divinity that created so many contradictions. I maintain the blatant factual differences exist to create the balanced/evolving characterizations of Jesus.

But wait! If God comes down here tomorrow and says, "Stocker, all four books were written by different scribes in different places," I'll accept it. My ego is in no way tied to the idea of how many writers are involved in the New Testament. My intent is to see Jesus the man. However, if God does come down here tomorrow, I'll ask, "Please, God, tell me which of the versions of Jesus' last moments and words are true?"

As I was struggling to understand who Jesus was, the word "portrayal" was key to me one day as I rummaged the library shelves for books of biblical commentary. One that caught my eye was Henry Coffin's *The Portraits of Jesus Christ in the New Testament*.

Coffin points out that much of what people remember about the Bible comes from Matthew. Coffin notes Matthew is the most important of all the portraits of Christ because it tells us more about him than we find in any other book, and being first in the New Testament, it is the section most often read. It is Matthew's version of the Lord's Prayer and his arrangement of the Beatitudes which are memorized and used in churches.

In **Matthew**, Jesus is linked to the Old Testament. There are at least sixty obvious examples with most of them coming from Isaiah and Psalms. But the entire Old Testament is represented. Time and again there are such expressions, "Now all this is come to pass...." In Matthew, Jesus is a revolutionary teacher out to change the entire world. Many times Jesus refers to what the "ancients" told or said, only to amend their words.

Matthew 5:

21   "You have heard how men of ancient times were told, 'Do not murder,'
      and 'Whoever murders is liable before the court.'
22   "But I say anyone who is angry with his brother without cause is
      liable before the court, and whoever speaks abusively of his brother is
      liable before the Sanhedrin. And whoever says 'You fool!' is liable to
      the fires of hell."

In Matthew, Jesus is the great new teacher who is juxtaposed to the
world. It is he who wants to find and save the lost sheep of Israel. It is he,
who, for the first time in the history of the world, will give us the truth.

Matthew 13:

34   Jesus said all of this to the crowds in parables and he only spoke in
      parables.
35   So that the saying of the prophet was fulfilled, "I will open my mouth
      in parables, and I will express what has been hidden since the creation
      of the world."

And of course, Jesus' big break from tradition was the spreading of
peace and not war.

Matthew 5:

43   "You have heard that it was said, 'Love your neighbor and hate your
      enemy.'
44   "But I say to you, Love your enemy and pray for your persecutors."

In **Mark**, there is a realistic portrait of a lively man named Jesus.
Jesus is portrayed more as a man of action, as Mark records his interviews
and describes his gestures. In Mark, Jesus' audience reacts to him as a man.
Their reactions range from amazement to fear, from puzzlement to bitter
hostility. Mark gives a greater depth to Jesus' miracles than the other Gospels.
    Luke gives an historical dimension to Jesus. He gives dates by tying
into other historical figures. "And it came to pass in those days, that there
went out a decree from Caesar Augustus, that all the world should be taxed."
(2:1)
    Also in Luke, there is an emphasis on doctrine. Salvation is in the
forefront of Luke's Jesus. "...the Son of Man came to seek and to save that
which was lost." (19:10)
    Luke dwells on Jesus' tenderness, and this is amplified by the fact

this Gospel is the most literary of the four, according to many scholars. Four poems in Luke have come down as modern day hymns.

Along with the doctrine in Luke comes emphasis on the Holy Spirit. There are more references to the Holy Spirit in Luke than in Matthew and Mark combined. In Luke, Jesus is characterized as the savior. The Holy Spirit emphasis ties into the prophecies which are not only abundant in Luke, but also in Acts, which biblical scholars believe Luke also might have written. By including Acts, my writer is the author of five books. It only makes sense that my one writer wanted to have commentary after Jesus' death.

In **John**, Jesus becomes the light and life of the soul. Jesus says,

I am the bread of life. (6:35)
I am the light of the world. (8:12, 9:5)
I am the good shepherd. (10:11, 10:14)
I am the resurrection, and the life. (11:25)
I am the way, the truth, and the life. (14:6)
I am the true vine. (15:1)

In John, the Gospels are ending so the relation of Jesus to the people who will carry on his works is emphasized. Readers are pulled back to this world as it were. There are 27 interviews by different individuals to accomplish this portrait. John gives the long details of Jesus' trial by Pilate which extends from John 18:28 to 19:22.

Rethinking the portraits of Jesus, I was certain the Gospels were written by one person. The one person showed us phases of Jesus' life: a teacher/revolutionary in Matthew, a man of action in Mark, a savior in Luke, and the eternal word in John.

THE TRIAL

What to look at next to see if my theory holds up? I assumed there would be some major differences of the trial scene in the Gospels.

Matthew 27:

11   Jesus stood before the governor and was questioned, "Are you the king of the Jews?" Jesus replied, "As you say."

There is no more dialogue as Jesus remained silent. Later, Pilate washes his hands of the deed of having Jesus crucified. (MT 27:24)

Mark 15, as is often the case, is a repeat of Matthew.

Luke 23:

2   And they started to accuse him, "We found this man perverting our
        nation and forbidding them to pay taxes to Caesar, claiming that he
        himself is Messiah, a king."
3   And Pilate asked him, "Are you the king of the Jews? He answered
        him, "You say so."

Pilate then sent Jesus to Herod.

8   Herod was very pleased to see Jesus, for he had wanted for a long time
        to see him because he had heard about Jesus, and Herod hoped to see
        Jesus perform some miracles.
9   But though he questioned him at length, Jesus never answered him.

"At length?" I really doubt this. I imagine Herod was quite adept
at interviewing and after three or four unanswered questions, consuming
one minute, two minutes at best, Herod would have sent Jesus back
to Pilate.
Does John's Jesus remain silent during the trial? Of course not;
he has to become the eternal word.
Peter has just denied Jesus the third time, and Jesus is led from
Caiaphas to the hall of judgment. Pilate is notified that Jesus has been brought
to trial.

John 18:

33   Then Pilate entered into the judgment hall again, and called Jesus,
        and asked him, "Are you king of the Jews?"
34   Jesus answered, "Are you saying this about me, or are others saying
        it?"
35   Pilate answered, "Am I a Jew? It is your nation and your chief priests
        who delivered you to me. Tell me, what have you done?"
36   Jesus answered, "My kingdom is not of this world. If my kingdom
        were of this world, then would my servants fight that I should not be
        delivered to the Jews. My kingdom is not of this world."
37   Pilate again questioned, "Are you a king?" Jesus answered, "You say
        I am a king. To this end was I born, and for this cause came I into the
        world, that I should bear witness unto the truth. Every one that is of
        the truth hears my voice."
38   Pilate remarked to him, "What is truth?"

Pilate's question sums up my observations regarding the penning of the Gospels, and my concerns about the relationship between materialism and spirituality--what is truth?

In Jesus' time, it was custom in the nation of Israel to release one prisoner at Passover. Pilate tried to have the crowd choose Jesus for release, but they chose Barabbas, a man imprisoned for robbery, murder, and sedition. Pilate pleaded with the crowd, stating Jesus had committed no crime. Finally Pilate made a last plea with Jesus to answer his question of who he was. Pilate implored Jesus to understand that he, Pilate, had the power to have him crucified.

John 19:

11   Jesus answered, "You could have no power at all against me, except if it were given to you from above; therefore he that delivered me to you has the greater sin."

Pilate was dejected. He did not want to crucify Jesus, and he returned to the crowd. Then the critical words were spoken from the crowd.

12   "...If you let this man go, you are not Caesar's friend. Whosoever makes himself a king speaks against Caesar."
13   When Pilate heard those words, he brought Jesus forth, and sat down in the judgment seat in a place that is called Gabba-tha--the Pavement.
14   And it was the preparation of the passover, and about the sixth hour. Pilate said to the Jews, "Behold your king!"
15   But they cried out, "Away with him, away with him, crucify him." Pilate questioned, "Shall I crucify your king?" The chief priests answered, "We have no king but Caesar."

If there were not one writer, then the trial scenes can be shuffled and there should be no difference in development. But if John were first, there would be a grandiose presentation by Jesus, only to get to the next version of the silent treatment. If this were the case, I hope most readers would say, "Hey, wait a minute, this order does not make sense."

However, if the silent treatment is first, we can then say, when we get to John, "I thought there would be more."

Thus in the end, we can make our own portrait of Jesus by taking those **famed lines** and **fragmented remembrances** that work for each of us. Some present-day Christian sects have done this. They focus on one or two famed lines to create their own interpretations of Christianity and then create a sect. Some individuals focus on speaking in tongues. "For he that speaketh in an unknown tongue speaketh not unto men, but unto God. For no man understandeth him; howbeit in the spirit he speaketh mysteries." (1 Corinthians 14:2)

Here is where I invoke my "Red Letter Law." A red letter edition of the Bible has the words of Jesus in red. I was raised with a red letter edition of the Bible. My red letter edition, given to me by my parents, is still at my mother's home in Pensacola, Florida. I tend to shy away from verses in the Bible that are not in red. My concerns are with what Jesus said, and he said nothing of unknown tongues.

Serpent handlers believe that by handling serpents and not getting bitten they have defeated Satan. The basis for this is an appended segment of Mark. In Revelation, Satan is referred to as "the original serpent." "And the great dragon, the original serpent of old, also called the Devil and Satan, the deceiver of all humans, was forced out and hurled to the earth, and his angels were flung out along with him." (Revelation 12:9)

MY SCIENCE

After I got to this stage in my analysis, I had reaped my share of criticism for even thinking one person wrote the four Gospels. I asked myself: If I am right, how would my writer end each of the four books? The same? Why should he? He wants to develop four distinct phases of Jesus' existence. He wouldn't want to end all the books the same. Maybe better said, he can't end them the same.

What would I expect at the end of each Gospel? From John I'd expect some type of grand farewell. It is the last of the four Gospels. **John's last words** are: "And there are also many other things which Jesus did, that which, if they should be written every one, I suppose that even the world itself could not contain the books that should be written. Amen." Well, in John, Jesus is characterized as the eternal word, thus the world couldn't hold everything about him.

Just what I wanted from John, a big *adios*. I won't get this from the other three. Which last words to look at next? Matthew? Being in the lead position, I would expect Matthew's last words of Jesus to contain a prediction or a direction since in Matthew he is portrayed as the teacher/revolutionary.

Matthew's last words are, 28:

18   And Jesus came and spoke to them, saying, "All power is given unto me in heaven and in earth.

19   "Go and teach all nations, baptizing them in the name of the Father, and of the Son, and of the Holy Ghost.

20   "Teaching them to observe all things whatsoever I have commanded
        you. And, remember, I am with you always, even unto the end of the
        world. Amen."

So, there are the initial instructions to go out and teach and a final
grand good-bye. What would I expect in between from Mark or Luke? One
of the two will have action.

Mark's last words are: "And they went forth, and preached
everywhere, the Lord working with them, and confirming the word with
signs of following. Amen." This fits perfectly for a characterization of a
man of action.

Now my work is cut out for me. What is Luke going to say?
There is instruction, action, and a farewell. What else is needed? What
is Christianity all about?

Luke's last words are, 24:

52   And they worshipped him, and returned to Jerusalem with great joy.
53   And were continually in the temple, praising and blessing God. Amen.

Christianity is about worship. The end of Luke is definitely one of the
savior.

Again, I thought about reordering the Gospels. I flip-flopped John
and Matthew. John's big good-bye wouldn't work well in the first book.
Also, in John there is no 40-day fast or temptations of Jesus by Satan. So,
there would be considerable confusion by placing John first; and then the
first three books would be read finally to be presented with Matthew's
opening genealogy connecting Jesus to the lineages of the Old Testament.
Reordering Matthew, Mark, Luke, and John doesn't give the orderly flow of
the developing character of Jesus that currently exists.

The flow of Jesus' representation is what leads me to believe there is
one writer. It's clever, and it presents a portrait of who Jesus was. That's the
one writer's job. In writing schools they say, "Tell them what you are going
to tell them, tell them, then tell them what you told them." Matthew, Mark,
Luke, and John are a superb example of this technique.

SOME DOUBTS

Additional evidence for my one-writer theory involves the structure
of the Gospels. Matthew, Mark, and Luke all have the crucifixion in the next
to the last chapter. The last chapter in each is Jesus appearing in a spirit

form to the disciples.

Doesn't it make sense that John is going to add one more chapter between the crucifixion scene and the last chapter? Remember, this is the last portrait of Jesus in the history of the world. Struggling to understand the flow of the Gospels, I tried to imagine what accounts would be placed between the crucifixion and the last chapter of John. Probably there would be a grand finale, one last push for faith.

One of the most well known verses to many, but somewhat perplexing to me, is Mary Magdalene going to Jesus' tomb after the crucifixion. She finds the tomb open. Mary is stunned.

John 20:

2   She runs to Simon Peter, and to the other disciple that Jesus had affection for, and said, "They have taken the Lord out of the tomb, and we know not where they have laid him."
3   Peter, the other disciple, went to the tomb.
4   They ran together; and the other disciple outran Peter, and came first to the tomb.

Is there some significance that Peter lost the race?

11   But Mary stood outside at the tomb weeping. As she wept, she stooped down and looked into the tomb.
12   She saw two angels in white sitting, the one at the head, and the other at the feet, where the body of Jesus had lain.
13   And they say unto her, "Woman, why do you weep?" She said unto them, "Because they have taken away my Lord, and I know not where they have laid him."
14   And after she spoke, she turned, and saw Jesus standing, and knew not that it was Jesus.

She sees Jesus, but doesn't recognize him? Had he changed forms?

15   Jesus said, "Woman, why do you weep? Whom do you seek?" She, supposing him to be the gardener, said unto him, "Sir, if thou have borne him hence, tell me where thou hast laid him, and I will take him away."

I don't understand. Why do the angels ask Mary why she's crying? I'm from the background that angels know everything. An angel doesn't need to ask Mary anything, unless the angel wants to hear her response. Of course, it could be argued that religious teachers ask questions to teach. But why doesn't Jesus recognize her? If he recognized her, wouldn't he have said, "Mary Magdalene, why are you crying?" Is there supposed to be some symbolism in Jesus looking like the gardener? What in the world was he dressed like? I want to understand. But there is no information to get answers. Then,

16   Jesus said, "Mary." And she turned herself, and said, "Rabboni," which means Teacher.
17   Jesus said, "Stop clinging to me; for I am not yet ascended to my Father. But go to my brethren, and say unto them, I ascend unto my Father, and your Father; and to my God, and your God."

Wow! Mary Magdalene got to see Jesus before God saw Jesus. But, she does what she is told and later that day Jesus appears to the disciples. But guess who isn't there? Didymus wasn't there. Didymus also had another name, Thomas.

25   The other disciples told Thomas, "We have seen the Lord." But he replied, "Unless I see in his hands the holes from the nails, and put my finger in the those holes, and thrust my hand in his side, I will not believe."
26   And after eight days again his disciples were within, and Thomas was with them. Then came Jesus, although the doors were locked, and stood in their midst, and said, "Peace be unto you."
27   Then saith he to Thomas, "Reach hither thy finger, and behold my hands, and reach hither thy hand, and thrust it into my side. Be not faithless, but believing."
28   And Thomas answered and said unto him, "My Lord and my God."
29   Jesus said, "Thomas, because thou has seen me, thou hast believed. Blessed are they that have not seen, and yet have believed."

Amen to this idea.

The ol' Doubting Thomas story. Only John has a chapter between the crucifixion and the last chapter. John had to get a little more in just before we leave the Gospels. The absence of Doubting Thomas in Matthew is suspicious. Matthew was with John and Thomas when Jesus returned, and Thomas was doubting him. Why would Matthew leave out this important event? Because the one writer needed the story in John. He needed it at a place where he was going to conclude the only passages we have on the life of Jesus, and in conclusion Jesus could say to Thomas, "Blessed are those who have not seen and yet believe."

I too am a Doubting Thomas. I doubt that Matthew, Mark, Luke, and John were all written by different people.

IS IT DOABLE?

In the beginning, some of my critics of the one-writer theory declare in a raised voice, "Come on, Stocker, you know how hard it would be to write and remember and keep all the stuff straight for four different books like that?" Nonsense. My one writer could have each completed scroll lying there before him as he worked on the next one. It would be no different than the parallel versions of the New Testament which abound bookstores today.

Besides, there are many writers like Truman Capote or Mickey Spillane, just to name two, who carried entire books in their heads word for word. They kept the characters and dialogue and setting cleanly separated. Then comes another set of critics. "Stocker, don't you think it would have been much more effective for your hypothetical writer to have just laid it out without repetition? Then we wouldn't have the contradictions which don't really add anything to our understanding."

I answer yes to the question and agree with the statement. But then you'd have everything about Jesus resting on the shoulders of one person.Then as now, there's safety in numbers.

Yet there is another set of critics, "Why didn't your one writer write all four books without the contradictions and give them different author's names? Then 2000 years later it would have been much easier on all of us."

Contradictions often lead us to believe there is more than one person writing. Without the contradictions, one writer may be suspect of writing all the Gospels.

I can only say that if I'm correct, my one writer accomplished the job of fooling an awful lot of people for a very long time. But he only fooled them in regards to the number of authors writing the four Gospels. He didn't fool them in regards to the existence of Jesus. Again, I am not questioning whether Jesus lived or not. I am trying to understand *who* Jesus was. After reading all the contradictions, I'm left to wonder who wrote what and why. Because of the contradictions, not only am I left to wonder who wrote what and why, I have difficulty creating an image of Jesus. Yet there is a common thread in the Gospels--Jesus is against the material world.

A WRONG MOVE?

Sometime in May of 1994, I began to put my ideas on the authorship of the Gospels in written form. By June, I had the outline of a book, this book. It became a compulsion. Was deciding to write the book a wrong move? Further, I had just completed an article for the *Hawaii Investor* on self-publishing, and I began formulating ideas for self-publishing *Vinegar on the Cross*. Suddenly, my 40-day fast had an attachment to the material world. Was the idea of writing this book a wrong move?

5

ALL IN A DAY'S WORK

Jesus had to endure life on earth as a mortal man. He worked, he ate, he slept, and he died. For each of these activities in Jesus' life, I wanted more information, but I am left to make certain suppositions.

One activity we all relate to is work. How many times have we said, "I don't want to work today," and wished we could just roll over in our warm bed and sleep? Did Jesus ever wish the same? I would guess that on an occasion or two he would have said something along those lines.

What was Jesus' occupation? If you ask ten people raised as Christians, a couple will respond he was a revolutionary. You might be amazed at how many say, "I don't know." And there will be about six who say he was a carpenter. If he were a carpenter, it was early in his life. There is only one reference to Jesus as a carpenter. It comes in the Gospel characterizing Jesus as an active man.

Mark 6:

2   On the sabbath he began to teach in the synagogue. Many were amazed at his words. They questioned, "Where did he get all this? What wisdom has been given him and why do miracles happen by his hands?

3   "Is he not the carpenter, the son of Mary and the brother of James and Joseph and Jude and Simon? And do not his sisters live here with us?" They took offense on his account.

Since Luke is to dwell on Jesus as the savior, a reference to carpentry isn't necessary, despite the fact that Luke and Matthew are supposedly copying from Mark. I say one writer is eliminating needless redundancies since in the entire spectrum of religion, Jesus' early occupation is not really important. Nevertheless, I would like to know.

Regardless of what occupation he held in his early life, after his 40-day fast, his life and occupation changed. What was his occupation after his 40-day fast? Let's approach the matter of Jesus' work from a different direction. During his time, how would one attract a large crowd?

Then as now, the propagating of a new philosophy is difficult business. Jesus had a new philosophy, but I can't imagine a group of people from a town quickly passing the word, "Hey, there's this guy with really fresh ideas who is going to talk tonight. You want to go and hear him?" Getting the attention of people is and was difficult--especially before the time of newspapers, radio, TV, and computers.

Few people would have just gone to hear Jesus talk. They went to get healed by him. Jesus was a curer. He healed the sick, and his preaching was tied to his healing. "And Jesus went about Galilee, teaching in their synagogues, and preaching the gospel of the kingdom, and healing all manner of sickness and all manner of disease among the people." (MT 4:23)

The matter of healing is well laid out in Matthew.

Matthew 10:

1   Calling his twelve disciples to him, he gave them power over depraved spirits to cast them out, and to heal every disease and every malady.
2   Now these are the names of the twelve Apostles: Simon, called Peter, and his brother Andrew; James, the son of Zebedee, and his brother John;
3   Philip and Bartholomew; Thomas and Matthew, the tax collector; James, the son of Alphaeus, and Thaddaeus;
4   Simon the Zealot, and Judas Iscariot, who also betrayed him.

Matthew, the supposed author of Matthew, listed himself as eighth. I find this strange if Matthew was supposedly writing Matthew. However, it is possible the listing has something to do with the order in which the disciples were chosen. But it is significant that he is provided additional non-kin identification, and such was also provided for Simon who was a Zealot. Both tax collectors and Zealots were considered unsavory people and it is probably for this reason that the information is given.

5   These twelve Jesus sent out with the charge, "Do not go to the Gentiles nor enter a Samaritan city.
6   "Rather go to the lost sheep of the house of Israel.
7   "And as you go, preach that the kingdom of heaven is at hand."

It would be nice if there were more details in the Gospels. Here, Jesus could have said, "Don't enter a Samaritan city because ..." and we would know more about his times and his thinking.

And what exactly is a lost sheep of Israel? Jesus focused much of his energy on the poor. Are all poor lost sheep of Israel? When he says the poor are evangelized, he doesn't say all the Semitic poor. (MT 11:5) Are some of the poor Gentiles? And is anyone ever "converted" without being healed?

8   "Heal the sick; raise the dead; cleanse the lepers; expel the demons. Freely have you received; freely give."

I find it interesting that cleansing lepers is placed after raising the dead. This might be a statement about the hideous position of lepers in Jesus' society.

9   "Provide neither gold, nor silver, nor copper to put in your belts.
10   "Nor a bag for the journey; neither two coats, nor sandals, nor staff. For the worker deserves his food."

How often did any disciple have to heal to obtain a week's worth of food and lodging? Presumably, a coat or a pair of sandals might be thrown in every now and then. Were the disciples sometimes given gold or silver for their healing?

Nevertheless, from these verses, we might derive a better understanding of Jesus' rejection of the material world. He obviously wasn't against eating, drinking wine, wearing clothes, or lodging. But he was against an accumulation of material goods.

How many people would have come to listen to Jesus if he only preached and did not heal? I think very few. Knowing that, I wonder what Jesus felt. What thoughts went through his mind each day when he looked at the world?

For the most part, he healed the sick by touch.

Mark 7:

32   They brought a deaf and dumb person to Jesus, and begged him to put his hands upon him.
33   Jesus took the man away from the crowd, put his fingers into his ears, and he spit and touched his tongue.
34   Looking up to heaven, Jesus sighed and said, *Ephphatha* which means, "Be open."
35   The man could hear and speak plainly.

Mark 6:56,

> And whithersoever he entered, into villages, or cities, or country, they laid the sick in the streets, and besought him that they might touch if it were but the border of his garment, and as many as touched him were made whole.

Jesus did not always have to touch in order to heal. In Mark 7, a woman asked Jesus to heal her daughter who was at home, and it was done. There is a different case of healing a non-present person in John 4:49-54.

There had to be much contentment in Jesus' heart to make a sick person well. But at the same time, he knew there was a world of sadness around him because of illnesses. So, there must have been times when there was consternation in his heart. Maybe the mix of the two emotions, contentment and consternation, caused Jesus to feel complacent some of the time. Or did these emotions confuse and frustrate him?

DEMONOLOGY

The matter of Jesus' curing brought me to the state of medical theory of that time. Why and how was he able to heal?

Jesus adopted the Jewish belief in the nature and activities of evil spirits. Throughout the Bible, demonic spirits are believed to be the sources of physical and psychological infirmities. We get to curing immediately in Mark.

Mark 1:

27 And they were all amazed, insomuch that they questioned among themselves, saying, "What thing is this? What new doctrine is this? With authority commandeth he even the unclean spirits, and they do obey him."

28 And immediately his fame spread abroad throughout all the region about Galilee.

29 And forthwith, when they came out of the synagogue, they entered into the house of Simon and Andrew, with James and John.

30 But Simon's wife's mother lay sick of a fever, and at once they told Jesus.

31 And he came and took her by the hand and lifted her up; and immediately the fever left her, and she ministered unto them.

32 And at evening, when the sun did set, they brought unto him all that were diseased, and them that were possessed with devils.

33 And all the city was gathered together at the door.

34   He healed many sick of divers disease, and cast out many devils; and suffered not the devils to speak, because they knew him.

Then we are told Jesus cured people by casting out demons.

> And he was casting out a devil, and it was dumb. And it came to pass, when the devil was gone out, the dumb spake; and the people wondered. (Luke 11:14)

Even today there are people who are pronounced medically incurable of something, but occasionally a person finds his way to some church and then he becomes well. I have witnessed this on more than one occasion in Korea where there are many religions that combine Buddhism, Christianity, and Animism. Did these sick people become well because of some spiritual blessing, or was it simply the problematic healing process of the body? The answer that the healed person gives is spiritual blessing. The answer of modern science is spontaneous resolution; that is, the body "simply" healed itself at that time through a matter of probability.

Of course in Jesus' cases, immediate results are viewed as spiritual blessings. If the demons were gone when Jesus healed, what was left? In Jesus' own words, "...if I cast out devils by the Spirit of God, then the kingdom of God is come unto you." (MT 12:28) The variation of Jesus' words in Luke 11:20 are, "But if I with the finger of God cast out devils, no doubt the kingdom of God is come upon you." Thus there is a supposed conclusion that through physical healing by Jesus there is spiritual growth. Said another way, the reason that individuals apparently are not healthy is because devils or demons haunt them, and by expelling the demons, an individual can then be well and holy.

One evening as I sat by the stream behind my Hawaii home, listening to the cascade of the small rapids, I wondered what the demons Jesus dealt with were like. It would be difficult to understand the dynamics of Jesus' healing without knowing the perceived source of the disease.

Consider lines in Matthew 12:28 and in Luke 11:14 where "...he was casting out a devil...." It doesn't say "the" devil, but a devil. The implication is that like angels, there were legions of devils. If there are devils, what are their physical manifestations? Angels have wings to move about. Do demons? Two demons characterized in the Bible are Behemoth and Leviathan.

Behemoth

One demon is called Behemoth. This guy could scare the hell out of some dinosaurs in *Jurassic Park*. This Old Testament entity is described in Job.

Job 40:

15   Behold now Behemoth, which I made with thee. He eats grass like an ox.
16   His strength is in his loins, and his force is in the navel of his belly.
17   He moves his tail like a cedar, and the sinews of his stones are wrapped together.
18   His bones are like iron bars.
19   He is the chief of the ways of God. He that made him can make his sword to approach unto him.

How to interpret this? In Hebrew tradition, everything under the sun was made by God including Behemoth. So, God can provide the device to destroy that which he has made. But why is this right in the middle of defining Behemoth? I would have expected it after the description.

20   Surely the mountains bring him forth food, where all the beasts of the field play.

Now, I have an idea as to where the saying comes from, "This leaves a lot to the imagination." Does this mean he eats the beasts of the field? Or does he eat only the vegetation where the beasts of the field play?

21   He lies under shady trees, among the reeds and fens.
22   The shady trees cover him with their shadow; the willows of the brook surround him about.
23   He drinks up rivers, and hasteth not; he trusteth that he can draw up Jordan into his mouth.
24   He taketh it with his eyes. His nose pierceth through snares.

Leviathan

This demon follows Behemoth in Job 41:

1   Can you draw out Leviathan with an hook? Or his tongue with a cord which thou lettest down?

2   Can you put a hook into his nose? Or bore his jaw through with a thorn?

3   If you can, will he make supplications of you? Will he speak soft words to you?

4   Will he make a covenant with you? Will you take him for a servant forever?

5   Will you play with him like you play with a bird? Or will you bind him for your maidens?

6   Shall the companions make a banquet of him? Shall they part him among the merchants?

7   Can you fill his skin with barbed irons? Or his head with fish spears?

8   Lay your hand upon him, remember the battle, do no more.

9   Behold, the hope of him is in vain; shall not one be cast down even at the sight of him?

10   None is so fierce that dare stir him up. Who then is able to stand before him?

11   Who hath prevented me, that I should repay him? Whatsoever is under the whole heaven is mine.

12   I will not conceal his parts, nor his power, nor his comely proportions.

13   Who can discover the face of his garment? Or who can come to him with his double bridle?

14   Who can open the doors of his face? His teeth are terrible round about.

15   His scales are his pride, shut up together as with a close seal.

16   One scale is so near to another, that no air can come between them.

17   His scales are joined one to another, they stick together, that they cannot be sundered.

18   By his nestings a light doth shine, and his eyes are like the eyelids of the morning.

What are eyelids of the morning? Is it a reference to the eyes of the crocodile? Or partly closed eyes like some people have first thing in the morning?

19   Out of his mouth go burning lamps, and sparks of fire leap out.

20   Out of his nostrils goeth smoke, as out of a seething pot or caldron.

21   His breath kindleth coals, and a flame goeth out of his mouth.

22   In his neck remaineth strength, and sorrow is turned into joy before him.

23   The flakes of his flesh are joined together. They are firm in themselves; they cannot be moved.

24   His heart is as firm as a stone; yea, as hard as a piece of the nether millstone.

25   When he raiseth up himself, the mighty are afraid. By reason of breakings they purify themselves.

26   No sword can wound him; no arrow or spear or lance can harm him.

27   He treats iron like straw and brass like rotten wood.

28   Arrows cannot make him flee, and he turns sling stones into rubble.

29   He considers darts stubble, and he laughs at the shaking spear.

30   Sharp stones are under him; he spreadeth sharp pointed things upon the mire.

31   He makes the deep to boil like a pot; he makes the sea like a pot of ointment.

32   He makes a path to shine after him; one would think the deep to be a hoary.

33   Upon earth there is not his like, who is made without fear.

34   He beholdeth all high things; he is a king over all the children of pride.

These descriptions gave me an idea what Jesus was up against when he was curing. He had to contend with the Leviathans and the Behemoths. But these are just two examples of demons Jesus inherited. Until Jesus' time, the constitution of demons was largely acquired from Jewish apocalyptic literature of the second and first centuries before Jesus. There were many evil spirits and many devils. Demons are a complex subject extending back a millennium before Jesus. Biblical scholars tell us the demons Jesus dealt with are an end result of a mix of many traditions: Judaism, Manichaeism, Greco-Roman, etc.

Where do the demons come from and how do they have the power to inhabit earth and cause illnesses? There are many versions. In one version of demonic origins, some angels cohabited with the irresistible daughters of men, and this resulted in a race of giants. The giants in turn gave birth to evil spirits, and thus there were many devils or fallen angels as the case may be.

A unique element was added to demonology during the time of Jesus. There were many devils for centuries, and then through the simple process of evolution, it became necessary to provide them with a single spokesman. Thus, Satan came into the picture. Some information is presented in Luke.

Luke 11:

15   Some said Christ casts out devils through the power given to him by
        Beelzebub, the chief of the devils.
16   And others, tempting him, sought of him a sign from heaven.
17   Christ, knowing their thoughts, said unto them, "Every kingdom
        divided against itself is brought to desolation; and a house divided
        against a house falleth.
18   "If Satan is divided against himself, how shall his kingdom stand?
        Because ye say that I cast out devils through Beelzebub.
19   "And if I by Beelzebub cast out devils, by whom do your sons cast
        them out? Your own sons prove you wrong!
20   "No, it is by the power of God that I expel demons, and this proves
        that the kingdom of God is already upon you."

In time, Satan was not confined to land like Behemoth or Leviathan.
He moved through air, on earth, and in the underworld.

> Wherein in time past ye walked according to the course of
> this world, according to the prince of power of the air, the
> spirit that now worketh in the children of disobedience.
> (Ephesians 2:2)

Satan had these powers to confront Jesus, because Satan was the
Antichrist. It is, according to most Christians, the Antichrist who is expected
to precede the next coming of Jesus at the end of the world. However, this
belief is only reached through a bit of contorted reasoning.

The term Antichrist is not used in Revelation. It is found only in the
First and Second Letters of John. John uses the term to refer to anyone who
denies the divinity of Jesus Christ. Most Christians believe the "Antichrist"
will precede the second coming of Jesus based primarily upon Paul's
discussion in II Thessalonians 2:1-12 of the coming of the "man of
lawlessness" or the "son of perdition" who "proclaims himself to be God"
which takes place before the next coming of Jesus.

Finally, in the evolution of monster imagery, I arrived at Revelation.
There the entire issue of good versus evil is encapsulated in a monumental
battle.

Revelation 13:

1   And I stood upon the sand of the sea, and saw a beast rise up out of
        the sea, having seven heads and ten horns, and upon his horns ten
        crowns, and upon his heads the name of blasphemy.

2　　And the beast which I saw was like unto a leopard, and his feet were as the feet of a bear, and his mouth as the mouth of a lion. And the dragon gave him his power, and his seat, and great authority.

3　　And I saw one of his heads as it were wounded; and his deadly wound healed before my eyes. And all the world wondered after the beast.

5　　And there was given unto him a mouth speaking great things and blasphemies; and power was given unto him to continue forty and two months.

11　And I beheld another beast coming up out of the earth; and he had two horns like a lamb, and he spake as a dragon.

12　And he exerciseth all the power of the first beast before him and causeth the earth and them who dwell therein to worship the first beast, whose deadly wound was healed.

13　And he doeth great wonders, so that he maketh fire come down from heaven on the earth in the sight of men.

14　And deceiveth them that dwell on the earth by the means of those miracles which he had power to do in the sight of the beast; saying to them who dwell on the earth, that they should make an image to the beast, which had the wound by sword, and did live.

15　And he had power to give life unto the image of the beast, that the image of the beast should both speak, and cause that any as would not worship the image of the beast should be killed.

HOW MUCH POWER?

Removing bad spirits from people was a real task for Jesus. During Jesus' time, people believed demons populated the world and caused illnesses. Sometimes I try to put myself in his place as he was laboring to remove bad spirits. Imagine pulling something like a Behemoth from someone. That's energy consuming.

Mark 5:

27　When she heard about Jesus, she came behind him in the crowd and touched his robe.

30　Then and there Jesus, conscious that power had gone from him, turned around in the crowd and asked, "Who touched my clothes?"

He was conscious that power had gone from him. Thus I could assume his powers were limited. I have of course encountered opposition to the latter statement. Some say that because he was aware that power had left him does not mean that his powers were finite. In physics, the rule is half of infinity is infinity. Of course, I could also propose that the healing of one individual takes almost an infinite amount of power and that Jesus' powers were rechargeable. What did it take for Jesus to heal someone? Jesus never said; thus, I don't know.

Often people see Jesus as some type of constant. I suppose Jesus had a finite amount of energy. Otherwise, he would have held up his hand and said, "All the sick people, in the village yonder, are now well." He didn't do that as far as is known. (Isn't it interesting that you and I accept the idea that Jesus might hold up his hand to accomplish this? Why wouldn't he just say it? Or just think it?). Nor did he have the apparent power to say, "There will be no more infirmities on earth." His job as a curer was labor-intensive.

On the other hand, maybe he could have healed all the sick in the world, but didn't. I don't think this was the case. If Jesus could have done that, he might have. And for me, this is again proof that Jesus had finite energy. Having a finite amount of energy, Jesus had his ups and he had his downs.

John 5:

1   There was a festival of the Jews and Jesus went to Jerusalem.
2   At the sheepgate in Jerusalem, there is a pool designated in Hebrew as *Bethza'tha*, with five colonnades.
3   In these a multitude of the sick, blind, lame and paralyzed lay.
4   (verse not in the original Greek Bible)
5   But there was a certain man who had been sick for thirty-eight years.
6   Seeing this man lying down, and knowing he had been sick for a long time, Jesus said unto him, "Do you want to become healthy?"
7   The sick man answered, "I do not have a man to put me into the stirring pool. While I try, another person always steps in front of me."
8   Jesus said to him, "Get up, pick up your mat, and walk."
9   With that, the man immediately became well and picked up his mat and began to walk.

Within the boundaries of finite powers and healing, what happens to devils once they are expelled? Do they inhabit other individuals? Why don't they make the entire world sick? While investigating Jesus the man, I am left with many questions for which I have no answers.

Once, Jesus was confronted by two demoniacs in the Garadene country.

Matthew 8:

30   Now at some distance from them a large herd of swine was feeding.
31   The demons begged of Jesus, "If you expel us, send us into the herd of swine."

32   He said to them, "Go!" And they, coming out, entered into the swine and the whole herd rushed down the precipice into the sea and perished in the waters.

33   The herdsmen fled, went off to town, and reported the affair of the demoniacs.

34   Then the whole town came out to meet Jesus and asked him to leave their district.

This still doesn't tell me about what happens to demons once they are driven out of a human. Did the demons drown with the pigs? If this is the case, then I can assume that demons must have air to live. This passage leaves so much to be desired. Jesus just left how many herdsman without a means of making a living by destroying their herd? Wasn't there another way he could have destroyed the demons? Further, why did he follow the demons' wish of being put into the swine? Readers may think Jesus was obeying the demons. But the point of this passage is obviously to show how powerful demons are. They can make a herd of swine, the number of which isn't told, drown themselves like lemmings. The epidemiology of Jesus' time rests on demons. It would be 2000 more years before modern medicine would demonstrate that such maladies are not the result of demons.

HOW IS HEALING DONE?

The miracles of Jesus are the essence of Christianity. How can they be explained? Science has one explanation and religion another. For religion, miracles are proof of the supernatural.

I first approached the scientific aspect of healing miracles from the matter of probabilities and biology. I'm mystified by people, like my wife, who think that the recordings of Jesus healing people are not true. Unfortunately, these skeptics have never been to a pilgrimage center and watched people being healed. People go to a pilgrimage center hoping to be healed from some infirmity. A certain percentage are healed. For the pilgrimage centers I have visited, there are no concrete figures, since no one has kept records.

There are curing figures for Lourdes, France. This is the second largest pilgrimage center in the world with an annual visitation of 15,000,000 people. The last recorded miraculous cure was in 1982. This doesn't bespeak a credibility of miracle cures. However there are those who propose that Lourdes has now been commercialized to the point that the power has left that site.

I point out I am constantly concerned that what I see or am told could be fraudulent. I have been to twenty pilgrimage centers. But I have only been to one annual, five-day ritual festival at a pilgrimage center. The festival was in a small town in Veracruz, Mexico. It lasted for three days, and there was an air of awe. I did talk to people who had been healed in previous years. However their ailments were minor. I have never talked to a person who was blind and later was blessed with sight.

But regardless of the percentage, is the healing of pilgrims a miracle? There are two answers: one from the healed and one from the observer. Some observers will say the healing was probability. Probability of what? If those people stayed home, would they have been healed there? Maybe so. But I do know from talking to pilgrims that some are awed by the experience of the pilgrimage and awe translates into a profound change in consciousness. I think this change in consciousness opens them to the healing powers of the mind and body. I know that the times my body was sick and became well, my consciousness went through some substantial shifts.

Dan Wakefield's *Expect a Miracle* documents many cases of individuals being healed of incurable diseases presumably as a result of prayer either on the part of the sick or by friends and family members. The medical community refers to most of these cases as "spontaneous resolution." In other words, whatever caused a body to malfunction stopped.

This still does not really explain anything. My concern is that a change in our consciousness or subconsciousness is capable of creating change in body chemistry. I know when I suffer from stress I get eye-ticks or stomach aches, and on occasion I get tremendous burning sensations in my thighs. If I meditate, my stress is diminished.

Can spontaneous resolution be created by altering consciousness? In our society, once a person is informed he is going to die, the result is negative energy pouring out from the mind. This is just the opposite of what is needed for healing.

There is a tremendous amount of potential in the human mind. But how can the potential be tapped when it is blocked with materialistic concerns? I doubt it can. I think this is what Jesus meant when he said, "How difficult a thing it will be for those having money to make their way into the kingdom of God. It is easier, in fact, for a camel to pass through the eye of a sewing needle than for a rich man to get into the kingdom of God." (LK 18:24-25)

When I was about 13 or 14 years old, I wrote an evangelist and asked how he could display his wealth in such a public way when Jesus said it would be easier for a camel to pass through the eye of a needle than for a rich man to enter the kingdom of heaven. I received a letter stating this was a metaphor. The evangelist maintained that during the time of Jesus small gates were referred to as the eyes of needles and with some difficulty, a camel could pass through them. However, my latest research shows that to be a modern interpretation, and there is no linguistic evidence that the eye of a needle was a reference to a small gate during Jesus' time.

Furthermore, the evangelist wrote that Jesus was making a reference to one person, and there was nothing in the Bible against being rich. Since then I have looked at the passage in the Greek Scriptures and I note that Jesus said a sewing needle and he uses the qualifier, "in fact."

If someone has negated his ego (emptied his mind), the state of consciousness would be different than if his concerns were constantly ego related. I think that those individuals who are capable of healing have denied the self, and are capable of using rarely tapped human energies to heal someone else.

Therefore, the assumption is that there is some type of energy flow between two people. One person has the power to change the consciousness of another. In Jesus' case, he was sending his energy to heal another.

If the consciousness of a healed person changes, what is expected to happen to the healer? How did Jesus feel at any given time? We are only ever told that he was conscious that power had gone from him.

PARADOX FOUND

There is an allusion in the New Testament that individuals had to have faith in Jesus for him to preform miracles, such as healing.

Mark 6:

4   Jesus said, "A prophet is not unhonored except in his home territory, among his relatives, and in his own house."
5   So he was able to do no powerful work there except to lay his hands upon a few sickly ones and cure them.

This matter presents a delicate problem. The assumption is that he could not do miracles because people rejected him (and thus God). His faith was only half of the formula.

But there was the exception of the blind man at the pool. That passage can now be completed. The blind man got up and was walking around with his mat as instructed by Jesus.

John 5:

10   The Jews said to the blind man, "It is the Sabbath. It is not lawful for you to carry your mat."
11   He replied, "But the person who healed me said to pick up my mat and go."
12   They asked, "Who is this person?"
13   But the man did not know who healed him.

Thus Jesus was able to cure a man who did not even know him, let alone believe in him. But, why didn't Jesus cure everyone there that day? Maybe he had limited powers.

There is a larger paradox. If Jesus couldn't perform miracles because people rejected him, then this is a statement that evil has power over good.

MEALS

Jesus worked. He worked hard. Working drains one of energy and creates hunger. Was he hungry after a hard day of healing and loss of energy? Jesus was a man who knew hunger. It is written that after his 40-day fast, he hungered. I would love to have a description of how he savored his first bite of food after 40 days. Did he hold a cool grape in his mouth and let the juices slowly glide down his throat? Is there a difference between a grape and a "cool grape?" Jesus is specific about a cold cup of water. "And whoever gives one of these little ones but a cup of cold water to drink because he is a disciple, I assure you he will not lose his reward." (MT 10:42)

Considering this, I can assume that Jesus did enjoy specific qualities of food. What did he eat? Jesus, in comparing himself to John the Baptist, says that the Baptist ate honey and locusts. Jesus elaborates that the Baptist came neither eating nor drinking. The leaders of the temples said the Baptist was possessed by a devil. Yet, Jesus himself, the Son of man, came eating and drinking. Was this eating and drinking to amplify his human qualities?

The temple leaders called Jesus a gluttonous man and a winebibber. So, Jesus drank wine. How much did Jesus eat? And how did he feel about the desire for food? And how much wine did he drink? Who ever wrote Luke 1:15 is adamant that John the Baptist's being filled with the holy spirit is directly related to abstaining from wine.

Matthew 21:

18   In the early morning, Jesus was returning to the city. He felt hungry.
19   Noticing a single fig tree, he walked to it. But it had no fruit; only leaves. He said to it, "Let there be no fruit from you any more forever." Instantly the fig tree withered.
20   The disciples marvelled, and said, "How did the fig tree wither so quickly?"

Several points can be deduced from this passage. First, Jesus ate figs. Second, he was at times provoked to anger. And obviously he killed the tree because he was famished, and the tree did not provide him food. I really don't understand why he had to kill that tree. Why didn't he turn a stone into a loaf of bread? Then he could have produced the miracle he needed to teach the disciples, satisfied his hunger, and let the tree live. I think his anger was lingering from the previous day when he overturned the tables of the money changers in the temple. Remember the portraits of Jesus my one writer created? This story of human anger is only in Matthew and Mark, where it would be expected since in those two books his humans qualities are emphasized.

What else did Jesus eat? What did he eat most of the time? When he was around the crowds, he confined himself to bread and fish.

This entire matter of diet needs a larger context. Cuisine is something not much discussed by biblical scholars or other social scientists. They talk about diet; not cuisine. Myself, I constantly wonder how people of the time period prepared their food, and especially how they might have savored it. I particularly wonder how Jesus might have savored food.

If I only had the foods mentioned in the Bible--wine, bread and fish--what could I say about cuisine? I once spent some time in southern France. The wine and bread were incredible. I can't say you would have needed more to eat. Yet Jesus sometimes asked for meat. After he had been crucified and resurrected, he at one point encounters the disciples and asked them, "Have ye here any meat?" They gave him a piece of a broiled fish and a part of a honeycomb. (LK 24:41,42)

Did Jesus ask for meat and receive fish? Or did meat and fish mean the same? The Israelites once complained to Moses, "If only we could have some meat. In Egypt we used to eat all the fish we wanted, and it cost us nothing...." (Numbers 11: 4-5) It is likely that meat meant meal or food in the language of the time.

Maybe the simplicity of dried fish, bread, and wine is the reason there's no description of cuisine in the Bible. The food was considered repetitive, but delicious.

THE RITUALS OF EATING AND HEALING

Then there is the matter of when the people of Jesus' time ate. The sabbath was a day for fasting. The last vestiges of fasting were by Catholics not eating meat, but fish, on Fridays. However, Jesus broke the rules. As a result, we are privileged to other information about his society.

Luke 6:

1   And it came to pass on the second sabbath after the first, that he went through the grain fields; and his disciples plucked the grain and did eat, rubbing them in their hands.

2   Certain Pharisees asked, "Why do you do that which is not lawful to do on the sabbath days?"

3   And Jesus answered, "Haven't you read what David, and those with
       him, did when he was hungry?
4   "They went into the house of God, and ate the shewbread which was
       lawful for only the priests."

Jesus and the disciples ate from certain fields. Were these state-owned
fields? I assume so. Otherwise they were stealing from private property.
The point of this story is apparently twofold. One, in some cases the
religious elite were privileged to certain foods and were able to eat while the
masses had to fast or go hungry. Second, since Jesus was for the masses he
reinterpreted the laws. If you are hungry on the sabbath, eat. He was fighting
rituals. Jesus had little use for ritual rules; he wanted spirituality. Luke 6
continues with Jesus healing in a synagogue on another sabbath. He healed a
man with a withered hand. Jesus was challenged by the Pharisees for healing
on the sabbath and he said,

9   "I will ask you one thing; Is it lawful on the sabbath days to do good,
       or to do evil? To save life, or to destroy it?"
11   And they were filled with madness, and communed one with another
       what they might do to Jesus.

FEEDING THE MASSES

How much did the people of Jesus' time eat? Today, most of us are
absolute gluttons. The matter of how much people ate and how quickly they
were full is a point that brings me full face to miracles.
On two occasions, Jesus is reported to have fed a multitude of people.
Once it was 5,000 and once 4,000. How did he do it? Often when this question
arises among lay Christians, they propose that it only took a little crumb
blessed by Jesus to feed someone.
This may not be the case. In Matthew 14, the disciples had five loaves
of bread and two fish. Jesus took the loaves of bread, looked up to heaven to
give thanks, broke the loaves, and gave them to the disciples to feed the
people. The number of people who ate were 5,000 men, not counting women
and children. The disciples then took up twelve baskets full of what was left
over. Thus, the five loaves of bread presumably somehow expanded.
Die-hard opponents say to me, "You don't know how big those baskets
were. Maybe they were only little baskets and he could still have fed 5,000
plus people with just minuscule crumbs and have crumbs left over." And of
course to begin to entertain this idea I have to know how big the loaves of
bread were. And how big were the baskets? Details to answer these questions
would be nice, but there are no details.
How did Jesus do it? Is it possible for someone to tap into a latent

human-energy field, like an adrenaline rush, and multiply food? Or is it possible for someone to tap into a latent human-energy field and have a crumb of food have the sustenance of an entire meal? Of the two questions, I believe in the latter, and I don't believe in the former.

Another example of a biblical prophet feeding a multitude of people on a small amount of food is in 2 Kings 5:

42   A man from Baal Shalishah brought Elisha twenty loaves of bread made from the first barley harvested that year, and some freshly-cut heads of grain. Elisha told his servant to feed the group of prophets with the bread.

43   The servant asked, "Do you think this is enough for a hundred men?" Elisha replied, "Give it to them, because the Lord says that they will eat and still have some left over."

44   So the servant set the food before them to eat, and as the Lord said, they all ate and there was still some left over.

One implication is that an extra energy force was added to the bread in both cases. Twenty loaves of bread for a hundred men is one matter, but five loaves and two fish for 5,000 is quite another. Here we could be up against the accuracy of the figure 5,000. Possibly it was 500?

However, in all four Gospels, the numbers reported are identical: 5,000, five loaves of bread, two fish, and twelve baskets of fragments. This bothers me. I would think if we have four people writing in different times and places we should have a bit of variation. There is no consensus on Jesus' last words, but the four specifics of feeding the masses are identical? I think my one writer has created this one consistent redundancy, amid ongoing contradictions, because he didn't want any controversy with this incident.

Regardless of the numbers, I need to ask why Jesus didn't feed more people with his powers. For me, this is additional proof that his powers were not infinite.

PHILOSOPHY

Jesus' philosophy instructs people to turn their backs on the material world. The more one is tied to the material world, the less one can develop one's spirituality. It is for this reason he told his disciples to go and report, "...the poor are evangelized. And happy is anyone who does not lose his faith in me." (MT 11:5-6)

However, Jesus never tells how a society can eat if everyone is poor, and I assume poor to be translated as non-materialistic. Is everyone to be farmers and fishermen? Of maybe if everyone has enough faith, a group can take a loaf of bread and make it feed many people. Here I have definitely arrived at the intersection of materialism and spirituality. Right now on our planet there are three countries having a similar message--an absence of conspicuous consumption for the benefit of society: Cuba, North Korea, and China. I don't see where there is any overriding spirituality in those countries. I don't see where by definition if I am obviously poor I am obviously spiritual. And I don't see many of the poor people I know who espouse a belief in Jesus as being spiritual.

For those who were not poor, Jesus wanted his disciples to "...preach that the kingdom of heaven is at hand." (MT 10:7) And they must keep the Ten Commandments. For the rich, their coveting of the material world would keep them from entering the kingdom of heaven.

Luke 18:

18   A man asked Jesus, "How can I obtain everlasting life?"
20   "You must keep the commandments," Jesus replied.
21   The man replied he had done that since a youth.
22   Jesus admonished, "Go sell all you have and distribute the money to the poor. Then you will have treasure in the heavens. Then come follow me."
23   The man was sad because he was rich.
24   Jesus said, "It will be difficult for those with money to make their way into the kingdom of God.
25   "It is easier, in fact, for a camel to get through the eye of a sewing needle than for a rich man to get into the kingdom of God."

Jesus is very specific that faith is tied into a rejection of the material world.

Jesus came to earth to start a revolution. In his own words, "... I am come to set a man at variance against his father, and the daughter against her mother, and the daughter-in-law against her mother-in-law." (MT 10:35)

It was a revolution. Like many revolutionaries, Jesus went beyond the known boundaries set by the state and became an outlaw. Sometimes the state kills for revolutionary acts. The revolutionary might be gone, but the words and works live on. Jesus even said, "Heaven and earth will pass away, but my words will not pass away." (MK 14:31)

I understand his words and his philosophy, but I still don't know how to implement the ideas in my life. I can't get to heaven if I'm rich. Jesus said sell everything and follow him. If I do that, society will brand me a kook. So, I still wonder how to balance spirituality and materialism.

6

YOU CAN'T ESCAPE TAXES

Jesus said, "Render unto Caesar the things which are Caesar's, and render unto God what is God's." (LK 20:25)

Luke 23:

1   They led Christ before Pilate.
2   They accused him, "We found this man perverting our nation and instructing them not to render tribute to Caesar. He claims himself a king."

What was Jesus' society like? He was born into a society that had been conquered by Rome only 65 years prior to his birth. Jerusalem was forced to pay tribute to Rome. Some segments of Jesus' society quietly accepted this; others openly rebelled against it. There was armed conflict over tribute paying. In this web of hostilities, Jesus was crucified. After his death, the radicals of Jerusalem escalated resistance against paying tribute to Caesar. Rome responded in A.D. 66, by destroying Jerusalem. This fact, 33 years after Jesus' death, provides a better idea of why Jesus was crucified.

The charge of sedition against Jesus was false, but he was crucified for that charge. Many people think that it should have been easy to exonerate Jesus and set the record straight. Yet, then as now, legal situations can become complex, and good does not always win out, especially for the poor.

Entering the entangled web of Jesus' society and trying to isolate a few strands helped me understand what it would have been like to stand in Jesus' place when he was charged with sedition.

TRIBUTE

What exactly was to be rendered unto Caesar? And why?

Before taxes, there was tribute. Before the existence of money, people paid tribute in goods or services to their leaders. Money greatly simplified economic transactions. Instead of having to carry 30 bushels of corn ten miles to a leader, a person could pay that amount of tribute in money.

The society around Jesus cannot be understood without a knowledge of tribute. Tribute was the bottom line of the economic structure. Tribute was the economic phenomenon that made everything work. Knowing about tribute helps one understand what was rendered unto Caesar and how Christianity began and grew.

While walking through the streets of Jerusalem, did Jesus ever hear, "There are only two things certain in life, death and tribute"? I wonder when this saying started.

Did Jesus ever pay tribute?

"And when they came to Capernaum, the tribute collectors came to Peter and said, 'Doesn't your master pay tribute?'" (MT 17:24). Jesus and Peter paid immediately. Not that day, but that hour! This should tell us something about both tribute and Jesus. In other words, tribute/taxes can't be escaped, and Jesus was living proof of it.

Like many things in life, tribute came in many sizes and forms. Obviously, the more tribute paid, the bigger and more ostentatious the receiving government could be. Some archaeologists define "civilization" as grandiose achievements in art, philosophy, and literature. One such achievement was the hanging gardens of Babylon. That is why it is one of the Seven Wonders of the ancient world. Any civilization was the result of tribute forced from the people.

Christians should not see Jerusalem's tribute paying as an isolated case. Tribute was an integral aspect of history. One area conquered another area and made the conquered people pay tribute. Peru and Mexico were conquered by Spain and paid tribute for centuries. Slaves, diamonds, copper, and vegetable oils were all tribute paid by Africa to England. The cotton, rubber, and spices of India and Malaysia were paid at gun point to European nations. Rome lived off of grain exacted as tribute from Sicily, Spain, North Africa, and Gaul--all conquered by Rome.

Looking at the above paragraph closely, the areas reduce to the First World and the Third World which we have today, thus the "haves" and "have nots." Who gets to be the First World and why? Was the Israel of Judea and Galilee of Jesus' time the First World or the Third World? They were the Third World; they paid tribute. Jesus lived in the Third World. The larger context of the Bible is not about Pilate against Jesus, but Jerusalem against Rome and Babylon.

THE BABYLONIANS

To begin my journey towards understanding Jesus' society, I delved a bit deeper into a broader context of the Old Testament. I knew I could never understand Jesus if I looked at him as an isolated individual. I needed to understand the society around Jesus to give texture to my picture of him.

In 587 B.C., Babylon conquered the southern kingdom of Judea, the capital of which was Jerusalem. Many of the upper classes were carried away as slaves to Babylon. In all, about 10,000 slaves were taken.

Revelation is one of the most important books in the Bible because it deals with the end of the world. Revelation is also about the Babylonians.

Revelation 17:

3   So he carried me as the spirit into a wilderness. There I saw a woman seated on a scarlet beast with seven heads and ten horns. It was covered with blasphemous titles.

4   The woman was dressed in purple, scarlet, gilded with gold, precious stones and pearls. She held a gold cup, full of abominations and impurities of her immorality.

5   On her forehead a symbolic title, "Babylon, the great, the mother of the harlots and of the abominations of the earth."

6   I saw the woman drunk with the blood of the saints and with the blood of those who witnessed for Jesus, and on seeing her I was utterly amazed.

7   An angel said to me, "Why are you amazed? I will tell you the mystic meaning of the woman, and of the beast...."

18   "And the woman represents the great city [Babylon] that has dominion over the kings of the earth."

We know Babylon as having one of the seven wonders of the ancient world. But the Babylonians were part of Jesus' world. Why are these bitter sentiments about Babylon expressed in Revelation?

TRIBUTE, OLD TESTAMENT ARCHAEOLOGY, AND REVELATION

During my presentations about biblical archaeology, people often comment, "There are too many tribes and it is hard to follow the story." I too have that problem. So, I try to simplify any presentation. The book of Revelation is about the hate the Israelis had for Babylon since Israel was conquered by Babylon in 587 B.C. and forced to pay tribute.

Before the era of Babylon, Israel fought with other nations. The boundaries of Israel shifted; sometimes contracting, sometimes expanding. During the reign of Solomon, Israel grew to its maximum. It conquered nations as far north as the Euphrates River. Those nations paid tribute to Israel, and since there were so many tributaries, Solomon was able to build his lavish temple. This temple was destroyed by the Babylonians.

It becomes imperative to understand that the Bible is not just about individuals but about conflicting groups. The main group is the "chosen ones." The relationship between the Jews and the Philistines was long and drawn out. David was an Israelite. Goliath was a Philistine.

The Philistines' and the Israelites' relationship began around 1200 B.C. when the Philistines settled on the southern coastal area of Canaan. They threatened the existence of the emerging Israelite nation. Many times the Old Testament tells of conflicts between the Philistines and the Israelites.

These two groups might be easier to remember if we keep in mind that Samson was an Israelite and Delilah was a Philistine. Delilah was offered 1100 silver shekels by her people if she could find the source of Samson's strength. Delilah quizzed him regularly. Although Samson tricked her several times, eventually she cut off the mighty Israelite's hair. It is the age-old story of betrayal, and it was, and still is, used by groups to show that one should not become romantically involved with an outsider.

The Philistines blinded Samson and took him to a mill in Gaza where he worked with other slaves. According to some biblical scholars, the "reward" money paid to Delilah supposedly prefigures Judas' betrayal of Jesus. If you ask me, 700 years is a long time. But we are dealing with the Bible.

The Philistines took Samson to a festival in the temple of their god Dagon. (The god Dagon was at constant odds with the Israelite god--Yahweh.) There, Samson was mocked by jeering crowds. While 3,000 people stood on the temple roof, Samson persuaded a boy to take him to the entrance of the temple. He told the boy to escape. Then Samson pushed down the temple.

The story of Samson was placed in the book of Judges 1. This book is about the lawless period of Israel's history ranging from the invasion of Canaan to the establishment of Israel's monarchy. The book contains the stories about "judges," most of whom were military leaders, not judges in the legal sense of the word. Military conquest translates as the loser paying tribute.

The ongoing clashes between the Philistines and Israelites have been popularized with Indiana Jones seeking the ark. The ark is a box in which Israelite power objects are kept. The mystique of the ark is nowhere better colored than in 1 Samuel 4:

1   The word of Samuel came to all Israel to go out against the Philistines to battle. They pitched beside Ebenezer and the Philistines pitched in Aphek.

2　　They joined in battle and Israel was smitten. The Philistines slew 4,000.

3　　In camp the elders of Israel asked, "Why has the Lord smitten us? Let us fetch the ark of the covenant of the Lord out of Shiloh so that it may save us out of the hand of the enemies."

4　　Eli sent the ark with his two sons Hophni and Phinehas.

5　　And when the ark of the covenant of the Lord came into the camp, all Israel shouted with a great shout, so that the earth rang again.

6　　And when the Philistines heard the noise of the shout, they said, "What meaneth the noise of this great shout in the camp of the Hebrews?" And they understood that the ark of the Lord was come into the camp.

7　　And the Philistines were afraid, for they said, "God is come into the camp. Woe unto us! For there hath not been such a thing heretofore.

8　　"Who shall deliver us out of the hands of these mighty gods? These are the gods that smote the Egyptians with all the plagues in the wilderness.

9　　"Be strong Philistines, that you be not servants [pay tribute] unto the Hebrews, as they have been to you. Fight like men."

10　　And there was another battle and every Israelite fled into his tent. And there was a great slaughter; for there fell of Israel 30,000 footmen.

11　　And the ark was taken. And Hophni and Phinehas were slain.

12　　An Israelite ran that day to Shiloh.

14　　The man hastily told Eli.

15　　Eli was ninety-eight. His eyes were so dim he could not see.

17　　The messenger told Eli of the great slaughter and that his two sons were dead and the ark taken.

18　　Eli fell from his seat backwards and broke his neck and died. He had judged Israel for forty years.

There's that number 40 again.

1 Samuel 5:

1　　The Philistines took the ark to Ashdod.

2　　They brought it into the house of Dagon. [Samson toppled this Philistine god's temple.]

3　　And when they of Ashdod arose early in the morning, they saw Dagon was fallen upon his face to the earth before the ark of the Lord. And they took Dagon, and set him in his place again.

4　　The next morning Dagon had again fallen and the head of Dagon and both the palms of his hands were cut off upon the threshold; only the stump of Dagon was left to him.

6   The hand of the Lord was heavy upon Ashdod and he destroyed them, and smote them with emerods [hemorrhoids].

7   And when the men of Ashdod saw that it was so, they said, "The ark of the God of Israel shall not abide with us. His hand is sore upon us, and upon Dagon our god."

10   And it came to pass, as the ark of God came to Ekron, that the Ekronites cried out, saying, "They have brought about the ark of the God of Israel to us, to slay us and our people."

12   And the men that did not die were smitten with the emerods; and the cry of the city went up to heaven.

I understand this incident shows Dagon did not have much power, otherwise there would have been no reason to butcher him. And I understand God was punishing the Israelites and teaching them that there is really no power in any earthly object without God's blessing. But couldn't the ark have been of more help that day, at least a little, during the second battle when 30,000 Israeli footmen fell?

Later in 1 Samuel 7:9, "And Samuel took a sucking lamb, and offered it for a burnt offering wholly unto the Lord. Samuel cried unto the Lord for Israel; and the Lord heard him." The next day the Israelites defeated the Philistines.

How much power was in the ark, and how much power was in the animal sacrifice? We may never know for sure, but what value is there in any ritual? Presumably the ritual of a burnt offering had some power at one time. However, the "laws" of the universe apparently changed. There was no more need for ritualistic animal sacrifice, or at least there was no need for such a ritual in the Judaeo-Christian world. Religious perspective continued to change as Jesus conveyed his message. Animal sacrifice slowly ceased. Jesus said, "I want mercy and not sacrifice." (MT 9:13) What is significant is that the rules of the religion changed and continue to change. What can be expected of religious change in the future?

About 700 B.C., the Philistines vanished from the historical record. Why they disappeared was for a long time a mystery. However, a papyrus letter was discovered about 50 years ago near modern day Cairo and was translated recently. The letter, written in Aramaic, Jesus' mother tongue, dated to the end of the seventh century B.C. The letter was written by King Adon of the Philistine city of Ekron, 30 miles northwest of Jerusalem. He begged his lord the Pharaoh to save him from the king of Babylon who was about to invade his territory. There is a great earthly reality for the Christian hate projected on Babylon in Revelation.

To understand King Adon's letter, I returned to the early history of the Philistines. In the 700's B.C., the Philistines were conquered by a larger group called the Assyrians resulting in the Philistines paying tribute to the

Assyrians. The Philistines only had to pay a little tribute; thus, the relationship was not too demanding. Both the Assyrians and the Philistines flourished.

Later, 600s B.C., the Babylonians conquered the Assyrians. The Babylonians wanted to conquer Egypt, and they would stop at nothing to achieve their goal. The Philistines lived between the Babylonians and the Egyptians. To ensure no problem in their attempt to conquer Egypt, the Babylonians annihilated the Philistines. Thus, the Philistines disappeared from the Bible and human history.

Now we can more thoroughly answer the question, "Who gets to be the First World?" Then, as now, the First World controls the world's economy and has the best military. It would be tough to collect tribute without a military. There is a latent message throughout the Bible: People come to earth to either pay tribute or collect it. Those paying tribute are often greatly impoverished. Jesus lived in that sector of society paying tribute, and his religious message should be viewed in that light. Jesus said, "Go and report to John...the poor are evangelized." (MT 11:5)

The book of Revelation cannot be understood without understanding Babylon and the groups paying tribute to Babylon. All of Revelation 18, four chapters before the Bible closes, is about Babylon.

Revelation 18:

2   And he cried mightily with a strong voice, saying, "Babylon the great is fallen, is fallen, and is become the habitation of devils, and hold of every foul spirit, and a cage of every unclean and hateful bird."

There aren't too many times in the Bible where a phrase is repeated within the same dialogue. Here the repeated phrase is "is fallen!" Revelation 18 continues,

6   Reward her [Babylon] as she rewarded you. Double unto her double according to her works, in the cup which she hath filled to her double.
24   And in her was found the blood of prophets, and of saints, and of all that were slain upon the earth.

A CAST OF CHARACTERS

Looking at Jesus' society we might begin to comprehend his juxtaposition to the material world. We can also expand our context for explaining the beginnings and the growth of Christianity. While Christianity is a religion, it is also a socio-economic phenomenon, and Christians may have more introspection of themselves as products of social forces.

Rome conquered Judea and Jerusalem 65 years before Jesus was born, and at that time Babylon was only a secondary city. We know what was to be rendered unto Caesar, but what exactly was the relationship between the First World of Rome and the Third World of Jerusalem? A very small portion of Caesar's empire composed the world of Jesus Christ.

Too often Jesus is visualized in Jerusalem living with about thirty people in some type of isolation. In the mental picture, there are always the three wise men, disciples, Pilate, Mary, a few other women, some Pharisees, and some Roman soldiers. Of course, the times Jesus fed the multitudes is remembered. But the multitudes seem to come out of the desert and then disappear back into it, as though they weren't really part of a society.

This is the mental image of Jesus' world with which I grew up. But as an archaeologist, I try to visualize the dynamics of ancient landscapes. Sometimes I imagine Jesus walking through the streets of Jerusalem. Whom did he see? Jerusalem was a large city. How did those people he saw perceive him? For me, this is a fascinating aspect of trying to complete a portrait of Jesus. If we don't try to visualize the society in which Jesus lived and functioned, it hampers our comprehension of him. However, a main problem with tackling this topic is that there is much important information that we will never know, such as details on the everyday lives of all the people involved.

These are the central characters who populated Jesus' world:

Caesar
Herod
Pilate
the Pharisees
the poor
the middle class
the Romans

the slaves
the Hellenists
the Hebraists
the Zealots
the Sadducees
the Essenes
the Egyptians
the Babylonians

Most Christians only know about the first group (Caesar through the Romans). Few know about the second group. However, the Zealots and the Sadducees were most responsible for Jesus' crucifixion.

How did Jesus relate to all these different groups? And how did the different groups relate to him? He was viewed differently by different groups around him. Some people revered him. Others crucified him. That's an extreme difference.

Zealots

The Zealots don't get much New Testament air time. They were political activists during the time of Jesus. Indeed, they advocated violence as a means of liberation from Rome. The focus of the Zealot's creed was Jewish tribute should only be paid to Jerusalem. More specifically, they proclaimed God as the only Lord, and it was to God they paid tribute. Therefore, Israel should pay no tribute to Caesar.

From the time of Herod the Great's death (21 B.C.), to the downfall of Jerusalem (A.D. 66), Zealots rebelled against Rome's domination. The Zealots fomented many small rebellions and sometimes were crucified.

According to Josephus, the Zealots were founded as a nationalistic Jewish party by Judas the Galilean in opposition to the census taken under Quirinius in A.D. 6. The Zealots modeled themselves on the "zealous" followers of Yahweh such as Phinehas and Elijah, as well as the Maccabean fighters who lived 200 years before Jesus.

It was because of the rebellions of the Zealots that Rome destroyed Jerusalem in A.D. 66. It was a message sent to the rest of the Roman world; pay tribute without complaint or die. "After him Judas the Galilean led an uprising at the time of the census, and raised a popular following, and he perished and all his followers were scattered." (Acts 5:37)

Jesus must have heard of, and maybe even witnessed, some of the Zealots' violent rebellions. One of his disciples was Simon the Zealot.

During all of Jesus' life, the cities in which he lived or passed through paid tribute to Rome. This is something the Zealots detested and protested against. If it hadn't been for the Zealots, Jesus may never have been crucified. If the Zealots had been paying tribute to Rome, there would have been little grounds for Rome to accuse Jesus of telling others not to pay tribute. Jesus was not on trial for some religious offense. His charge was political. He was accused of being the king of the Jews. Were he a king, he might receive tribute that rightly should have gone to Caesar. For the mere pretense of claiming something that belonged to Caesar, one could be crucified. We know Jesus was falsely charged. Jesus already told his disciples "render unto Caesar what is Caesar's." And Jesus paid tribute.

Jesus surely understood the roots of the Zealot's philosophy, drawn from the Old Testament. He often referred to and quoted from the Old Testament. For example, his statements to Satan at the end of his 40-day fast were taken from Deuteronomy. In Matthew, Jesus replied after the first temptation, "It is written...." Concluding the second temptation Satan says, "For it is written...." To which Jesus began his reply, "Furthermore it is written...." And in the third temptation there is a final, "...it is written...." (MT 4) The "it is written" refers to the Old Testament: Deuteronomy 8:3, Psalms 91:11-12, Deuteronomy 6:16, Deuteronomy 6:13.

ENTER PILATE

Pilate was appointed by the emperor Tiberius to serve as governor of Judea, Samaria, and Idumea from A.D. 26 to 36. Imagine, only for the last six years of Jesus' life did Pilate hold this position of governor. Interestingly, he was appointed to that position during the years that Jesus was missing. Jesus resurfaced during the fourth year of Pilate's administration.

Much like our present society, politicians often had a military background. Pilate served as an officer in the Roman Army. Civil leaders originating out of the military is a cogent commentary on civilization and its economic base of tribute.

When Pilate first marched into Jerusalem, his military escort displayed standards with the image of Tiberius. The Jews, led by the Zealots, detested idolatry and retaliated by besieging the governor's palace. Pilate threatened violence to end the demonstration. However, the Jews were prepared to die rather than accept pagan images in their city. They lay down in the streets. When Pilate saw the Jews would indeed accept death, he had to acquiesce or lose his tribute payers; the latter choice Rome would not have appreciated.

But Pilate was not a man to be denied. Eventually, he raided the temple treasury to fund the building of a new aqueduct. Thousands of people were prepared to accept death and did die in the ensuing riots. Rome was "somewhat tolerant" of these deaths because the underlying motive of aqueduct construction would mean a more productive life in Jerusalem, and this in turn would mean more riches going to Rome.

In A.D. 33, Pilate sentenced Jesus to death. Pilate was irritated with the Jews' willingness to accept death. Around A.D. 36, he ordered the annihilation of a Samaritan mob. He was recalled to Rome for that. The rulers in Rome didn't want their tribute payers to die. Religious differences were tolerated for economic reasons. Killing taxpayers was hard on the cash flow. Rome's toleration of religion has to be viewed economically.

Yet the demonstrations against Rome grew, and the acceptance of death by the Jews likewise grew. Finally, by destroying Jerusalem in A.D. 66, Rome sent a message throughout the empire that those who rebelled against tribute payment did so at their peril.

ELITES

There were those who did not pay tax in the Roman Empire. Why? The ruler did not; rather, all tax and tribute were received in his name. The ruler to whom Jesus paid his tribute was Tiberius Caesar. Caesar was a surname. "The Caesar," otherwise known as Gaius Julius Caesar, died 44 years before Jesus was born. But no ruler of Rome paid tax.

Matthew 22:

15   Then the Pharisees took counsel on how they might entangle Jesus in his talk.
16   And they sent out unto him their disciples with the Herodians, saying, "Master, we know that thou art true, and teachest the way of God in truth, neither carest thou for any man; for thou regardest not the person of men.
17   "Tell us therefore, what thinkest thou? Is it lawful to give tribute unto Caesar, or not?"
18   But Jesus perceived their wickedness, and said, "Why tempt ye me, ye hypocrites?
19   "Show me the tribute money." And they brought him a coin.
20   Jesus asked, "Whose is this image and superscription?"
21   They said that it was Caesar's. And Christ said, "Render unto Caesar the things which are Caesar's."

Throughout the Roman Empire, there were certain free citizens, and only a small percentage were citizens with full rights, such as voting rights. Rome's voting system was restricted to the free and mostly the upper and middle classes.

SLAVES

Still, half of the Roman Empire did not pay tax. Who were the 50 percent so lucky as not to pay taxes? They weren't so lucky because at the time of Jesus, half of the Roman empire was made up of slaves. Half of the Roman Empire's population were slaves!

As an archaeologist, I am fascinated with ancient societies like the one in which Jesus lived. I'm very interested in how those societies viewed slavery. According to Paul's early documented letters to the Asian churches, Christians were both slaves and slave holders.

Slaves were treated somewhat differently in various societies. Among the Aztecs, children were often taken from other tribes and kept in isolation without clothing. By being kept in isolation, many lost the ability o to communicate through language since the slaves spoke a language different than the Aztecs. While they were made to do labor, their ultimate function in that society was to be sacrificed. The slaves of the United States were often brutalized. Nevertheless, they did keep some remnants of their African culture alive in the new land, and sometimes families survived together.

However, many of the slaves in the time of Jesus were doctors and craftsmen. The Babylonians carried off many of the elite of Jerusalem. One of the better documented cases of these slaves is the conquest of Tyre by Alexander the Great.

The city of Tyre is mentioned often in the Bible. Tyre was situated on a small island 25 miles south of Sidon, close to the borderland of the Israelite tribe of Asher. "And he [Jesus] came down with them, and stood in the plain, and the company of his disciples. A great multitude of people out of all Judaea and Jerusalem, and from the sea coast of Tyre and Sidon, came to hear him, and to be healed of their diseases." (LK 6:17)

The Israelite kingdom extended to Tyre under both David and Solomon. King Hiram of Tyre (981-947) sent tribute of cedar lumber, along with carpenters and masons, to help build David's palace. During Solomon's reign, Hiram sent more cedar and cypress.

The Old Testament prophets prophesied Tyre's destruction.

Ezekiel 26:

9   Tyre's wall will be pounded by battering rams, and the towers will be torn down with iron bars.
10   The clouds of dust from the destruction will cover everyone.
11   The noise of the horses and chariots will shake the walls as they go through the gates of the ruined city.

Alexander the Great came to Tyre around 333 B.C. His policy: If a town agreed to pay tribute, the people were not harmed. If they resisted, punishment was imposed. Tyre refused to pay tribute. To reach the island of Tyre, Alexander built a mole, a road under the water that could be walked or rode on, two hundred feet wide and half a mile long. For seven months, he attacked Tyre. Finally it fell. The numbers vary, but the high figures are that 2,000 of its leaders were hanged and 30,000 were sold as slaves.

When a city like Tyre fell, those taken slaves were from many walks of life. There were doctors, accountants, and craftsmen. Epictetus was a renowned Stoic philosopher and a slave. Most of the slaves worked on agricultural estates. Some worked as household servants, others were clerks in businesses, and still others worked as copyists for publishers.

Some of the slaves Jesus saw in his life might have been descendants of those slaves taken from Tyre.

Matthew 11:

20   Then Jesus began to reproach the towns in which most of his wonders
      had been accomplished because they did not repent.
21   "Alas for you, Chorazin! Alas for you, Bethsaida! Because if in Tyre
      and Sidon the wonders had been done that were done in you, they
      would long ago have repented in sackcloth and ashes.
22   "I tell you further, it will be more endurable in the Judgment Day for
      Tyre and Sidon than for you."

Many of the slaves lived under a bond of fear, but some lived under a
bond of friendship. Of the latter, some were able to amass enough material
wealth to obtain their freedom. As a consequence, there was a stream of
freemen entering the social structure of the empire. A few of the freed slaves
became prominent in the government. One of these was the Governor Pallas
under Claudius.

Some scholars say that there is no statement in the New Testament
against the institution of slavery. But this might be a matter of translation.
Where would such a positive statement be made? In Luke, Jesus is the savior.
"Jehovah's spirit is upon me, because he anointed me to declare good news
to the poor, he sent me forth to preach to the captives and a recovery of sight
to the blind, to send the crushed ones away with a release." (L 4:18) Here
captives might be read as slaves.

One slave has an interesting status in the Bible. On the night of Jesus'
arrest, it was a slave girl who asked Peter if he were with Jesus. Peter made
his first denial of Jesus to a slave girl. (MT 26:69)

THE CRIMINAL ELEMENT

Crime in Jesus' time was substantial. However, the concept of crime
is relative. There was no political freedom of speech in the Roman Empire.
One could not speak against Caesar. Jesus' charge was for claiming to be
"King of Jews." This was a claim of Caesar's. Often the cross was the ultimate
punishment for sedition.

Historians place the beginnings of crucifixion in the 6th century B.C.
It might have been started among the Persians, but crucifixion became a
common practice among the Seleucids, Carthaginians, Romans, and Jews.

Crucifixion was usually reserved for political or religious agitators
and thieves. In 519 B.C., King Darius I of Persia crucified over 3,000 political
opponents in Babylon. In 88 B.C., the Judaean king and high priest Alexander
Jannaeus had 800 pharisaic opponents crucified. (The Pharisees are the priests
who argued with Jesus about biblical interpretations.) In 71 B.C., 6,000 slaves,
the followers of Spartacus, were crucified along the Appian Way to Rome.

A person to be crucified was usually stripped, whipped or scourged, and made to drag the crossbeam to the site of punishment. There the hands were either tied to the crossbeam or nailed to it. The nailing was usually done through the wrist. Next the crossbeam was raised up, set on, and fastened to an upright pole rising about 10 feet above the ground. The feet of the person were then bound or nailed. Thus the cross was usually "T" shaped and not the cross as we think of it. It would have been too much work to place an individual on a cross, then dig a hole, and steady the cross with the person tied to it. It was simpler to have the upright pole already in the ground.

Some scholars think that at Golgotha, the site of Jesus' crucifixion, permanent large upright stakes of the crosses were in place with grooves at the top of the stakes. The crossbeam was lowered into the groove. Jesus would have probably only dragged the cross beam, not the entire cross. An entire cross would have been too heavy to drag.

Sometimes a notice of the crime was hung around the neck of the victim as he walked to the crucifixion site. This was then placed over the victim's head upon crucifixion. Over Jesus' head hung the words, "King of Jews."

THE POOR

Who were the people with whom Jesus shared his new philosophy? Who heard his message? Who followed him and why?

Jesus broke from a religious tradition of Judaism that was centuries old. Breaking from Judaism, he started a new religion--Christianity. Jesus' life and death were special moments in the communications network of the world. That is why we have the major chronological markers of B.C. and A.D. Christianity had a profound impact on Western Civilization. Some would even argue that Christianity is Western Civilization.

When Jesus broke from Judaism, he needed followers. Who, besides the disciples, were Jesus' followers? More importantly, why did they follow Jesus? Jesus told the disciples, "Do not go to the Gentiles nor enter a Samaritan city, but rather go to the lost sheep of the house of Israel." (MT 10:5-6) Yet in the end we only really know "...the poor are evangelized." (MT 11:5)

Many Christians think Jerusalem at the time of Jesus was the center of the world. Jesus paid tribute, and he saw Jerusalem pay tribute to Rome. Can we say Rome was the First World and Jerusalem was the Third World? The Vatican was placed in Rome and not Jerusalem for a reason, and the reason is economics. While all roads may not actually lead to Rome, enough of the roads did lead to Rome to place the Vatican there. Jesus lived in the Third World. And the Third World was and is a very impoverished place. Any American need only travel to Latin America to understand what the difference between Rome and Jerusalem might have been at the time of Jesus.

This brings me back to my thoughts about what Jesus saw when he glimpsed at all the kingdoms of the world in a moment of time. Rome had to be in the forefront, didn't it? Or approached like this: Of all the civilizations to have existed, which is the one that still stands out among the rest? Yes, people go to see the Great Wall of China, but there's no city or other cultural event that we look to as the epitome of Chinese culture. But there is something special about Rome. One special thing is the Vatican.

Obviously no labor laws applied to slaves. More properly stated, there were no laws protecting the laborer. In the entire span of history, industry seeks the lowest possible payment of wages. That is why some modern name-brand sports shoes are made in Thailand, where the average worker makes an estimated $5 a day. Because of slavery, the great agricultural estates of Jesus' time didn't have to hire laborers; they bought them.

By understanding the slave element in Jesus' society, we can begin to understand that the poor were quite numerous. The economic conditions of the poor were pitiful. Slaves were often better off since they at least had the assurance of food and clothing. The poor had no hope. But Jesus, with his message of non-materialism, gave them hope in another world. The poor often were willing to follow any man who would give them some food. These people were easy prey for demagoguery of every type.

Everyone wants more information about the poor. So do I, but as Harry S. Truman said, "History is always written by the winners...and they had to justify what was done."

HEBRAISTS AND HELLENISTS

Jesus' view of the world was not restricted to Jerusalem and Rome. The Assyrians conquered the Philistines, and later the Babylonians conquered the Assyrians. In 607 B.C., Babylon conquered the southern kingdom of Judea, the capital of which was Jerusalem. Judea had to pay heavy tribute to Babylon. Also many of the upper classes were carried away as slaves to Babylon. This is known as the Diaspora. I began to learn about this on my trip to Spain in 1970.

In time, some of these people would return to the Jewish homeland, but others remained in Assyria and Babylon. This should give anyone a better understanding of why Babylon receives acrimonious comments in Revelation. Many Jews of Jesus' time carried a grudge against Babylon.

The Jews of the Diaspora developed into two distinct groups: Hebraists and Hellenists. Both are mentioned in Acts 6.

The Hebraists retained the use of Hebrew, the Aramaic language, and often spoke a second language. Paul, a Hebraist, was born in the Greek city of Tarsus, and he wrote in Greek. He proudly claimed Roman citizenship according to some scholars.

Many other Jews lost the use of their mother tongue and spoke Greek or other languages. These are the Hellenists. Hellenists dressed like the inhabitants of their host country. They were only Jews in matter of race and faith, but even in faith they adopted some of the elements from other religions. In a synagogue at Dura-Europos on the Euphrates, there are elements of heathen mythology depicted in the mosaics and wall paintings.

Greek colonies dotted the Near East landscape 300 years before Jesus. This was in part due to the Greeks who had been carried off by the Persian leader Xerxes in 480 B.C. Many Greek mercenaries also fought for Xerxes. However, the Greeks heavily colonized the Near East because of the successful campaigns of Alexander the Great about 330 B.C. He united the Near East under one military power resulting in more commerce between areas. The Ptolemaic and Seleucid successors of Alexander encouraged the outward migration of Jews by offering citizenship and tax exemptions to those who would migrate to the larger Greek cities of their domains.

In Rome, there was also a growing number of Jewish inhabitants. The Jewish slaves, whom Pompey brought to Rome from Palestine 65 years before the birth of Jesus, were ultimately given freedom. Just before the birth of Jesus, there were 8,000 Jews in Rome. The 'render unto Caesar' line is always remembered, as though Caesar was always the bad guy. It was under Julius Caesar (and Augustus) that the Jews were given legal standing in Rome. In the city of Corinth, as well as a few other cities, the Jews were freed from military service and the jurisdiction of heathen (non-Jewish) courts.

Most Jews of the Diaspora clung to their religion of believing there was only one God based on the laws of Moses, and most Jews paid the yearly tax of half a shekel to the temple at Jerusalem.

How did the Romans see the Jews of the Diaspora? The Jews were considered odd because they wouldn't worship the Roman gods and goddesses. The Romans considered the Jews as atheists. The Romans did not understand why the Jews worshiped an invisible God. However, the Romans greatly tolerated the Jews because they were hard working, sober, and moral.

Under the Romans, the Jews didn't fair too badly. They had religious freedom. However, while some Jews didn't fair too badly, others were impoverished. Jesus saw both the Hebraists and the Hellenists because they came from throughout the Roman empire to make a pilgrimage to the annual feasts at Jerusalem. However, Jesus could only speak to the Hebraists since his mother tongue was Aramaic.

RELIGION

What was the religious world into which Jesus was born? Most people think he broke away from the Jewish tradition, thus creating a two religion system: Judaism and Christianity. It was more complex than that.

At the time Jesus began his mission, the Jewish people did not exist as a sovereign political nation. Rather they paid tribute to Rome. Rome, while pantheistic, tolerated other religions. As long as the tribute was paid, Rome was not in the business of religious conversion. Rome only became involved in religious conversion when the ruler of Rome, Constantine, in 313 A.D. was converted to Christianity. It was he who "saw" a large cross in the sky with the accompanying words *in hoc signo vinces*, "by this sign thou shalt conquer." Subsequently, Christianity became the dominant religion of the European world and the Vatican became autonomous.

Judaism

If one does not understand the Judaism of Jesus' day, it is quite difficult to develop an idea of who Jesus was. Jesus was born into the lineage of David, the great Jewish king. Some perceived Jesus as the prophesied Messiah of the Old Testament; others did not. In Jesus' time there were three major branches of the Jewish faith: the Sadducees, the Pharisees, and the Essenes.

The Sadducees

The Sadducees were a powerful priestly group governing the religious life of Judea under the Herods. They traced their names from the Sons of Zadok who was high priest in the days of David and Solomon. The Sadducees allied themselves with the dominant power structure, Rome, to maintain religious control.

The Sadducees were conservative in religious doctrine. They accepted only the five books of Moses (the first five books of the Bible, known as the Torah) as religious dogma. Their religion could not change or evolve. Based on the five books of Moses, they rejected the idea of the resurrection of the dead, they didn't believe in angels, and they didn't believe in personal immortality.

Matthew 22:

23   That same day, the Sadducees, who say there is no resurrection, approached Jesus and asked,
24   "Teacher, Moses said if someone dies childless, his brother shall marry his widow and raise descendants for his brother.

25   "There were seven brothers in our community, the first of whom
        married and died, and, having no children, left his widow to his brother.
26   "So the second, and the third, down to the seventh.
27   "Following them all, the woman died.
28   "At the resurrection, then, whose wife will she be of the seven. For
        they all had her."
29   Jesus answered, "You are mistaken. You do not understand the
        scriptures or the power of God.
30   "In the resurrected state they neither marry nor are given in marriage,
        but are like angels in heaven.
31   "And about the rising of the dead, have you never read what God said
        to you,
32   "'I am the God of Abraham, the God of Isaac, and the God of Jacob'?
        He is God not of dead but living beings."

These passages obviously show the extreme in religious interpretation,
even in the days of Jesus. The Sadducees certainly gave Jesus an advantage
by asking him about something he, but not they, believed in. To take it any
further would have reduced it to name calling. They came from two entirely
different religious perspectives, almost akin to Buddhists and Christians.

While Jesus might have silenced the Sadducees, it was them--in
religious friction--who silenced him. When Jesus was on trial for his life,
Pilate asked of the chief priests, "Shall I crucify your king?" The chief priests,
the Sadducees, answered, "We have no king but Caesar."

Rome protected the Sadducees. But, when Jerusalem was destroyed
by Rome in A.D. 66, it spelled the end of the Sadducees. Why? As far as
Rome was concerned, the Sadducees were a failure at governing the civil life
of Judea; otherwise, Rome would have had no problem from the Zealots.

The Pharisees

Unlike the Sadducees, the Pharisees believed in angels, the immortality
of the soul, and the resurrection of the dead
Two individuals were responsible for burying Jesus, Joseph of
Arimathea and Nicodemus. Nicodemus was a Pharisee who sought out Jesus.
The Pharisees are mentioned throughout the New Testament. In many
passages, they are in conflict with Jesus. They strictly observed the sabbath
by denying earthly concerns. Thus, they fasted, and they did not heal the
sick on the sabbath. Jewish law forbade non-observance of the sabbath. The
Essenes believed it, the Sadducees believed it, and the Pharisees believed it.
However, Jesus radically reinterpreted the scriptural laws, and he healed the
sick on the sabbath.

Luke 11:

37   During his discourse a Pharisee invited him home to dine. Jesus went
      and sat at the table.
38   The Pharisee noticed Jesus had not washed before the meal.
39   Jesus said, "Now you Pharisees cleanse the outside of the cup and of
      the plate, but inside you are full of robbery and wickedness.
40   "Fools! Did God not make both the outside and the inside?
41   "You had better bestow in kindness what is inside and everything will
      be clean for you.
42   "But alas for you Pharisees, because you tithe mint and rue and every
      vegetable, while disregarding justice and love for God. You should
      practice these things without omitting others.
43   "You Pharisees cherish the prominent pews in the synagogues, and
      the salutations in the markets.
44   "Because you are like unseen tombs over which people walk and you
      are unaware of them."
45   One of the teachers of the Law replied to Jesus, "When you say this,
      you insult us too."
46   Jesus said, "It is for you too. You pack the people with loads that are
      too heavy to carry, while you yourselves do not touch those loads with
      even one finger.
47   "It is for you too because you build monuments for the prophets your
      fathers killed.
48   "In that way you are consenting to your fathers' works. They indeed
      killed them and you build their monuments."

While Jesus often paralleled the Pharisees in religious ideology, he
differed greatly in the social orientation of his message. His message: To
develop spirituality, one had to avoid materialism. It is more blessed to give
than to receive.

The Essenes

The Essenes were one of three major groups of Judaism Jesus saw
and interacted with as he was growing up. Some scholars believe Jesus might
have spent his "missing years" with the Essenes.

But the Essenes aren't mentioned in the Bible. Of course, this fact
leads to comments like, "If they aren't in the Bible, they are not important
for knowing Jesus." The Bible is by no means a complete record of social or
religious history. The book of John ends with "And there are also many other
things which Jesus did...if they should be written...I suppose that even the
world itself could not contain the books that should be written." I think most

Christians would love to have these materials, and in them might be mentioned both Jesus' missing years and the Essenes.

The Essenes were a closed, Jewish society. We don't know much about them, although they appear in the accounts of Philo of Alexandria, Pliny the Elder, and Josephus.

Their self-containment was somewhat like the Shakers of the eastern United States. Their community allowed for no differences in wealth. They did not believe in a massive accumulation of the material world, quite similar to Jesus. They ate plain food, and their meals were taken in silence. They dressed in white garments when not working. Members of the community were recruited by receiving converts or adoption. They abstained from marriage. Their energies were directed to studying conical law. The new members underwent a period of probation lasting several months and then they were purified by baptism.

With few exceptions they shunned temple worship. They advocated hatred of falsehood, love of the truth, and justice toward all people. The latter social component of their beliefs parallels the teachings of Jesus.

The Essenes believed the conflicting qualities of good and evil wage war within the human spirit. Humans become subject to those conflicting qualities, thus becoming "sons of light" or "sons of darkness." Individuals who control their own lives will have a righteous life ending in personal happiness. Those who don't control their own lives succumb to evil and live lives of disgrace and doom. Anger was a manifestation of evil. For the Essenes, however, evil is no match for good, and not eternal. Therefore, eventually good will win out.

Unlike the Pharisees, the Essenes denied the resurrection of the body. The Essenes believed a person has an immortal soul which was imprisoned in a perishable body. At death, good souls went to a place of sunshine and cool breezes, but it wasn't called heaven. Bad souls went to a place of continual torment.

Some scholars believe John the Baptist and Jesus might have resided with the Essenes for a time. Certainly there are many parallels in beliefs of all three. If true, this would make Christianity an outgrowth of Essenism.

Other scholars like Merrill Tenney, with whom I agree more often than not, think this is not the case, because the Essenes focused on strict ritual conduct. The Essenes believed one had to conduct a proper life to be rewarded in the afterlife. Jesus, however, emphasized grace. One could be a criminal, but in the last mortal minute, the criminal could accept God and go to heaven. This is exemplified by one criminal crucified with Jesus.

Luke 23:

39   One of the criminals reviled him, "Are you not the Christ? Save
      yourself and us."
40   But the other reproved him and said, "Do you not fear God, when you
      are suffering the same punishment?
41   "We, however, are suffering justly, we are getting what we deserve for
      our misdeeds, but he has done nothing amiss."
42   And he asked, "Jesus, remember me when you come in your kingdom."
43   Jesus said, "I assure you, today you will be with me in paradise."

And here is where Jesus finally divorced himself from Judaism. Ritual
cannot help one enter heaven, only the grace of Jesus himself.

Ritual was one aspect of religion Jesus opposed, yet it is heavily
emphasized in most modern day churches. What else are most present day
churches but ongoing statements of ritual? But Jesus said, "I want mercy and
not sacrifice." (MT 12:7)

Baptism was not practiced by the other two branches of Judaism, but
it was practiced by the Essenes and John the Baptist. Both the Essenes and
Jesus rejected the material world. Jesus in his rejecting ritual did not baptize.
In the words of John the Baptist, "Whereas I baptize you with water for
repentance, the one who comes after me is so superior that I am not fit to
carry his sandals. He will baptize with the Holy Spirit and fire." (MT 3:11)

Jesus said, "If you want to be complete, go and sell what you have and
donate it to the needy, and you will have treasure in heaven; then come and
follow me." (LK 18:22) Like the Essenes, Jesus was non-materialistic.

Could Jesus have been an Essene? Many times the offshoot of an
ideology resembles little appearance to its roots. If we didn't have historical
records and we were to attend a Catholic service and then a Methodist service,
we might find it hard to believe that the latter was an offshoot of the former.

Some scholars are also concerned that the Essenes aren't mentioned
in the New Testament. I think this supports my theory of one writer. What
we have in the four Gospels is a perfectly dovetailed caricature of Jesus as
though one person were sculpting an image with words. That person wouldn't
want too much extraneous social history to detract from the overall effect,
especially since the Essenes didn't believe in resurrection. However, if there
are four writers, I would expect to find a tidbit or two of other aspects of
Jesus' society. We have four supposed writers, and yet there is not one little
morsel of information as to how Jesus spent his missing years? And not one
mention of the Essenes who are so much like him?

Maybe my one writer never mentioned the Essenes because they didn't
fit with his idea of dramatic tension. He didn't want us to think Jesus'
philosophy was influenced by a worldly source. But he wanted us to believe

it was only inspired by God.

We should keep in mind that the Dead Sea scrolls were found near the Essenes' living quarters around Jerusalem.

Christianity

The interaction between all of the groups of Jesus' time was complex and sometimes involved conflict. Of the three sects of Judaism, only Pharisism survives. Modern orthodox Judaism traces its roots to the Pharisees.

One should not consult the Bible as a good source to understand the dramatic tension that existed between all of these groups, especially since the Bible doesn't even mention the Essenes. I recommend for serious perusal *Jesus and the Politics of His Day*, edited by Ernst Bammel.

But it was Christianity that came out big. One man changed the social complexion of much of the world, mainly because Christianity somehow became divorced from race. While Jesus told his disciples to go to the lost sheep of Israel, it was the poor, regardless of race, who were evangelized.

A second critical point is that Jesus' message was as much social as it was religious. He emphasized doing social services for the poor. Like Confucius before him, he broke a tradition by taking his disciples without regard to social status.

Of all of the groups of Jesus' time, it can be argued that the Hebraists were best equipped to carry Jesus' message to the "outside" world since they had already been exposed to it. They spoke Jesus' mother tongue, so they could understand him, and they spoke another language, often Greek. Paul was a Hebraist as we see him speaking in Acts.

Acts 21:

25　　"As for the Gentiles who believe, we have written that they keep themselves from things offered to idols, and from blood, and from strangled meat, and from fornication."

26　　The next day Paul took the men, and after undergoing a purification ritual with them, he entered the temple to announce the completion of the purification period, which would be when an offering had been made for every one of them.

27　　But when the seven days were almost ended, the Jews which were of Asia saw him in the temple. They stirred up all the people, and laid hands on him.

28　　The Jews cried out, "Men of Israel, help. This is the man, that teacheth all men everywhere against the people, and the law, and this place, and further brought Greeks also into the temple and hath polluted this holy place."

It would then appear from this that it was the later followers of Jesus who began to inject Jesus' message with ritual. Paul, while emphasizing grace, also speaks of ritual conduct. Christianity thus began and was carried to the outside world as a mass of ritual. Something Jesus himself was against.

7

LEARNING TO DIE

With taxes behind us, we can deal with the second part of the cliché that only two things in life are certain--paying taxes and dying. One thing is certain, according to the Bible, Jesus did both.

A main reason there are religions in the world is because of a concern about what might happen after death. I'm from a family of morticians. My family's funeral home also provided ambulance service. I had, at the age of 17, the experience of riding in the back and holding the oxygen mask on a writhing stroke victim. The victim was my good friend Gene Harshbarger's grandmother. The stench of vomit, the wailing of the sirens, and her frail body going through convulsions while gasping for air are ingrained somewhere in my subconscious. Every now and then the incident pops into the forefront of my consciousness as if it were 1964 again. She died about an hour after arriving at the hospital.

I'm also an archaeologist. People sometimes say I went from putting the dead in the ground to digging them out. That is not exactly true. I excavated one person, and I will never do it again. She was a Native American who probably died about 1400. She was about 30 years of age and almost six foot tall. While I was slowly brushing the dirt away from her bones, I had misgivings, but I couldn't articulate them. Later I thought, that woman would have wanted to remain buried. Now her skeleton is divided into separate bones, wrapped in some 1968 Missouri newspaper, and placed in cardboard boxes archived in Missouri. I never touched another human skeleton since.

These two experiences with death did much to formulate my ideas of religiosity. The Native American woman was an animist. After digging her up, I began to read about animism. I regret what I did to her, but she was fundamental in my acceptance of animism and leaving Christianity. I hope our spirits cross someday so I can apologize. Would she accept the apology?

In the Christian world however, I have come to see much of people's religiosity as a hedge against being condemned to some type of hell and not as a spiritual awakening in the living flesh.

GETTING TO HEAVEN

It was a beautiful autumn day in Manhattan as I made my monthly stroll from the American Museum of Natural History through Central Park to upper 5th Avenue to visit my friend Bernie. The year was 1975.

In apartment 4T, I casually glanced at the pond in the upper part of Central Park as Bernie was telling me a joke. Bernie was much older than I. He died not long after that get-together. Bernie had a glowing, warm personality. I think he might have been the humblest individual I have ever known. He spun this elaborate joke, and the punch line was, "Everybody wants to go to heaven, but nobody wants to die."

I didn't laugh. I simply nodded. So, he proceeded with, "You don't get it?" He repeated, "Everybody wants to go to heaven, but nobody wants to die."

I slowly shook my head. I could feel my eyebrows folding in as I spoke, "That's a line from a Black Oak Arkansas song. They're a rock n' roll group." Bernie wasn't an *aficiado* of rock and roll. Then I repeated the line adding the tune from the song, "Everybody wants to go to heaven, but nobody wants to die."

Perhaps that is true. I have never done a survey, so I can't say for sure that "everyone" wants to go to heaven. However, most Christians want to go to heaven, but many don't want to die; though many profess they are prepared to die and accept the consequences of their earthly actions. Some Christians dream of Jesus returning in their lifetime, thus allowing them to skip death and go directly to heaven. I have heard more than one Christian not only pin-pointing the year of Jesus' return, but predicting the day. Jesus has been gone for 2,000 years, and every generation of Christians since his death has expected his return.

Of the three great religions, Christianity instills a tremendous fear of death through the concept of hell. Is it time to rethink teaching the scary ideas of hell to children? How nice it would be if we would teach children about living and dying. If we wanted to, we could teach ourselves about dying. Few people have learned how to accept death. Most of us are struggling with it. While most of us are frightened by death, we should begin to explore the possibility that it could be a tranquil, pleasant, and meaningful experience.

Religions exist because of the great unknown after death. Trying to understand more about the Christian view of death, I studied for many years some non-Christian ideas surrounding death and contrasted those thoughts with those of Christians. I am still in the process of learning.

BUDDHISM

Buddha lived 500 years before Jesus. Buddha said there are three types of vanity permeating our lives: the vanity of youth, the vanity of health, and the vanity of life. Because of the last vanity, there is a fear of death. Part of Buddha's message was to get people to realize the existence of those vanities and destroy them through awareness and meditation.

Some Christians say Buddhism is devil worship. However, this type of name calling is diminishing. Of course, the foundation for the idea that Buddhism is devil worship is the biblical reference, "Do not worship any other god, because I, the Lord, tolerate no rivals." (EX 34:14) We should understand that the Jews said this before Christians and that it is a Jewish creed.

Buddhism is not about gods; it is about how a person lives and dies. Buddhism is about how each person must find his or her own salvation. To do this, a person must be aware of Noble Truths.

Noble Truth One: Most of life is suffering. Buddha said there are more tears in the world than water in the ocean.

The reason that Buddhism replaced Confucianism in many areas is because the latter did not address the issue of suffering. Indeed, the growth of Christianity was and is also in part because Jesus' message addressed suffering.

Noble Truth Two: All suffering derives from an attachment to this world.

Noble Truth Three: Suffering can only stop by destroying attachment to this world.

Noble Truth Four: Suffering can cease through being moral, meditating, and attaining wisdom.

It is documented that heavy meditators produce greater alpha (pleasure) waves in the brain. Through daily meditating, according to the Zen Buddhists, one can learn to shut out pain. Dying is one of the biggest events in our lives, and to treat it summarily is not part of the Zen creed. One tenant of Zen is to die sitting up and experiencing death coming into one's being.

Many Christians find it hard to believe that one could shut out all pain and watch death come into one. However, there are documented examples of the shutting out of pain to deal with death.

The Buddhists of southeast Asia are from the branch called Theravada. For them the essence of life is to deny the self and find enlightenment. When they say pain does not exist, they mean it. In 1971, I saw the movie *The Year of the Pig*, an expose of the Vietnam War. In the movie, there were news clips of Lyndon Johnson that didn't do him much justice as a thinking human being. At one point, the scene went to a street and a Buddhist slowly positioned himself in lotus. He then poured gasoline over himself and lit a match. It slowly dawned on me that he was going to be sitting there for some time. This wasn't the five second news flash of American news coverage I was used to. I wanted a time marker. I could hold my breath for about 2 minutes. I gulped air and watched. I had to breathe and the monk still sat. I've been burned from the waist up when a high school chemistry experiment went awry. The burns were extremely painful. I spent one week in the hospital. Finally the stiff monk fell. I considered what I had just seen to be a miracle--a total denial of self. That man went to a level of consciousness I will probably never know anything about.

There is the argument that suicide is not a denial of self since it violates the highest of all laws, the respect for life. The monk was not committing suicide to eliminate life, but to make a statement to the U.S. government that was napalming innocent men, women, and children. Many monks immolated themselves to try to save the lives of others. It was a statement to the U.S. government, "We are not afraid of your fire. It does not hurt."

After seeing the movie, I asked Vietnam vets if they ever saw a monk burn himself. Few had. But those who had were impressed that the monks' faces never showed signs of torture; rather, there was a countenance of serenity. Most Americans indoctrinated into the philosophy of conspicuous consumption didn't understand the symbolism of those acts of self-denial by Third World Buddhist masters. Instead, most of the Americans interpreted the monks' acts as stupid religious fanaticism.

When I walked out of the Zen temple in Chicago in 1969, I thought I would never enter another one, but the movie *The Year of the Pig* was one reason I reconsidered. I was deeply impressed that religion could be more than simply sitting in a church and praying one's way to heaven.

The type of denial of self and control I saw in *The Year of the Pig* is the foundation for my belief that one can heal a sick person. Regardless of the implication for miracles, there is really no reason meditation cannot be incorporated into the educational system for American youth. Previously, the main problem was the matter of "devil worship," but enough people are now beyond that. Aren't they?

JAINISM

Jainism, centered in India, is a religious offshoot of Hinduism. There are around 2,000,000 Jainists, and some estimates go as high as 3,000,000. Jainism was founded by Mahavira. He was a contemporary of Buddha, and so, he too lived 500 years before Jesus. But most Jains consider Mahavira to be the last in a long line of teachers, not the originator.

The name Jainism comes from the Sanskrit word *jina* meaning "conqueror" or "victor." The idea of *jina* is to have spiritual victory over the material world. (Sounds like Jesus.)

Mahavira was hailed as *jina* because he had overcome earthly desires to the point that he was prepared to fast to death.

In the beginning, the Jainists turned their backs on the material world. There are still monasteries in India where they go naked, so there is never a worry about what clothes to put on each morning. Nakedness in certain contexts can help destroy vanity. The extreme Jainists also practice *ahimsa* which involves not injuring any living creature, even insects. The orthodox Jainists constantly sweep the ground in front of them every time they walk so they can avoid stepping on bugs.

Because of *ahimsa*, Jainists are vegetarians. They avoid occupations such as farming because the tools might be injurious to small creatures. All Jains are not monks. Some have gravitated into banking, law, and commerce. As a consequence, they are rather prosperous, and they generously contribute to monasteries.

As with any religion, the further one moves from the roots and the basic foundations, the more one finds the encroachment of the material world. I had the opportunity to talk to a few Jains in New Delhi, and I'm not convinced they would fast to death. They seem as if they would continue to grasp the material world until death became imminent.

CHRISTIANITY

Looking at Christianity as an outsider, much like I looked at Buddhism and Jainism, gave me new insights.

Christianity is named after a man, Jesus Christ. Jesus was a Jew. He was raised, lived, and died in a Jewish environment with several sects of Judaism having different and sometimes conflicting ideas.

Jesus was born of a virgin in a manger. His name Jesus was bestowed upon him by an angel before he was conceived. (LK 2:21) Christ, meaning "anointed one," is the Greek equivalent of the Hebrew word Messiah. It is from the word Christ that Christianity is derived. Thus the name Christianity is of Greek origins and not Jewish. Sometimes Jesus forbade people to tell others that he was the Messiah since if this title should be used freely, the populace would expect him to be a political messiah and help them become free of Rome. (MT 16:20) The fact that he didn't free Jerusalem from Rome is the basis for the Jewish community not accepting him as the Messiah.

Jesus mysteriously disappeared from the time he was about 14 to the age of 30. At the age of 30, he went into the desert alone to do a 40-day fast. Like Buddha and Mahavira, Jesus advocated abstinence from the material world. Jesus advocated a pure mind. He said that if adultery is even thought of, then it is committed in the heart. He spoke in parables and this gave, and still gives, some latitude to interpretation of his words.

Unlike religious leaders before him, Jesus began to preach that he was the Son of God, at least according to the only written source on him, the four Gospels. Jesus promised a blissful heaven where one would live for eternity should one accept him as the Son of God. Anyone not believing Jesus is the Son of God was to be condemned to an eternity of torment. Yet Christians are not taught how to die.

Jesus only ministered three years. Christianity began in A.D. 33 with the crucifixion of Jesus Christ. Recent sects focus on Jesus as a prophet and not the Messiah. This is the tenet of many New Agers.

THE WORST DEATH

The act of dying for most Christians becomes worse than death when we consider the crucifixion of their savior. Of what did Jesus die? It was either suffocation or heart failure. A crucifixion victim could hardly breathe because of a build up of carbon dioxide in the blood. The victim would have to push up with his legs to breathe. That's why the soldiers broke the legs of the two thieves who hung beside Jesus. Broken legs hastened the death. I've never quite figured out if breaking the thieves' legs was humane or not. The time on the cross wouldn't be as long. I don't think the Roman soldiers who monitored the crucifixions were into acts of humanity. Suffocating would be bad enough, but then to feel the pain of broken legs? Since the main point of crucifixion is to torture someone to death, I assume that the pain of broken legs just before death was one last bit of torture.

We know from historical facts that many Zealots were crucified, yet only Jesus as a "good" figure dies by crucifixion in the New Testament.

It would be interesting to know how many people died in the Bible and how they died. How many of them died a natural death? How many of them were killed? Such data might give some new insights into the relationship between Christianity and death.

One biblical individual, Elijah, went to heaven without dying. He went to heaven in a whirlwind in a chariot of fire. (2 K 2:11) I am fascinated by Elijah, this Old Testament John-the-Baptist type. At one point, Elijah took refuge in Cherith Brook, and he was fed by ravens. (1 K 17:6) I'd like to find that spot on the brook. But my main fascination with Elijah is that he appeared, with Moses and God, at the Transfiguration--where his face was shining like the sun and his death was revealed to him. At the Transfiguration, it was Elijah who talked to Jesus. This is a mighty privileged position in Christianity. So, Elijah not only escaped death, but he was one of the messengers to inform Jesus he would be crucified. Now, I better understand the Christian premise for believing one can escape death. Everybody wants to go to heaven, but nobody wants to die.

It is also interesting that of the three human counterparts at the Transfiguration--Elijah, Moses, and Jesus--all did 40-day fasts.

There are also individuals in the Bible who wanted to commit suicide. At one point, Moses asks God to kill him because he felt too much pressure in having the responsibility for the Israelites. (Numbers 11) Elijah too felt a moment of doubt and pain. After defeating Baal's prophets, he fled into the wilderness and while sitting under a broom tree he implored God, "It is enough now, O Lord, take away my life." (1 K 19:4) It is interesting that both former earthly figures at the Transfiguration contemplated suicide.

How did Moses die? We don't really know for sure. God took his life and buried him in the land of Moab. God was angry with Moses because he disobeyed God's order to speak to a rock; instead, Moses smote the rock. (Numbers 20:2-13) The location of his burial is not known either. The moral of Moses' death: Do what God says. I wonder if Moses got to go to heaven. This is a ticklish problem in Christianity. Moses lived according to the Torah, the first five books of the Bible, and as we know the Sadducees upheld these books as proof that there was no personal immortality.

In the history of Christianity, we go from people who escape death to the Messiah being crucified and being resurrected. This total package gives Christians the illusion that death may be defeated. I think this is why Christians have a hard time accepting death. It is as if they believe they can escape death. And what is the basis for this belief? The fundamental core of Christianity is the Resurrection which promises eternal life. For as Paul wrote, "If Christ has not been raised from the dead, then our preaching is in vain, and your faith is worthless." (1 COR 15:14)

This is the reason that Christians, unlike Buddhists and Jainists, are not taught how to die. There is no reason for such a teaching since the main point of Christianity is that one isn't really going to die, but one is going to go to a blissful heaven to live forever. So the earthly death is unimportant. But some people will have to suffer tremendously in their earthly deaths. More liberal Christians argue that the Resurrection is a metaphor. Jesus was resurrected in the thoughts and actions of his followers. The body of Jesus is the church, not a reconstituted physical body. Nevertheless, liberal Christians are not taught how to die either.

THE MASTERS AND THE MASSES

Looking at the history of religions, there are a few masters, then there are disciples who spread the masters' messages, and there are the followers. How do masters become masters? In some cases, they turned their backs on the material world. In some cases, masters achieve tremendous religious insights through intensive meditation or prayer, as with Mohammed.

For many reasons, not everybody can turn his back on the material world or spend long hours in solitary prayer. It would be a different world indeed if everyone did nothing but sat along the river banks contemplating the essence of existence.

Overall there does seem to be a rejection of the material world by the masters. One accomplishment from denying the material world is an acceptance of death. And with the acceptance of death, there is a different view of life. Life becomes transitory, not permanent and material.

The problem becomes that the followers live a paradox. They are firmly attached to the material world, and that attachment includes a denial of death. This group includes Buddhists, Jainists, and Christians.

Whatever we are as humans, we are certainly religious. And I think as religious people, the first thing we need to do in analyzing ourselves is to witness that the masters of the great religions we have today all lived around 2000 years ago.

There are many variables which can be used to explain this. However, I believe that 2000 years ago the human mind was profoundly different than it is today. This is the poignant message of Julian Jaynes' *The Origins of Consciousness in the Breakdown of the Bicameral Mind*.

Perhaps *one* of the reasons we no longer have masters is the ongoing encroachment of noise. The world was a much quieter place 2000 years ago. Of course, this does not explain why the masters popped out of the woodwork about 2000 years ago since it was quiet for a long time before that.

Compassion for the poor is embodied in the message of the three great religious leaders--Buddha, Jesus, and Mohammed. Until these three, religion was not a social service but a mass of rituals designed to result in favors from the deities.

Regardless of the messages, the masters were much more accepting of death than the masses, and this is amplified 2000 years later.

ACCEPTING DEATH

What is death? As defined by many religions, death is an intermediate step in our existence. Death is the entry to another realm. For Christians, this means if they lived a righteous life, they should not fear death.

Several people have told me that a fear of death is the reason scientists search for cures for diseases like cancer and AIDS. Curing diseases will not give us immortality. It seems to me we try to find a cure for diseases so that we can have a healthy, extended life before dying.

In the United States, we try to deny death. But we still die. After we went to the moon, there was an attitude that we could do anything, even escape death. There is an American cliche, "Ignore it and it will go away." Looking into the American psyche, I see both a denial and a fear of death.

Is death something we have to learn to accept? I say yes. When I started studying anthropology, the Eskimos were used for many examples of culture. I was impressed that when it was time for the group to move on and an old person could no longer make the journey, he or she chose to remain behind, sitting alone on the ice. Accepting death, not avoiding it or refusing to think of it, is something we can learn.

LET THE DEAD BURY THE DEAD

Some people asked if I was afraid of dying during my 40-day fast. It was obvious certain people thought I was going to die of starvation during the fast.

While I was writing this portion of the book, the headlines were filled with Dr. Jack Kevorkian assisting people to commit suicide. I feel that these people were not accepting death, but escaping intolerable pain. Is there a difference? When a person is in such pain or anguish, will the person accept anything? Why don't people fast themselves to death when they know death is near? Maybe the suicide would be obfuscated if one fasted himself or herself to death? Would fasting to death really be a peaceful death? Would it allow a person to "watch" death enter the body? Or would the person have organ failure and resulting pain?

If I were told I was terminally ill, I hope I could go alone and fast to death. I would want the quiet time to reflect on my life, and that yet to come. Of course, how we accept death in part depends on our age. If one is young and terminally ill, there is hope of recovery, and I would not advocate fasting to death. However, the older one is, the greater the likelihood of death no matter what.

Through conversations, I have learned that for some people fasting to death seems like crucifixion. It is too slow. They seem to prefer a quick death. Again, there is the big fear of death. On occasion I've heard, "Oh, he died of a heart attack. Thank goodness it was quick and not drawn out." Well, heart attacks are very painful. Another interpretation is that if a person has a heart attack while sleeping and dies, it will be quick and nothing will be felt. I have a hard time believing this. But since we don't have any of those people around to ask, the possible pain will remain a debated point.

If one fasts to death, one presumably gets to experience the entrance to the next phase of one's existence. I would prefer to die like a Zen Buddhist or the Eskimo sitting and waiting for death to arrive. Some might be concerned that freezing to death would not be pleasant, but the extant accounts, like Robert Scott's 1912 diary, indicate that it is slow and peaceful. (Scott froze to death in Antarctica.)

Encapsulating my point, I ask, "What way can I die and experience the most?" I hope I am sensitive to my time of death, and I will be able to go in solitude and fast to death. The isolation and the absence of food will both be necessary, just like Jesus' 40-day fast.

If I don't get to go alone and fast to death, I could be the victim of a funeral. I don't go to funerals anymore. I don't believe in what they represent. Funerals are a way to benchmark one's accomplishments in life. Many people wonder, "How many people will come to my funeral? How plush will my casket be? How will I be remembered? How will I look in the casket?" Most people like the idea of a grandiose funeral. Jessica Mitford's *The American Way of Death* is an insightful commentary on this point. Part of the grandioseness is the fact that all one's friends will be there, talking. Why isn't the focus on what actions are taken now, not how much materialism can be displayed after death?

The American way of dealing with death began to strike me at the funeral of my paternal grandmother. It was the largest funeral in the history of my family's funeral home. The flowers literally overflowed the place. The next week, with that image, I walked into the funeral home, and there was a casket with one lonely arrangement of flowers. The difference stunned me. It was an Amish funeral. Somehow, I thought the friends and family of the deceased didn't care. Then I thought maybe they were poor. About eight years later, I learned the differences between Asian and Western style still-life paintings. In the latter, there are beautiful vases full of flowers and in the former only one beautiful flower is shown on the branch as it grows. So, twice in my life, I have seen parallels between the non-materialistic Amish and the Buddhists.

Some feel my interpretations of the commercialized treatment of death are too harsh. It would be hard to turn one's back on the material world if one is worried about one's great modern funeral.

Matthew 8:

21   And another of his disciples said unto him, "Lord, suffer me first to go and bury my father."
22   Jesus replied, "Follow me; and let the dead bury their dead."

EPITAPHS

As for a treatment of death, who thought up epitaphs? I wonder which culture had the first tombstones, and how these stones relate to our vanity.

Not too many people know about potter's fields. It is mentioned in the New Testament. After betraying Jesus, Judas flung the 30 pieces of silver in the temple and went to hang himself.

Matthew 27:

6   The chief priests picked up the money and said, "It is not right to put
       this in the treasury because it is blood money."
7   Instead, they bought with it Potter's Field as a cemetery for strangers.
8   Therefore that place is called "The Field of Blood."

Potter's fields still exist. There is one right outside of Bradford, Ohio.
But I don't think it functioned much after the 40s. Bradford was a rather
bustling railroad center before the depression. Where there are railroads,
there are hobos, and hobos don't carry money for a funeral.

I went by Bradford's potter's field hundreds, probably thousands, of
times in my life. But I never walked through it to look at the small head
stones. Maybe I'll get back there someday.

CONVICTIONS

Some early Christians were willing to die for what they believed in;
although, there weren't too many during the night of Jesus' betrayal. Even
his main disciple betrayed him because of fear of death. Jesus forewarned
Peter he would deny Jesus on the night of Jesus' arrest.

Matthew 26:

35   Peter said, "Even if I must die with you, I will never betray you." And
       all the other disciples said the same.

Then Jesus was arrested.

58   Peter followed them from a distance. He went to the high priest's
       courtyard and sat down with the attendants to see the end.
67   Then they spat in the face of Jesus. Others slapped him and others
       struck him with their fists.
68   They mocked Jesus, "Prophesy to us, Christ! Who struck you?"
69   Peter was outside in the courtyard and a slave girl approached him,
       saying, "And you were with Jesus the Galilean."
70   Before them all, Peter made a denial, "I do not know what you mean."
71   As he was leaving the courtyard, another girl noticed him, and she
       said to those present, "This man was with Jesus the Nazarene."
72   Peter gave an oath, "I do not know the man."
73   A little later some bystanders came and said to Peter, "Your accent
       reveals that you are one of them."
74   Peter began to curse and to swear, "I do not know the man."

Why did Peter deny Jesus? Because of a simple fear of death. Everybody wants to go to heaven, but nobody wants to die. Yet Jesus said, "Whoever finds his life will lose it, and whoever on my account loses his life will find it." (MT 10:29) Christians seem to focus on the second part of this statement.

RAISED FROM THE DEAD

People sometimes say I read too much into the modern day Christian fear of death. Yet when I ask for an example of a miracle most people respond with Jesus' Resurrection and next Jesus' raising people from the dead. Raising someone from the dead seems like a major miracle since it is tantamount to the creation and continuation of life. However, the act of raising people from the dead is not unique to Jesus. In social history, being raised from the dead is a widespread phenomenon.

Marquesas

In the following account from the Marquesas, it is interesting that this story is divided into two sets of three days, a highly symbolic number in Christianity. It is possible that this story has been influenced by Christianity.

***

As two uncles, Tikaue and Namu, were going to get some crabs, Tikaue stubbed his foot on a stone. At that very moment he was struck with horror and he said to Namu, "Come, we must return. Our niece has strangled herself." When the uncles arrived at the house, the girl was dead.

They both suffered so much grief they wanted to die. Each climbed a coconut tree and jumped head first. But they did not die; nor did they hurt themselves. They climbed the trees and jumped again. They did not die.

Three nights after the girl died, her spirit came to her husband in Nukuhiva. Upon seeing the spirit, the husband wept openly. "Please stop," she said to him and they embraced and pressed noses. Finally they both wailed.

The husband did not understand, "How are you here like this?"

She replied, "My husband, I have died."

"But you can't be dead since your body is here."

"Nevertheless, I have died. You must tell your family to gather certain fruits and plants and squeeze them all together. Put the juice of the plants in that trough." The husband addressed his family. When the family members had gone to look for the plants, the woman told her husband, "Please shut off our room with a piece of cloth. After three nights assemble the family and take away this curtain."

After three nights, the husband assembled the family and removed the cloth. The woman was alive. The family marveled greatly and they were pleased.

***

The "average" Christian is going to say, "Hey, wait a minute. This is a myth. No one jumped head first from a tree and didn't get hurt. This has nothing to do with individuals coming back from the dead."

The matter at hand is: What are we going to accept as proof of someone coming back from the dead? What would someone from the Marquesses think about the Christian individual, Elijah, going to heaven in a chariot of fire? Did this really happen?

Most Marquesans, of a century past, probably would believe the chariot of fire story. And apparently some present-day Christians continue to believe it.

Roman

While Jesus was working miracles in his little section of the Near East, a Pythagorean philosopher named Apollonius of Tyana was working miracles further to the west in the Mediterranean. Apollonius is described as one who healed the blind, the lame, and the paralyzed. He also performed similar miracles on himself.

Once, it is told, while he was in Rome, he brought a girl back to life. The girl died just before she was to be married. All of Rome was grieving over her death because she was from a prominent family. Apollonius went to the funeral and told the people to put down her body, and he would end their grief. He brought her back to life.

Christian

In Christian history, there are many reported cases of people bringing a dead person back to life. St. Ignatius Loyola brought a man back to life who had hung himself for losing a lawsuit. St. Philip Neri resurrected a 14 year old boy. Father Vincent Bernedo brought back a widow about to be buried and a boy who drowned. Blessed Margaret of Castello brought at least three people back to life at different times. These are only a few of the "raising the dead" stories. An apparent key to all the incidents is a belief by the "resurrector" that he or she could bring the people from a dead state to a living form.

In *Raised from the Dead*, Father Albert J. Hebert provides details of 400 individuals being resurrected from the dead. There are several perplexities in these cases. Most important, why do all the cases take place before the 20th century?

WHY DON'T WE RAISE 'EM FROM THE DEAD ANYMORE?

A main problem with accounts of being raised from the dead is verification. Many Christians claim that the cases from the non-Christian world lack verification and are mythological accounts.

I then confront Christians with the problem of why I no longer hear of such cases in the industrialized/Christian world. To date, the only answer I have is, "I don't know."

Well, I don't either, but have we perhaps lost so much spirituality, that people are no longer capable of this "miraculous skill" of raising the dead? Or did it ever happen?

My explanation of the miracles of raising the dead is an extension of my explanation of curing. There is a transfer of energy from one person to the next and/or a change from some state of unconsciousness to consciousness in the apparently dead person. My ideas receive support from Sherwin Nuland's book, *How We Die*. The core of Nuland's perspective is that until this century, death was an element of the home. People didn't go to hospitals to die. They died in the home, and the immediate family was there to watch and to interact with the dying person. The sights, sounds, and smells of death were as ordinary as those of a baby being born in the home.

The family was there when grandma died. They remembered her for who she was; not necessarily for what killed her. And in such cases, if someone were there with the ability or power to transfer energy to someone not really dead, this could account for resurrection. Nobody, not even Jesus, could resurrect an embalmed body.

Now, in industrialized countries, most people die in hospitals removed from the basic humanity which surrounded them all their lives. The dead slowly become medical statistics with a room number. If dying people are taken straight to the hospital for some modern treatment, saints or traditional curers have no opportunity to try healing the person. This might account for why the dead are no longer raised.

But is this the real answer? Maybe through time we as humans have lost some of our spirituality. We have become much more materially oriented, and much less involved with nature. We are more concerned with having a high priced car than a spiritual self. As a consequence, maybe there are fewer individuals capable of raising people from the dead.

According to Nuland, most dying patients are so awestruck by the authority of medical science and so frightened of dying that they grab whatever shreds of hope are held out to them.

Again the ugly question raises its head, "Why should Christians be frightened of dying? Aren't they going to heaven?"

One of the more insightful things I learned about Nuland and death came from a review of his book by Michele Ingassia (*Newsweek*). Nuland characterized himself as "...a Jewish agnostic, chuckling at the incongruity of belonging to a temple when he's not even sure he believes in God."

His honesty brings home a familiar point: We do things and often don't know why we are doing them. If we are agnostic, why go to a temple or church? Is our attendance because of social pressure? Going to a temple or church, when we don't know if we believe God exists, may mean we are frightened of dying not only because life stops, but because of the great religious unknown. Nuland said people are so frightened of dying that they grab at shreds of hope from science. It comes back to a statement made in the beginning: We have religions because of a fear of what will happen to us after death. Everybody wants to go to heaven, but nobody wants to die.

AT THE CROSSROADS

Three types of miracles have been discussed. I call these three types of miracles "other-dependent" miracles. These miracles require one or more people. (The healer needs someone to heal.) We have to be in a certain situation to either witness or induce such a miracle.

1. Healing the sick. This can be explained by the healer transferring energy to the sick, and/or the sick having a changed state of mind by believing he or she has been healed.

Again the only way we might be able to experience this type of miracle is if we were sick or we believed we had the power to heal.

2. Feeding the masses. This can be explained by a person infusing energy into the food or the consumer/ practitioner believing a small amount of food would feed them.

3. Being raised from the dead. Here we might assume that an individual was not really dead, but in a state of suspended animation, and the touch of a super-energetic person (or the voice of a stranger, as in hypnosis) brought him or her out of the state of suspended animation.

However, two miracles are totally individual oriented: walking on water and seeing the future. We have arrived at the crossroads. How are we going to explain those miracles?

Which way are we going to go? We have one of three choices. We can take the road of blind acceptance; or we can take the road of the skeptic who doesn't care to talk about it; or we can take the road of the skeptic who tries to explain. I care to take the latter path, and in doing so, I constantly ask myself, "Why do I believe what I believe?"

8

MYTHOLOGY OR RELIGION?

WHY DO WE BELIEVE WHAT WE BELIEVE?

Do you believe what you believe because your parents told you so?
Do you believe what you believe because a friend told you so?
Do you believe what you believe because you read it?
Do you believe what you believe because of something you experienced?

We all have one thing in common--being born into a belief system about the world around us. We have another commonality: Most of us do not know much about the history of our religion. Somehow we accept our religion as correct because our parents and/or society indoctrinated us. Often we accept it because it's the path of least resistance. Investigating religious beliefs requires a tremendous intellectual energy investment. Ask a Methodist, for example, when the Methodist church began and why, and most times the answer will be, "I don't know." So, why are Methodists Methodists? By far the great majority are Methodist because of their parents. It would be a complex household if the children went to a Catholic church while the parents went to a Methodist church.

Most of us have another religious commonality. We are not taught much about other religions, except that they are probably wrong or weird, or at least, they are not "ours." The further we get from similarities of our own religious beliefs, the more likely we are to label other religions as mythology.

SEMANTICS?

When I passed this chapter around for review, one friend suggested I entitle it "Religion or Mythology?" My friend felt that as a matter of validity, religion should be placed before mythology. So I asked my friend if I were discussing science and religion, should science be placed first in the title? For some people it is right to place science first. However, the validity of religious beliefs are often different. Most Christians don't find the shaministic beliefs of the Eskimos valid. Some people think the Eskimo religion is false. We are back at my childhood experiences of Methodists versus Catholics.

Validity is not an idle point since it involves the creationism/ evolutionism debate. What do the creationists say about the Paleolithic cave paintings of Europe? Most social scientists feel these must figure into the chronology of human existence somewhere. But we can go back to the Scopes Trial in Dayton, Tennessee, and understand why creationists do not want to accept science or its endeavors. For them, there was a Garden of Eden, and then sometime chronologically later, there was Jesus. And they believe, one day Jesus will return, and there will be no need for science in heaven or hell. In the meantime, what we find as scientists is irrelevant.

As an archaeologist, I am concerned with social evolution and religious diversity on many levels. If Adam and Eve and the Garden of Eden were in the beginning, where did all the other spiritual beliefs populating the globe come from? Religious diversity is an intellectually consuming point for me. I am not interested in hearing other religions explained away as "the work of the devil." Once people do this, they deny themselves the opportunity to gain something beneficial from other religions. For example, I can see no reason why Christians don't incorporate meditation into their doctrine. But many people to whom I suggest this idea insist I am influenced by sacrilegious beliefs from the orient. Then they suggest that prayer is meditation. However, most prayer is not meditation. Most prayer is a form of chanting. Silence is a form a meditation.

What is mythology and what is religion? Mythology has a special function in religion. Myth is a collection of stories addressing the needs of a group. The basic needs of every group are an explanation of origins, gods, heroes, and history, much like the Old Testament. Religion, however, is a belief in and reverence for supernatural beings, sometimes regarded as the creator(s). Religion is a code of ethics, often dictated by the creator(s) through a human master or leader, by which we should live our lives to enter another existence after this lifetime.

Yet, the difference between mythology and religion depends on whom you ask, "us" or "them." Anthropologists quickly learn that most groups have a name for themselves which translates as "people." The names they have for other groups of people are often less complimentary. The Cheyenne Indians don't call themselves "Cheyenne"; they call themselves "Tsistsistas." This can be translated as "our people." The Sioux call the Cheyenne "people of alien speech." Often a group will refer to its spiritual beliefs as religion and the spiritual beliefs of others as something untrue, mythology.

Hinduism has a similar etymology. Persians referred to the Indus Valley as *hind*. Eventually, Muslims referred to the peoples of South Asia as *hindu*. The people of South Asia did not refer to themselves as hindu.

Another distinction is temporal. Historic groups such of the Aztecs and Greeks are seen to believe in myth, while present day groups have "religions."

Thus, mythology is one means of categorizing the religious beliefs of others. In the 1940s, the "average" American thought Buddhism was mythology. Today the "average" American is a little more open-minded. Nevertheless, even today religions are designed to protect themselves. Leaders of religions are in the business of perpetuating their positions. Otherwise they jeopardize their incomes. Sometimes perpetuating a belief system requires that everything outside of the belief system be considered false.

Religion is a way humans feel about the nature of the universe. I look at religion as something in the human spirit. There is something in the human spirit battling good and evil. Obviously Satan tempting Jesus is an example of the battle between evil and good.

Buddha had a similar experience. Siddhartha Gautama (Buddha) left his life as a prince and gave up the material world. He became a wandering ascetic. As part of his intellectual quest to understand himself, he had to analyze the battle between good and evil that waged in his head.

In Buddhist mythology, when Buddha became a wandering ascetic, Mara, an evil temptress, followed him and promised him an empire if he would desist from his intention of becoming enlightened. No Buddhist monk believes that any female spirit offered Buddha an empire. This is a myth which adults can use to teach young children so that they can begin to understand the battles between good and evil and between materialism and spirituality. In terms of Buddhist religion, *mara* is a Sanskrit word meaning hindrance. There are many hindrances which keep one from becoming a moral and/or enlightened person.

This is an interesting parallel between Buddhism and Christianity. Mara offered Buddha an empire and Satan offered Jesus kingdoms. Yet, Mara made her offer to Buddha 500 years before Jesus was born. The significance in both religious versions is a poignant message that materialism can destroy spirituality. Buddha and Jesus both rejected the offers.

AN IMPORTANT FACT

What do we know about the written sources on which Islam, Buddhism, and Christianity are based?

Consider this: Buddha died when he was 80; Mohammed died when he was 62; Jesus died at the age of 33. This is probably one reason we know less about Jesus than the other two religious figures. Had Jesus lived longer, we might know more about him and his philosophy. Maybe we would know where he spent some of his missing years and if his philosophical message was influenced by someone else. We might know if Jesus ever baptized. As it now stands, we can only say that in the four Gospels, there is no record of him ever baptizing anyone.

Furthermore, of the three great religious figures, Jesus is known only from one written source, the New Testament. Buddha and Mohammed are known from different sources of their times. Thus, outside of the Bible there is no proof that Jesus ever existed. Some Christians are quick to argue that we don't need more proof. Maybe we don't; but for me, it would be nice to know more about Jesus. For example, I would like to know if he ever laughed. Remember, the Gospel of John ends with, "And there are also many other things which Jesus did, the which, if they should be written, I suppose that even the world could not contain the books that should be written." I want to know those "many other things."

CHANGE

Buddha, Jesus, and Mohammed all symbolized change. Each presented a philosophy of religion different from their society. Each must have asked himself at one time or another, "Why do I believe what I believe?" Each in a very profound way rejected the religious cannons of his day.

Some people worry about change. But I wonder: Can't the philosophies of any of these three great teachers be refined? If I try to reinterpret the words of Jesus, I am considered by some to be a heretic and a heathen. Since Jesus himself didn't write his own words, I assume there was some reinterpretation of his philosophy from the very beginning. I assume the same for Buddhism and Islam, since Buddha and Mohammed didn't write anything either.

Nothing escapes change. Christianity today is not what it was 200 years after the death of Jesus. At that time, the various Protestant groups of today's globe did not exist. Christianity continually changes.

The changes and directions of American religions are outlined in *Megatrends 2000*. The point of the chapter "Religious Revival of the Third Millennium" is that Americans are looking for spiritual fulfillment and traditional organized religions are not providing it. In other words, our traditional churches have become a depot of ritual with little emphasis on what each of us can do to become a more spiritual person. It would be a fundamentally different church if the minister espoused, "Don't come here next Sunday. Go sit alone in the woods and wonder about your existence."

In *Megatrends 2000*, it is reported there is a tremendous decline in mainstream religions. The United Methodist Church dropped from 11 million members in 1965 to 9 million in 1990. In the Roman Catholic Church, there were about 176,000 nuns in 1968 and by 1988 the number had dropped to 107,000. In 1987, an average of 15 nuns a day left the cloisters.

In attempting to create a complete picture of religion today, one must include all the variations that exist. For example, how many people know there are 4 million followers of Islam in the United States? How many people know that Buddhist chaplains are recognized by the U.S. armed forces?

Looking at the great diversity of religious beliefs, I am not surprised that "New Agers" originated. While many individuals see New Agers as detached from the foundations of Christianity, New Agers have correctly perceived the loss of spiritual fulfillment on the part of organized religion. Constantly, I'm asked by life-long Methodists and Catholics, "Who are New Agers?" Simply put, they are a diverse group maintaining the underlying principle of individualism of religious beliefs. Most despise the herd instinct. They basically feel that one must arrive at one's own salvation. They ask: Is Christianity becoming merely ritual without personal meaning?

On occasion when I am discussing religion, I find it hard to find a line between some New Agers and some Buddhists. In Buddhist countries, most Buddhist don't participate in a Sunday group exercise of reading from a book, and then group singing, and then group prayer, and then group responsive readings, and then group offerings of money. Rather they will go to any of a number of temples in the country. They will walk outside and reflect on nature. They will eventually make their way to the main temple, and they will bow to the main statue of the Buddha, and they will perhaps deposit money in an offering box. They spend their religious time quietly reflecting. Many New Agers likewise go the countryside for quiet reflection.

I, too, believe each person must seek his or her own salvation. Over time, we have become much more materially oriented, and much less involved with our inner selves. Most people are more concerned with the clothes they wear to church than their spiritual self.

As far as change, if any person deviates just a little from "the accepted Christian dogma" he or she is branded as a "cult" member by many Christians. Josh McDowell and Don Stewart explain this well in *Understanding the Cults*. The bottom line of that book is there are the "we's" and the "they's." The "we's" have religion and the "they's" have cults, not a "real" religion. I think Jesus would have understood how some New Age groups feel when they are branded as cults.

Matthew 21:

45   When the chief priests and the Pharisees heard Jesus, they knew he was talking about them.
46   They wanted to arrest Jesus, but they were afraid of the crowds since they considered him a prophet.

I think about this passage when I try to tell people that the four Gospels were written by one person. Why do some people act as if they want to have me arrested? And for what? If we really had good written representations of Jesus' life, Christianity would not have the problems it now has.

BACK TO THE PHARISEES

Changes in Christianity are all built on one basic principle going back to the Pharisees: Apply the principle of the law to new questions. People have the right to interpret and reinterpret any scriptures within the context of Judaic Law and the times they are living in. After all, Christianity is 2000 years old. It's useful to reinterpret the scriptures for today's society. If you are a Catholic, you now hear mass in English. Your great grandparents, assuming they were Catholic, would be stunned to go to mass with you. If you are Protestant, your grandparents would be stunned to go to churches in drive-in theaters which gained some notoriety in the 1970s.

These are matters of form. As for changes in spiritual content, the New Age movement is yet another reinterpretation of the Christian scriptures. Consider Jesus' words, "Alas for you, scribes and Pharisees, hypocrites; you resemble white washed tombs which appear beautiful on the outside, but inside they are full of dead mens' bones and every impurity." (MT 23:27)

I have asked many people what Christianity is, and the most common comment is: It's the belief that Jesus is the Son of God. Those I ask sometimes add that they also feel one can have everlasting life by believing in Jesus. Nowhere in this statement is there a requirement to go to a church or to belong to a church. Indeed, until Jesus came along, there were strict rules about ritual behavior, such as going to the synagogue every sabbath and observing ritual behaviors in the home. Jesus broke the rules. He drew part of his belief from the Pharisees and possibly part of it from the Essenes and he added the rest.

Was what Jesus added of his own will or was it inspired by God? I don't have an answer, but I do know it will be a point of debate until he comes back.

Jesus was quite adamant in his rejection of ritual, unlike the Pharisees and Essenes. Early in his ministry, Jesus made a cogent statement about fasting and ritual.

Matthew 6:

16   "When you fast, do not be sad-faced like the hypocrites, for they disfigure their faces to let others know they are fasting. I assure you, they have received their full reward.

17   "When you fast, wash your face and grease your head.
18   "In this way, only your heavenly Father who is there in the secret place may notice your fasting. And your Father who sees in secret will reward you."

OLD TO NEW

There are three major phenomena in the New Testament not found in the Old Testament. All of these phenomena Christians hold up as proof of the divinity of Jesus: the virgin birth, Jesus walking on water, and his resurrection. Almost every other event in the New Testament is found in the Old Testament. For example, Jesus fed many people with a little food; Elisha of the Old Testament did the same.

Knowing almost everything in the New Testament is in the Old Testament, I was forced to ask: What acts and events are in the Bible that do not exist in other religions? The question then begs: What is particular to Christianity? Is virgin birth only found in Christianity? No. Is walking on water only found in Christianity? No. Is the raising of the dead only found in Christianity? No. Is building temples on holy sites only found in Christianity? No. Are the mystical qualities of mountains found only in Christianity? No.

Joseph Campbell said it best. There are a series of themes found in the human consciousness: stealing fire from the gods, the global flood, the land of the dead, virgin births, resurrected heroes, being sired by god, dying on a hill, ascending to heaven, etc.

Looking at what some call myth, and comparing it to Christianity, gives me a deeper background for understanding Christianity. There are many motifs and themes common to most religions. By exploring common motifs, Christians may deepen their understanding of what a particular motif means in Christianity.

Most elements of Christian ideology are found in other religions. However, three beliefs that are not commonly found in other religions are feeding the masses, the Christian beliefs that Jesus is the Son of God, and that he is coming back to Earth.

So, why does anyone believe what he or she believes? If I accept being part of a greater system, then I must, at this point in time and space, accept being part of a great unknown. Looking at myself in terms of a larger context should help me examine myself and my beliefs. On a personal level I have found four themes fascinating: virgin births, the mysticism of mountains, consecrating specific earthly events by building temples, and fasting.

VIRGIN BIRTHS

The virgin birth of Jesus is offered as proof of his divinity by many Christians. However, the concept of "virgin birth" or of a woman giving birth without impregnation as we know it is reported in many religions.

The Inuit trickster Raven was born by a woman who ingested a feather that was floating in the sea. The Water Jar Boy of the Tewa Indians was conceived when a piece of clay went into his mother while she was making a pot. The Changing Woman story of the Navajo tells of a woman who gave birth to twins through conception by contact with the sun. In Hindu religion, Karna was conceived and born by a virgin who was impregnated by the sun. In Buddhism, Buddha's mother, Mahamaya, was circled by an elephant three times, struck by the right side of the elephant, and later Buddha was born. Zoroastrianism recounts the story of the conception of Zarathustra by light.

Often Christians assert that virgin births in other religions are mythology and didn't actually transpire. Many Christians believe they have the only "proven" virgin birth. Any virgin birth is difficult to prove.

MOUNTAINS

Mountains have a mystical place in most religions, and Christianity is no exception.

> Jacob solemnly vowed to keep this promise. He killed an animal, which he offered as a sacrifice on the mountain and he invited his men to the meal. After they had eaten, they spent the night on the mountain. (Genesis 31:53-54)

> The Lord came down on the top of Mount Sinai and called Moses to the top of the mountain. (Exodus 19:20)

> The dazzling light of the Lord's presence came down on the mountain. To the Israelites the light looked like a fire burning on top of the mountain. The cloud covered the mountain for six days, and on the seventh day the Lord called to Moses from the cloud. (Exodus 24:16-17)

> Moses went on up the mountain into the cloud. There he stayed for forty days and nights. (Exodus 24:18)

> Elijah got up, ate and drank, and the food gave him enough strength to walk forty days to Sinai, the holy mountain. (1 Kings 19:8)

The Lord said, "Mortal man, speak to the mountains of Israel and tell them to listen to the message which I, the sovereign Lord, have for them. Israel's enemies gloated and said, "Now those ancient hills are ours." (Ezekiel 36:1-2)

And before Jesus walked on water, he went to a mountain to pray.

I once asked Zen Master Kando Nakagima why the Zen built their temples high in the mountains. He contemplated for some time then replied, "I don't know, but the animals in the mountains seem more friendly to me."

As I began to study world religions in greater detail, the mountain motif appeared time and again.

Aztec

There's a mountain story in Aztec religion that goes something like this: The fifth Aztec king, Moctezuma the Elder, spoke to his prime minister, "O ancient father, I want to know the true story. Tell me from the knowledge hidden in your books on the seven caves from which our ancestors came forth. I wish to know about the place where our god Huitzilopochtli was born and where the Aztecs hailed from."

"O mighty lord," answered the prime minister, "Our forbearers dwelt in that blissful, happy place of Aztlan, which means 'whiteness.' In that place, there is a small mountain in the midst of the waters. It is called Colhuacan, Twisted Hill, because its summit is twisted. On its slopes are caves where our grandfathers lived.

"However, after our forbearers came to the mainland and abandoned that delightful place, everything turned against them. I have seen it painted in our ancient books."

Moctezuma then appointed 60 sorcerers to go seek that small mountain that had given birth to the Aztec people. Laden with rich gifts from the king, they departed to the north. Some time later they reached a small mountain called Coatepec in the province of Tula. There they conducted secret rituals, traced magic symbols upon the ground, and smeared themselves with their ritual ointments.

Finally they invoked the spirits. The sorcerers begged the spirits to show them the home of their ancestors. Through the spirits the sorcerers became birds or wild beasts: ocelots, jaguars, jackals, and wildcats. In these forms they arrived, together with their gifts, at the land of their forbearers.

On reaching the shores of a great lagoon from the midst of which emerged the hill called Colhuacan, the sorcerers resumed their human forms. They stood on the shore of the lake and they saw fishermen going about in canoes. The sorcerers called to them. The natives, seeing the strangers and hearing them speak the same language, rowed to the shore and asked what they wanted and where they came from. An Aztec soothsayer answered, "Sir, we have come from Mexico and we are the envoys of the authorities there. We have come to seek the homeland of our ancestors."

The people of the place asked, "What god do you adore?" To which they answered, "Huitzilopochtli." They added that Moctezuma had sent them to find Coatlicue, "She of the Snaky Skirt," mother of Huitzilopochtli, and the seven caves, Chicomoztoc. They also wished to deliver gifts to his mother.

The natives welcomed the sorcerers into their canoes and took them to Colhuacan. The old priest, caretaker of the Lady of the Snaky Skirt, lived at the foot of the hill. He welcomed them, and asked, "Who sent you?"

"Moctezuma," they replied.

"I know not this name. Those who departed from here were Tezacatetl, Acacitli, Ahuexotl, Ocelopan, Ahuatl, Xomimitl, Huicton, and Tenoch."

"Sir," responded an Aztec soothsayer, "We never met those people, but we know of them, for we are their grandchildren. Those leaders you have mentioned have gone from earth."

The old man was amazed. "Why is it that all of us are still alive here in the place they abandoned? Why is it that none of us have died? Who is now the custodian of Huitzilopochtli?"

"The great priest Cuauhcoatl is the custodian of Huitzilopochtli. Only he can speak with our god."

The old man said, "Take what you have brought and follow me."

They put their gifts on their shoulders and followed the old man. He climbed the hill with ease. They followed, but as they went up their feet began to sink as though they walked in soft sand. The further they walked the more difficult it was. The elder turned to see that the sand had almost reached their knees. The elder beckoned them to make haste. Finally, they sank to their hips, and they yelled for help from the old man who was walking with such lightness that his feet did not seem to touch the ground.

He chastised them, "What is wrong with you, O Aztecs? What has made you so heavy? What do you eat in your land?"

"We eat the foods that grow there and we drink chocolate."

"Those foods and drink have made you heavy, and they make it difficult for you to reach the place of your ancestors. Those foods will bring death. The wealth you have we know nothing about; we live simply. Give me your loads and wait. I will call the mistress of this land so that you may see her."

The mistress appeared from her mourning, "Know that since your god, my son, Huitzilopochtli, departed from here, I have awaited his return. Is it true, my children, you have been sent by the eight leaders whom my son took with him?"

The envoy was filled with fear. One soothsayer spoke, "O great and powerful lady, we have never seen the heads of the tribes. We were sent by your servant Moctezuma to visit you and seek the place where our ancestors lived. We wish you to know that Moctezuma now rules over Mexico. He is not the first king, but the fifth. The previous ones lived with great hunger and poverty until they conquered other provinces and made them pay tribute. Please accept these gifts in the name of your son."

"What have you brought me?"

"Great lady, it is food and chocolate."

"This is what burdens you. This is why you cannot climb the hill. Go and tell my son to have pity on me and to observe my loneliness. Look at me; life has become fasting and penance because of him. So that he may remember me please take him this mantle and loincloth of simple maguey fiber."

As the envoy descended the hill, the old woman beckoned them, "Stop so that you can see how people never die on this mountain. Do you see my old servant? As he climbs down, he becomes younger."

The old man descended, and as he ran he became younger and younger. Standing in front of them, he said, "I am now a youth of 20. Watch as I climb and grow older." Halfway up the hill he was 40. The further up he went, the older he became. "Behold the virtues of the hill. Anyone can climb to the point on the hill he wishes and there he will acquire the age he seeks. That is why we live to old age, and that is why none of the companions of your ancestors have died since the departure of your people. We become young when we wish. You have become old; you have become tired because of the chocolate you drink and the foods you eat. You have been spoiled by the mantles of rare feathers and the riches that you wear. All of this has ruined you."

The envoy returned to Mexico and told Moctezuma what they had seen and been told. Moctezuma wept at not being able to see the land of his origins. The maguey fiber mantle and loincloth were sent to the temple and placed on Huitzilopochtli.

****

This story is more than an example of the mountain motif. This is the exact message of Jesus, materialism corrupts; or in the words of the Aztecs, it spoils and ruins. This is a succinct encapsulation in story form of the precarious balance between materialism and spiritualism.

With this story as a background, I continue to wonder: What did Jesus feel like as he went up a mountain? Did he feel wise or older? Was he able to relate to mountains in a way we are incapable of? The message of Jesus is: If one rejects the material world, one can experience a spirituality that is otherwise denied to one.

Maya

For the Maya-Q'Equchi' of Guatemala, mountains are alive. Mountains are thought to have the quality of personhood, and this applies only to mountains and people. While animals and plants have spirits, they are not imbued with the spirit specific to people and mountains. The mountains' spirits are believed to have human form and to live in caves.

The mountains' spirits own the land and everything on the surface. The spirits guard the plants, animals, and people. The mountains' spirits are the original owner of corn. People only hold corn on an extended loan. Because of the mountains' spirits, the Maya go to the mountains in hope of a cure for sickness and other placations.

Do the Maya really feel something in the mountains? Or do we of the scientific First World who export Christianity to them tell them that it is all in their minds? I think both. Thus I am forced to deal with whether the something the Maya feel in the mountain is real. There is little I can say to the skeptic that will be convincing.

Mohammed and Reverend Moon

Jesus went to mountains for some type of spiritual rejuvenation. It was on an "unusually high mountain" that Satan showed Jesus all the kingdoms of the world.

Matthew 17:

1   Now after six days, Jesus took Peter, James and John up into a lofty mountain.
2   And there Jesus was transfigured. His face was like the sun and his raiment was like white light.
3   Simultaneously Moses and Elijah appeared and talked to Christ.
4   Then Peter spoke to Christ, "Lord, it is good for us to be here. If you care, we can make three temples here. One for you, one for Moses, and one for Elijah."

Why did Jesus have to take Peter, James, and John up to a mountain? Only for solitude? What is important about mountains? Couldn't one have visions at an isolated place on the coast? What is so essential about mountains that significant biblical events, such as the Transfiguration, occured there? Are there documented cases of any other religious leaders obtaining spiritual enlightenment in mountains?

Soon after his 40th birthday, Mohammed was praying in solitude on a mountainside near Mecca. He had his first vision. The angel Gabriel ordered him to reform the faith of his people.

About 1936, Sun Myung Moon had a vision while praying on a Korean mountainside. In the vision, Jesus appeared to Moon and informed him that Moon had been chosen to carry out the task of converting the world, thus the title of his Unification Church. Moon came to the United States at the end of 1971, and today the Unification Church claims 2,000,000 members.

Some people blast Moon as a "cultist." At the bottom of this accusation are the fundamental questions: When is a vision real? What gives any vision credibility?

Heading into my attempt at a 40-day fast, I had some concerns for what I might see. What was I to do if Jesus appeared to me in a vision and said, "Terry, Reverend Moon did not complete the mission I set forth. You are now my chosen one." This isn't funny. What would I do? What am I supposed to do?

When is a vision religious and when is it a meaningless hallucination? I don't have the answer, and I doubt I ever will. One would have to ask the individual who had the vision and decide for oneself. Certainly, we are back to myth and religion. Within the confines of Christianity, a vision of Jesus is acceptable, but a vision of Buddha is not.

An Incident

I am still left with one question. Do mountains have a spiritual quality that humans can tap into under certain psychological circumstances? Or is it the solitude of mountains with silence that redirects human thoughts? I think Jesus could have obtained isolation without going up on mountains; thus, I am left with the idea that mountains do have a spirituality quality.

An incident occurred in Iowa in 1976 that showed me that it might be possible to tap into the spiritual energy of the earth. I was excavating a site in southeastern Iowa. There were four individuals with me. While we were excavating, an old man came by with a water-witching rod. He asked if he might walk over the site. We welcomed him. I watched as he traversed the land. Suddenly at one spot the V-shaped rod went quivering to the ground. He continued and he came back upon the same spot from a different angle, and sure enough it happened again. "Something is under the ground here," he said matter-of-factly.

I walked over to him and probably in a tone too blunt, I asked, "May I see that?"

He handed it to me and off I went. I walked around randomly. When I got to where the rod had bent for him, a power pulled it to the earth. I glanced out of the corner of my eye and smiled at the old man. He simply shrugged.

I was off again. Again, as I came over that spot, the earth pulled the rod toward it. This time I looked squarely at the old man, and slowly shaking my head I conceded, "That's amazing."

"Maybe a burial," he replied.

We dug on that spot. There was no burial. And we dug deep. We were far below any cultural deposit. The man stayed with us and after we finished digging, he walked over it again. The rod pulled to the earth.

I have no explanation, but it was a spiritual experience for me to feel that inanimate object suddenly move with ongoing force. I've always wondered if an individual could tap that power source. I think it's possible.

TEMPLES

In many cultures around the world, temples are built at the site of a religious experience. Many people want to build something as a physical remembrance of an event. The event sometimes becomes codified as religion or mythology. Later, people visit the site as a personal confirmation of religious belief. If enough people visit the shrine, it becomes a pilgrimage center.

The matter of economics of temples and pilgrimage is documented in the birth of Islam. The angel Gabriel ordered Mohammed to reform the faith of his people. At that time, Mecca was a "pagan" religious center and pilgrimages contributed heavily to its wealth. In A.D. 630, Mohammed entered the city with an army of 10,000 and the Meccans surrendered. Mohammed ordered all pagan idols destroyed except two: a meteorite called the Black Stone and the Kaaba, the temple housing the Black Stone.

By keeping the temple and the Black Stone, Mohammed insured that people would still come for pilgrimages. And to insure further monetary flow into Mecca, four chief duties of each Muslim is ordained in the *Koran*. They are prayer, alms giving, fasting, and pilgrimage to Mecca. Pilgrimage, or the *Hajj*, to Mecca is required at least once by all able Muslims.

After Jesus' Transfiguration, Peter asked if they should build three tabernacles; one for Jesus, one for Moses, and one for Elijah. In the Jerusalem version of the Bible (the oldest existing Bible), the word tent, not tabernacle, is used. However, the implication is not of camping, but of ritual.

In 1970, I was part of an excavation team that excavated the smallest temple known in ancient Mexico. It was 4 meters by 4 meters. It came complete with the sacrificial remains of a baby. It could have been built in one day by several people.

A parallel to building temples and the Transfiguration is found in the Aztec religion. This is one of my favorite passages in religious studies. *General History of the Things of New Spain*, by the Catholic monk Bernardino De Sahagun, written about the Aztecs not long after the Spanish conquest in 1521, gives a good understanding about the event from the Spanish point of view. Soon after the Spanish landed and began their conquest of Mexico,

King Moctezuma the Younger sent a group of sorcerers to cast spells over the Spanish so the Aztecs might defeat them. Among the group that went as messengers were soothsayers, magicians, and incense-offering priests.

Not long after leaving the Aztec capital of Tenochtitlan, the group of sorcerers came upon a drunk man in the road. The wizards were confused by him. He was dressed like someone from Chalco, a city to the south. He had eight grass ropes bound around his chest. He walked toward them.

Nearing them he asked, "What is it that you hope to gain in this journey? What is it that Moctezuma wishes? Has he still not come to his senses? Is he living in great fear?"

The messengers did not know what to think of the Chalcan. They remained silent as he continued talking, "Understand that Moctezuma, your king and leader, had committed a great fault. He abandoned and destroyed the common people. Because of Moctezuma, the common people have been struck on the head, and they are now wrapped in funeral garments. They have been laughed at; they have been mocked."

The company of messengers knew this person was not a commoner. But who was he? To pay him homage, they quickly built a small clay temple with a straw bed. In quiet did the Chalcan watch, and when they had finished, he spoke with great passion. "Do you not yet understand that the fate of Mexico has been decided? Mexico is gone forever. Look behind you and see what already has come to pass."

When they looked, they saw a vision of the large temples, the schools, and the houses of their Aztec capital being consumed with flames that leaped high into the heavens. The demise of their culture was reflected in their eyes, and the soothsayers were speechless. Their hearts went from them. They could no longer speak in a clear manner. They swallowed in choking agony. Finally, one soothsayer spoke, "This was not meant for us to see. Moctezuma should have seen this. It was meant for him. And truly, this messenger appearing as a Chalcan, who accosted us, was not just anyone; he was the youth, the trickster, Tezcatlipoca."

When they turned around, Tezcatlipoca, disguised as a Chalcan, had vanished. At that moment the group of wizards abandoned their mission. They went to notify Moctezuma.

Upon hearing their words, Moctezuma slowly bowed his head. For speechless hours, he sat dejected. He had lost hope. Finally, raising his head, he spoke, "What now? It appears our fate has been cast. Will we go into the mountains for our refuge? What now will be done in vain? What will happen to the unfortunate ones? The old men and women and the young children do not understand. While we go to the mountains, where will they be taken?"

Later, while addressing a crowd of Aztecs, an individual threw a stone hitting Moctezuma in the head. He died. He never escaped to the mountain. But did the soothsayers? I believe they did.

FASTING

Fasting is found in religions throughout the world. Jesus never ministered until after he fasted 40 days. He was definitely not concerned with the material world. By rejecting the material world enough, one can void oneself of certain mental constraints. Fasting emphasizes what is and what is not important in the material world. After three days of fasting, most people realize that their normal daily food consumption is too much. Some people often eat the amount they do because of oral displacement, because of commercial influence, and because they are too often being consumed by the material world.

With the subject of fasting in mind, we can continue with the Transfiguration in Matthew.

Matthew 17:

5   While Peter was speaking, a bright cloud overshadowed them. And a voice said, "This is my beloved Son, in whom I am well pleased; listen to his words."
6   The disciples fell face down in fear.
7   Jesus touched them and told them not to be afraid and to get up.
8   When they looked there was only Jesus. [Moses and Elijah were gone]
9   And as they were going down the mountain, Jesus told them not to tell anyone about the vision until the Son of Man be risen again from the dead.
10   And the disciples asked, "Why then do the scribes say that Elijah must come first?"
11   Jesus answered, "Elijah truly shall first come, and restore all things.
12   "But I say unto you, Elijah is come already, and they knew him not, but have done unto him whatsoever they listed. Likewise shall also the Son of Man suffer of them."
13   The disciples understood that he was talking about John the Baptist.

This is quite complex. Apparently, the Messiah would not be taken until Elijah had come to restore everything. But he had already come under the alias of John the Baptist, and nothing was restored? What just happened? The disciples thought he was talking about John the Baptist, when he said the name Elijah? Finally, if things were not restored, what conviction do we have for the truth of any biblical passage?

14   Down from the mountain they encountered a multitude. One man approached, knelt and asked,

15   "Lord, have mercy on my son, for he is a lunatic and sore vexed. Sometimes he falleth into the fire and sometimes into the water.

16   "I brought him to your disciples, but they couldn't cure him."

17   Jesus said, "O faithless and perverse generation, how long shall I be with you? How long shall I suffer you? Bring him to me."

18   And Jesus rebuked the devil; and he departed out of the lunatic, and the boy was cured that very hour.

19   The disciples asked Jesus why they couldn't cure the boy.

20   Jesus said, "Because of your lack of faith. If you have faith in the amount of a mustard seed, you can say unto that mountain, remove hence to yonder place; and it shall remove, and nothing shall be impossible unto you.

21   "However, you cannot do that without prayer and fasting."

My immediate aside would be, "Wait a minute!" It is stated in Matthew 10:1, "Calling his twelve disciples to him, he gave them power over depraved spirits to cast them out, and to heal every disease and every malady."

What happened? He gave them the power, but it didn't work? It is of some interest that there is no specific case of the disciples healing in the Gospels. Why? On the whole, the disciples seem like a pretty poor lot.

Luke 22:

45   And he rose from prayer, went to the disciples and found them slumbering from grief.

46   He asked them, "Why are you sleeping? Rise and continue praying so you do not enter into temptation."

"When the disciples crossed to the other side of the lake, they forgot to take any bread." (MT 16:5) This could be an explanation for the contradictions in the Gospels; the writers, including two disciples, are forgetful.

My second aside is why didn't the disciples fast? Or did they and it just wasn't recorded? Maybe fasting would have done them some good since Jesus preordained them as a perverse generation. He also called them hardhearted. (MT 19:8) And on another occasion he rebuked them for their non-understanding. (LK 9:55)

DID JESUS MOVE A MOUNTAIN?

Of greater substance, on the issue of nothing being impossible, can one make a mountain disappear? Or can one only move it?

Jesus said one only needs faith in the amount of a mustard seed and one can move a mountain. I sometimes wonder if Jesus moved a mountain. Maybe he had limited powers. We do know he was conscious that power left him when a person touched his clothes. Maybe he didn't need to move a mountain. Maybe he moved a mountain, and we don't know about it. Maybe the reason Jesus even said anything about moving a mountain is because he had done it. Jesus seems like the kind of person who would have accomplished certain acts and not talked about them.

Possibly when Jesus said one could move mountains, he didn't mean move them on the landscape, but move them in one's own mind. It would be a matter of interpretation, like the eye of the needle.

For parallel explanations of moving a mountain, I explored other cultures. Shamans exist in many groups throughout the world. Shamanism is one buzz word in many New Age circles. Shamans can be likened to healers, and for the most part they heal, like Jesus, by casting out evil spirits or demons.

Generally, shamans have to endure some type of physical hardship to obtain the power necessary to deal with the spiritual world. Among the Aranda of central Australia, a healer is initiated into the circle of medicine men through hardship rituals. An older medicine man uses a magical wand to pierce the index finger of a novice healer. This ritual enactment enables the novice to drive out objects from future patients.

Some North American Indians conduct vision quests to make contact with the supernatural world. Once a shaman has made this contact and journeyed in the supernatural world, he or she is capable of going to the supernatural world to find the wandering spirit of a sick person. By helping the spirit return to the body, the person becomes well.

Some groups have very rigorous physical trials to obtain powers. Among the Manchu of China, eight holes are made in the ice during the winter. The person trying to become a shaman has to dive into the first hole, come out through the second, dive into the third and come up through the fourth, continuing until he passes through the eighth.

Among the Labrador Inuit, the title of *angakkoq* is bestowed on a novice after remaining five days and nights in an icy sea and then demonstrating that his skin is dry. Frequently when discussing this case, individuals inform me that I'm crazy. Such disbelievers assert that scientifically one could not stay alive in those waters for more than an hour. I can only say that it is proven scientifically that if one walks on hot coals, one's feet will burn; but people do it, and they don't burn their feet.

I think Jesus' 40-day fast was a test, a test to obtain power. Here is a question to consider: Would it be better to fast 40 days in the deserts of Jordan or would it be better to spend five days and nights in the icy seas of Labrador?

One of the earliest recorded instances of shamanism is of the Baffin

Island Eskimos and the Hudson Bay Eskimos. Franz Boas described these groups around the turn of the century. These shamans were said to be covered with light and have light shining within. The stronger the light the further they were able to see into the supernatural world. The light guided the shaman and enabled him to see into the future and into the past.

An anthropologist named Knud Rasmussen lived with the Igtulik Eskimo. He recorded the name *qaumaneq*, or mystical light. When a shaman first encountered this light, it was as if the house he was in suddenly rose, and he could see far ahead. He could see through mountains, as if the earth were a great plain. His eyes could reach the ends of the earth.

Is this what is meant when Jesus says, "...ye shall say unto this mountain, remove hence to yonder place; and it shall remove; and nothing shall be impossible unto you"? Does remove mean the mountain moves as we understand the verb remove and move? Or could move in Aramaic have had a different meaning such as the ability to see through a mountain?

LINGUISTICS

Bruce Malina's *The New Testament World* helps with the problem of New Testament word meaning. The oldest Bible that exists is in Greek. Looking into any given passage, Malina implores us to imagine walking down the streets of a Syrian Hellenistic city and we overhear a conversation identical to a passage in the Bible. There would be several problems in understanding the conversation.

First, we would have to find a translator for Greek spoken 2000 years ago. Second, we would have to determine the meaning of the translation. What would the translation offer? It would let us know what those first-century Greek-speaking people were saying. But, Malina emphasizes, what a person says and what he means are often quite different. For example, Shakespeare's use of many words are quite different from the way we use them today. For example, homely meant homebody, still meant always, fond meant foolish, jealous meant suspicious, careful meant full of care, brave meant fine, and kind meant natural. Those differences have shifted in only 500 years. With the words of Jesus, we are talking 2000 years.

So, when Jesus says something about removing a mountain, the meaning might be more in line with the example of the Igtulik Eskimo in which removal means seeing through.

Buddhist scholars also point out the problem that the first written records of Buddha (*Tathagata*) were not done in the Buddha's native language, but in Pali, a Central Indian dialect; not to mention that it was 200 years later. Some specialists point out that this language difference is not as great as between the Greek of the Gospels and Jesus' mother tongue, Aramaic. So, even if we did get the 2000 year old Greek part of the word "remove" correct, we would still have to go through Aramaic of 2000 years ago.

Nevertheless, perhaps remove does mean remove as we think of it. After he made the fig tree wither, and the disciples asked how he managed it, he replied, "I assure you that if you have faith and do not doubt, you will not only do what was done to the fig tree, but if you say to that mountain, 'Be lifted and thrown into the sea,' it will happen." (MT 21:21)

Here I must say that I think Jesus is using a metaphor. I think he meant if you have faith you can accomplish great feats. However, I think he was capable of killing a tree. Like healing, this is transferring a spiritual power from one living entity to another. I have made the argument that mountains may have spiritual powers, and if this is the case, then by extension one could affect a mountain like a fig tree.

BORROWING FROM OTHERS

It is possible that Jesus meant one could perhaps create shamanistic powers to see through mountains. What will most Christians think of this explanation of moving a mountain? Sometimes it is easy for Christians to close their eyes to other religions. That is what they have been taught, "You shall have no other gods before you." I feel Christians don't have to have other gods before them to explore other religions for an explanation of their own spiritual existence.

Nonetheless, borrowing from one religion for an explanation in another religion is a delicate business. Once one entertains this idea, one is in jeopardy of opting for the mythological.

Faith

Jesus exhorts: If one has enough faith, one can move a mountain. But nowhere does he say how one can get that faith. This has been one of the valid criticisms of Christianity; the Bible lacks in instructions on how one might develop faith. Most Christians blindly accept Jesus as the savior. There are, however, guidelines for developing a moral character and thereby gaining spiritual depth. The guidelines are the Ten Commandments.

Yet, Christians repeatedly tell me that all one needs for faith is to accept Jesus Christ as the Son of God. I have asked people how much faith they have. And one repeated answer is, "Oh, I believe with all my heart and soul." Then I ask each individual to move a mountain. None ever has. So I guess their hearts and souls are smaller than a mustard seed.

What is faith? A 1987 Gallup poll found 94 percent of Americans believe in God, and 84 percent believe in the divinity of Jesus Christ. A 1993 cover of *Time* showed 69 percent of Americans believe angels exist. If people believe in these types of powers beyond earth, why don't they try to void themselves of the earthly or material world in order to tap into those spiritual realms within themselves and beyond earth?

It appears many people want to believe in another realm. However, most of those same people simultaneously satiate themselves in conveniences, and this, I believe, dissipates any focused powers and keeps them from really tapping those spiritual realms around them or inside of them.

It seems to me that if one has enough faith, one would turn one's back on this world. I keep trying to promote this idea as central to Jesus' message for creating faith. "I tell you do not worry about your living, what you are to eat or drink, or about your body, what you are to wear. Is not life more important than its nourishment and the body than its clothing?" (MT 6:25)

Jesus had no particular attachment to the material world. He said, "The foxes have holes, and the birds of the air have nests; but the Son of man hath no where to lay his head." (MT 8:20) Rejecting the material world is part of what Jesus meant by faith. The more one thinks about having a bigger house, or finer jewelry, the more one consoles the self and negates faith.

What of the centurion who asked Jesus to heal his servant boy? The centurion who had slaves! He had faith?

Matthew 8:

6   "Lord, my servant boy lies paralyzed at home. He is in great agony."
7   Jesus replied, "I will come and heal him."
8   The centurion answered, "Lord, I am not fit to have you under my roof. Only speak the word and my servant boy will be healed.
9   "I am under authority and have soldiers under me. To one I say, 'Go!' and he goes; to another, 'Come!' and he comes."
10   As Jesus listened he marveled and said to those following him, "I assure you, I have not found anyone in Israel with so much faith."

Where did the centurion get such faith? We are never told. But one thing is for certain, Jesus' statement about the amount of faith was aimed directly at the disciples. If a mustard seed's worth of faith will move a mountain, then the disciples were in pretty poor shape. I must conclude that being in the presence of the master and being void of the non-material world will not necessarily generate faith or spirituality. When the eyewitness disciples were not capable of healing difficult cases because they lacked faith, what then can be expected of Christians 2000 years later?

Again, Jesus did provide a cogent commentary on developing faith. The more non-material one is, the more one's mind can be opened to a spiritual realm; and by experiencing that spiritual realm, faith is generated. Jesus had entered a cycle in which he was continually expanding in faith by continually recognizing the corruption of the material world.

Prayer

Most Christians maintain that faith can be obtained through prayer. Are there different ways to pray? Will some prayer result in a greater faith?

Jesus said little about prayer. "When you pray, enter your inner room and with the door closed, pray to your Father who is there in the secret place, and your Father who sees in secret will reward you." (MT 6:6)

Jesus also said, "I assure you that if two of you are agreed on earth about anything for which you pray, it will be done by my Father in heaven." (MT 18:19)

During the Sermon on the Mount, Jesus informed his followers that when they prayed they should not repeat and repeat (chant) as pagans do (MT 6:7). Then he gave the Lord's Prayer, which somehow gets repeated and repeated and repeated. Jesus' commentary before the Lord's Prayer baffles me. "Do not be like them [the pagans], for your Father knows your need before you ask Him." (MT 6:8)

If this is the case, then why are we asking "give us," "forgive us," "lead us," "deliver us"?

What if one goes into the mountains to pray? Does that enhance the communicative value of a prayer? Maybe that is why Jesus was going into the mountains to pray.

Right after Jesus tells the disciples they can tell a mountain to jump into the sea and it will happen, he says, "And everything you ask in prayer, having faith, will be granted." (MT 21:22) So, it appears that we need to have the faith before we pray.

I'm back to the Swami asking me, "Where did the tree come from?"

What happened to Jesus when he prayed? What went on in his mind when he prayed? I imagine Jesus' praying may have been profoundly different from ours. It is even possible that during the time of prayer Jesus was being talked to. But we might assume he had to be in a certain state of mind to receive those messages. That state of mind might be translated as faith. Maybe the greater the faith one has during prayer, the more one is talked to. The less the faith, the more one has to talk. The latter I call the exertion of self. One has to negate one's ego to open oneself to the spiritual realm. Negating one's ego is problematic with any attachments to the material world. As a consequence of being talked to during prayer, maybe Jesus underwent a radical change in consciousness, possibly analogous to self-hypnotism.

A RUDE AWAKENING

Fasting is a short-term means of voiding the material world.

Matthew 9:

14   Then came to him the disciples of John, saying, "Why do we and the Pharisees fast oft, but thy disciples fast not?"
15   And Jesus said unto them, "Can the children of the bridechamber mourn, as long as the bridegroom is with them? But the days will come, when the bridegroom shall be taken from them, and then shall they fast."

What does Jesus' response mean? Does it mean that while he is alive, there is no need for the disciples to fast; but when he is dead and they have to live without his daily word, they will need to fast? Or does it mean they will fast during the funeral? I favor the first interpretation, but the vagueness of the Bible certainly allows for the validity of the second interpretation.

Trying to resolve this problem one day in Provo, Utah, I was talking to someone knowledgeable about the Bible. I mentioned Matthew 17:21. Jesus had just cured the boy who the disciples were unable to cure. The disciples question Jesus as to why they were unable to cure the boy. Jesus admonishes them that they lacked faith and indeed if they had faith in the amount of a mustard seed, they could move a mountain. Matthew 17:21, "But such faith can only be achieved through prayer and fasting."

My knowledgeable friend nonchalantly said, "Oh, but verse 21 was added later. It was not in the original biblical documents written in Greek." I checked a parallel version of the Bible. (*The Six Parallel Version New Testament* published by Christian Life Publications.)

In Matthew 17:20 of the Jerusalem Bible, Jesus answered, "Because you have little faith. I tell you solemnly, if your faith were the size of a mustard seed you could say to this mountain, 'Move from here to there,' and it would move; nothing would be impossible for you." There is no Matthew 17:21 in the Jerusalem Bible.

I was angry to learn I was reading an amended version of the Bible. I long held up Matthew 17:21 as symbolic of what fasting meant in Christianity. I couldn't help feeling deceived and betrayed. Not that I didn't know other versions of the Bible existed. But to me this section on fasting was important. By not existing in the original version of the Bible or by being added, I felt I had a distorted view of the "truth" or teachings of Jesus. I no longer read the King James Version.

We don't know for certain as to when the fasting part was added, but it is in the King James Version. The question is why would someone add these words? Maybe the individual putting words into Jesus' mouth, in the King James Version, was trying to show techniques for developing faith. Regardless, it shows that individuals can later amend content without disturbing style. This should be kept in mind when considering the one writer theory.

FULL CIRCLE

I have come full circle. Why do I believe what I believe? After I read the words of Jesus in the King James Version of the Bible, I found out they were not even the words of Jesus. So, for many aspects of Christianity, I don't know what I believe. This creates, in me, disillusionment. But my disillusionment with much of the Christian world does not influence what I believe about Jesus. He was a very spiritual being. I look at the Christian world and in many places I see anguish. There is an ongoing concern with materialism and the compassion for materialism creates a void of spirituality. I obviously don't believe this about the Trappists monks. But what is truth?

I said in the beginning, we all have one thing in common--being born into a belief system about the world around us. Many individuals have the tendency to believe his or her religious system is the only correct one--at least when he or she begins to worship in that religious system. Over time, some people's religious convictions become stronger. Some people alter their religious beliefs to suit certain needs. Some people reject the tenets of a religion they once held dear. So, all of us somehow change along the way. The second thing we have in common is change.

9

WHAT'S IN A MIRACLE?

Jesus took five loaves of bread and two fish and fed about 5000 people.

Matthew 14:

22   Then he told his disciples to get into a ship and go to the other side while he sent away the people.
23   Once everyone was gone, he went into a mountain to pray.
24   At evening the ship was in the midst of the sea and was being tossed because the winds were contrary.
25   And in the fourth watch of the night Jesus went unto them, walking on the sea.
26   And when the disciples saw him they thought it was a spirit and they cried out.
27   Jesus said, "Be of good cheer. It is I. Be not afraid."
28   Peter was doubtful and said, "If it is you, Christ, bid me come to you on the water."
29   Christ said, "Come Peter. Get out of the boat and walk on water."
30   But once out he showed fear and began to sink. He cried out, "Lord, save me."
31   Jesus stretched out his hand and said "O thou of little faith, wherefore didst thou doubt?"

An answer is never provided. The Gospels as they are written don't give many needed answers. Why did Peter doubt? What is doubt? How can one overcome it? If Peter could not erase his doubt in the presence of Jesus, what is the present-day Christian going to do about doubt?

32   And when he got to the ship the winds stopped.
33   And those that were on the ship came and worshipped him, saying, "Of a truth thou art the Son of God."

34   On the other side they landed in Gennesaret.

When they landed, a group of sick people, not a group of healthy people, came to hear his philosophy. Jesus promoted himself through curing.

Mark has a very different version of Jesus walking on water, but it starts with Jesus taking five loaves of bread, two fish, and feeding about 5000 people.

Mark 6:

45   Then he told his disciples to get into a ship and go to the other side,
        Bethsaida, while he sent away the people.
46   Once everyone was gone, he went into a mountain to pray.
47   At evening the ship was in the midst of the sea.
48   The wind was against them, and Christ saw them toiling in rowing.
        And about the fourth watch of the night he cometh unto them, walking
        upon the sea, and would have passed by them.

Why would someone, who was walking on water, not be capable of seeing the boat? Why would he have passed by them? It is in Mark that Jesus is portrayed most as a man. Maybe this is why he's going to err and is going to pass the boat while walking on water.

On the other hand, maybe it is the responsibility of the disciples to see Jesus.

49   But when they saw him walking upon the sea, they supposed it had
        been a spirit, and cried out.
50   Christ said, "Be of good cheer. It is I; be not afraid."
51   He walked to them, and the wind ceased, and they were sore amazed
        in themselves beyond measure and wondered.
52   They considered not the miracle of the loaves; for their hearts were
        hardened.

How was I to interpret, "their hearts were hardened"? There are two messages. First, there are levels of miracles, and the disciples should have clearly understood walking on water based on the feeding of the multitudes. However, Jesus certainly has not outlined what should be expected in the way of miracles, be it moving mountains, feeding multitudes, or walking on water. Second, the disciples cannot accept nor understand what Jesus was doing because they were attached to this world. Their hearts were hardened. Possibly he was saying, "They are so hard to teach." Of course, one could adhere to the literary posture that in all "real" interaction there must be an opening vulnerability. Thus, Jesus will refer to the disciples as the perverse generation, and in the case at hand, they are filled with fear.

It's hard to understand why Peter wasn't getting out of the boat in Mark's version. But then Jesus almost walked by the boat. Maybe Mark was written first and my single mystery writer realized his mistakes and rectified them in Matthew. (There is some merit in this idea since Mark is the shortest of the books.) John's version is abbreviated.

John 6:

16   As evening came, his disciples went down to the sea.
17   They boarded a boat and crossed the sea toward Capernaum. Darkness came and Jesus had not arrived yet.
18   A strong wind was mounting the sea.
19   They sailed about three or four miles when they saw Jesus walking on the sea and getting close to the boat, and they were afraid.
20   But Jesus said to them, "It is I; have no fear."
21   Then they were quite ready to take Jesus into the boat and at once the boat was at the shore to which they were sailing.

Ask my wife if Jesus walked on water and she'll say, "It was an illusion." I have to ask, "What is an illusion?" But then she'll ask, "How far did he supposedly walk?" The specifics bother my wife, and me too. But that brings us back to Jesus going up on a mountain. After feeding the multitude and before walking on water, Jesus goes up on a mountain. Did he walk back down from the mountain to shore and then walk on water? Or did he levitate out of the mountain to the sea of Galilee? Also, in Mark, Jesus saw the boat from up in the mountains. Is this possible? Did he have night vision? What was the distance? If he saw the boat from up in the mountains, how was he going to miss it?

Many of the answers to these controversies go begging, and can only be answered by blind faith. However, the distance should not have been a problem. If he walked on water, the distance was unimportant.

Now, I have to attempt an explanation of how Jesus might have walked on water. Is walking on water possible? Walking on water as a recorded event is unique to Jesus, but the yogis mention it. Is walking on water a miracle? It depends on how a miracle is defined.

DEFINITIONS

How to define a miracle? In *The Future of the Body: Explorations into the Further Evolution of Human Nature*, Michael Murphy observes, "...the concept of miracle is encumbered by the Christian and especially the Catholic view as dispensed by a God who is separate from us. I say this power is both inside and outside. Buddha believed Dharama is accessible to us from inside and outside. It's the same in the Hindu *Upanishads*." Jesus preached, "The kingdom is within."

Imagine a drug dealer. His shipment is concealed in one box of 50 look-alike boxes. The police go through the boxes, and open all but five. The drugs are in one of the five. Is it a miracle he didn't get arrested because the police didn't check all the boxes? Or is it luck? (We don't know the criminal wasn't praying that if he wasn't caught, he wouldn't deal in drugs anymore.) The average reader, not liking criminals, may disallow criminals from experiencing miracles.

However, one of the two criminals crucified with Jesus said, according to Luke 23:43, "...remember me when thou comest into thy kingdom." Jesus replied, "Verily I say unto thee, today thou shalt be with me in paradise." I think it is safe to say that criminal experienced a miracle, assuming I accept the incidence as true since it is reported only in Luke--where Jesus is portrayed as a savior. In Mark and Matthew, the criminals mocked Jesus.

If I could go to heaven and find the angelic spirit of that thief, I would ask, "Do you consider the fact that you were crucified beside Jesus that day to be a miracle or just luck?" He might say, "Well, the fact that I was crucified beside Jesus was luck, but the fact that I am in heaven is a miracle." And if I accept the statement of the "good" thief, then I have to assume the same for the "bad" thief; being crucified with Jesus was luck and being in hell is a miracle. Some critic will pop up and say, "The "bad" thief got what he deserved!" Well, I assume they both got what they deserved.

My point is that perception, feelings, and knowledge are key in determining what is and isn't a miracle. The drug dealer probably felt it was a miracle the drugs weren't found. Notice the word "felt" in the last sentence. A miracle has many facets, but I think one facet that is too often overlooked involves human feelings. This is the message of Dan Wakefield's *Expect a Miracle* where miracles are quite broadly characterized. But for Wakefield, feelings, are likewise a component of miracles. He considers it miraculous when an individual stops being an alcoholic. Some might label this as a fortunate event. But we could maintain that the label is in the eyes of the beholder. I'm not sure I would categorize all recoveries from alcoholism as miracles; however, I knew an Otomi (Mexican Indians) family where the husband was an alcoholic. He never had any intention of stopping. His wife made one pilgrimage to a Catholic shrine and the husband stopped. I witnessed that, and I considered it a miracle.

There are levels to miracles. Walking on water is considered by most a miracle. (By others impossible.) "Credible" miracles usually require a crowd, or at least other people to witness the miraculous event. If my wife walked on water, and I were the only witness, I doubt too many people would believe the feat actually happened. But if she did it right along Waikiki Beach, in front of thousands of tourists, I'm sure my wife and I could begin a very lucrative church. And if she could do it a second time; well.... Of course, this has been my point about needing four names to open the New Testament. The more witnesses the higher the credibility.

Now, if my wife did walk on water in front of other people, there would be, I hope, a big commotion about how she did it. I suppose I would first ask, "How did you do that?" But my basic instincts tell me she wouldn't know the answer. So I would then ask, "How did you feel while you were walking on water?" I think she would have experienced a profound change in consciousness. She might say, "I have never been that focused before. My entire essence, my life force was expanding in my mind and my feet. At first I thought I would be excited, but I wasn't. I was totally calm. The reason I came back is because my essence began to contract."

Like many concepts and words, miracle has more than one dictionary definition. For the scientist, a miracle is something out of the ordinary that cannot be explained by the laws of science. So, the scientist says, "Never mind how Jesus felt; tell me how he defied the laws of gravity." Here we have a big problem. Much of how Jesus felt might be part of the explanation of defying gravity; and once feelings are left out, I am in the realm of science.

For a scientific attempt at explaining miracles, I continued to look at human energy and potential. I have already proposed that Jesus had a finite amount of energy, and to refuel his spiritual powers he went into the mountains to pray. Jesus had his ups and downs in energy. Walking on water would have to be one of his ups. Again we might think of human energy as quantifiable.

How did Jesus experience changes in consciousness? I think we might best understand a change in consciousness through a few influences on human energy: adrenalin, self-hypnotism, and faith.

HUMAN ENERGY

Human energy is real. Today we have 18-year-old women swimming faster than Johnnie Weismuller (of *Tarzan*) did when he won the Olympics in the 1920s. What are the peaks of human energy? Will there one day be humans who can run 100 meters in 5 seconds? Our physical prowess has become greater through time, but people are no longer raised from the dead.

Perceptions of what miracles are is somewhat bound by time. If I could go back to Jesus' time and ask the people if someone could run a four-minute mile, I think the response would be; "That would be a miracle. It is not humanly possible." And that is precisely the reason Roger Bannister's sub-four-minute mile was called, "the miracle mile."

Today people want to run a miracle mile. In Jesus' time, they wanted to raise people from the dead. This point can't be overemphasized. That's why there are abandoned monasteries throughout the world. When those monasteries were built, people were abandoning the material world. As people left them, they returned to the material world.

Can human energy be focused to the point where physical behavior defies the laws of "western" physics? There are accounts of people picking up cars that fell on other people. Scientists say these acts are the results of tremendous rushes of adrenalin. A rush of adrenalin produces a change in consciousness, and the change in consciousness produces a change in human energy. Maybe Samson was able to push down the pillars of the Philistine temple because of a rush of adrenalin. But it could have been an insertion of power by God.

Adrenalin can explain some events that don't occur under normal circumstances. What about hypnotism? I've seen some incredible feats done while a person was hypnotized. Hypnotism is real. That's why it's against the law to hypnotize someone on television. If the act of hypnosis were aired on TV, some viewers might become hypnotized.

I once saw a good friend hypnotized. It was astounding. Two friends, Robert and John, and myself were in my hotel room at the Hotel Sharon in Tula, Hidalgo, Mexico. One friend, Robert, said he could hypnotize me and I said he couldn't. So, for a moment of truth, I said, "Okay, let's try."

Robert told me to close my eyes and think about a pleasant place. Then he told me to hold my hand over my head and slowly count backwards from one hundred while he talked some more. Then he said, "When I snap my fingers you'll wake up, and I'll ask you how you are. You'll reply, 'Fine.' I'll ask, "Are you thirsty?" And you'll go to the water jug and get some water. The water will taste like beer and you'll spit it out."

Robert snapped his fingers and asked me how I was. I said, "Fine." He asked, "Are you thirsty?" I shook my head slightly. But John got up, went to the water jug, filled a glass, drank some, and spit it out. I blurted out, "John, you're hypnotized." He loudly denied it. I turned to ask Robert his opinion. He said, "Well, while you were counting backwards, John had his arm over his head and his head was bowed. I would say he was hypnotized."

It was at that point I knew that I could have been hypnotized at a younger age because I realized that when the Robert snapped his fingers, I had a memory of the suggestion, but I didn't act on it either positively or negatively. In other words, I didn't go to the water jug, but I also didn't immediately say, "Hey, come on, I know what you are up to."

The most phenomenal event I every saw was a lady hypnotized and told to lie on three chairs; one under her head, one under her feet and one under her back. The lady was told her body would be as stiff as steel. The middle chair was removed and the lady was absolutely suspended by her feet and head. The hypnotizer then placed a block of ice on the woman's stomach and broke the block with a sledge hammer. She didn't move. He put the middle chair back and brought her out of the trance. (I saw this incident on film, and it could be a hoax, but hypnosis experts tell me it was probably true.)

An incredible case of hypnotism I read involved two individuals who were hypnotized and taken into a large room full of talking people. The individuals were placed in opposite corners. They were instructed to whisper to each other and maintain a conversation. They accomplished the feat.

Superaudition is commonly talked about by yogis of India. Yogis believe that if one is free of the ego, "supernatural" hearing, tasting, smelling, seeing, and feeling will occur.

So, both an adrenalin rush and an hypnotic state produce changes in consciousness. I know a specific change in consciousness allows one to accomplish extraordinary feats. In the background of my mind I might ask: Can a person be hypnotized and then walk on water?

In my quest to understand human energy, I happened upon an anecdote. Huston Smith and Joseph Campbell both attended a conference on human energy. Both are well known authors of myth and religion. Smith wrote *The Religions of Man*, and Campbell became the master of myth which spawned *Star Wars*. After days of discussions among swamis, yogis and gurus, it was concluded Joseph Campbell possessed the most energy. When asked his regimen, he replied, "Rare roast beef, good Irish whisky and 44 laps in a pool." (*Newsweek* 11/14/88) When asked if he had faith, Campbell responded, "I don't need faith; I have experience." I think it is of more than passing interest that this article appeared in the society column and not the religion column. But maybe that is where energy belongs, with society, not religion.

BACK TO FAITH

As an example of faith, many Christians hold up Jesus walking on water. When Jesus told one of the disciples to walk to him, Peter got out of the boat, and began to sink. At that point there is the famed line, "Oh, ye of little faith." Thus, we can translate this to mean that if one has faith, one can perform supernatural feats. The more faith one has, the greater the supernatural feat that can be performed. Thus, faith can be quantified such as in the amount of a mustard seed. Otherwise Jesus would have said, "If you have faith, you can move a mountain."

Jesus also used the line of "Oh, ye of little faith" in another context of human energy. Matthew 6 is about human energy in the form of worry and stress.

27   "Which of you by taking thought can add one cubit unto his stature?
28   "And why take you thought for raiment? Consider the lilies of the field, how they grow; they toil not, neither do they spin.
29   "And yet I say unto you, that even Solomon in all his glory was not arrayed like one of these.
30   "Wherefore, if God so clothes the grass of the field, which today is, and tomorrow is cast into the oven, shall he not much more clothe you, O you of little faith?
31   "Therefore do not be anxious saying, 'What will we eat?' 'What will we drink?' or, 'What will we wear?'
32   "Pagans focus their interests on all these things. But your heavenly Father knows that you need them all.
33   "If you seek his kingdom and his righteousness, all these things will be provided to you.
34   "Therefore, don't worry about tomorrow since it will have its own anxieties. Each day's peculiar troubles are sufficient for it."

If most of us didn't worry about tomorrow, it would be miraculous in and of itself. And while this might seem simplistic, it is at the bottom of the formula. How can one have a clear mind to step beyond the boundaries of the present into other possible realms of consciousness? This is central in my attempts to understand the balance between materialism and spirituality.

What Jesus is dealing with here are feelings. I asked myself: How do I feel about tomorrow? If I worry about what clothes I'll wear and what I'll have to eat, I cannot attempt walking on water. If one is preoccupied with even a minuscule problem, could one perform a miracle? As stated, for most, if not all of us, not worrying about tomorrow would be miraculous. Thus, it would take a miracle to produce a miracle.

Of course, Jesus is advocating one remedy, faith, for resolving our worldly problems. Faith is quantifiable and comes in degrees, as does consciousness. Otherwise Peter would have sunk all the way. Imagine the feeling of somehow being half sunk in water, but yet somewhat buoyant and upright.

Matthew 6:33 might be a statement for developing faith. We must *seek*. It is true that mental direction has to be in the formula for developing faith. This might seem vague, but Jesus is clearly saying to empty the mind of the mundane and focus on a spiritual realm. Emptying one's mind can often be expressed as nothing more than apathy. But one must empty the mind and seek.

In Christianity, denial of self can translate as faith. Jesus told the disciples, "If anyone wants to walk after me, he must deny himself, take up his cross and follow me." (MT 16:24)

I maintain the greater the denial of self, the greater the change in consciousness. By being void of self, Jesus developed, I contend, a different consciousness; a consciousness that allowed him to walk on water and accomplish other miracles. Consciousness is part feeling. Jesus had to be emotionally charged to accomplish what he did.

The counter argument to the nonmaterial life is, "If I lead the nonmaterial life of Jesus, where are the clothes coming from I will wear the next day?" Again it is a matter of degree. How many clothes do I need for the next day? Better yet, how many clothes do I want for the next day?

CONTROL OF CONSCIOUSNESS

The yogi concept of *Pranayama* gave me ideas for understanding Jesus the man. Pranayama means to control (*yama*) the life force (*prana*). One means of controlling the life force is by controlled breathing. Through pranayama some yogis have reputedly broken chains placed around their bodies.

As with many things in life, there are degrees. I'm not particularly interested in breaking chains. But I am interested in knowing how it can be done.

The very advanced yogis live in isolation so they avoid the material world and its illusions. By avoiding the material world, an individual can better control the life force. By living in isolation one can have a clear or an empty mind, a different state of consciousness. I assume Jesus had an empty mind when he was tempted by Satan after his 40-day fast. The more muddled the mind, the greater the deviance from spirituality. And of course, Jesus was in isolation, like the advanced yogis, when he was tempted by Satan.

Tai Chi masters develop an internal energy, *chi*. It is converted into internal controlled power *jing*. Projecting internal power is *fah jing*. (*Fah* means transfer or projection.) Fah jing was developed by monks, not movie stars. The important thing here is that fah jing is consciously controlled. When a Tai Chi master uses it to maneuver or throw another human being, he is consciously controlling an internal power. Perhaps Jesus used fah jing when he threw the money changers out of the temple, and likewise when he was lead from Nazareth by a hostile group that wanted to throw him down a hill. But according to Luke 4:30, "He made his way straight through their midst and went away."

Luke 4:

16   He came to Nazareth, where he had been raised, and he went to the
      synagogue on the Sabbath and stood up to read.
17   The book of the Prophet Isaiah was handed to him. On opening the
      scroll, he found the place where it was written,
18   "The Spirit of the Lord is upon me, for he has anointed me to preach
      the gospel to the poor. He has sent me to announce release to the
      captives and restoration of sight to the blind, to set free the
      downtrodden.
19   "And to proclaim the year of the Lord's favor."
20   Rolling up the scroll, he handed it back to the attendant and sat down.
      The eyes of all those in the synagogue were fixed on him.
21   He began by telling them, "Today this scripture is fulfilled in your
      hearing."
22   They remarked about the gracious words that flowed from his lips.
      They said, "Is not this Joseph's son?"
23   Jesus said, "You will doubtless quote me this proverb, 'Physician,
      heal yourself. Do in your own home town what we hear you did in
      Capernaum.'"
24   He continued, "I assure you that no prophet is acceptable in his home
      town.
25   "I tell you that in the days of Elijah there were many widows in Israel,
      when for three years and six months the heaven was closed up and a
      severe famine visited all the land.
26   "But to none of them was Elijah sent except to a widow at Sarepta of
      Sidon.
27   "There were also many lepers in Israel in the time of Elisha the prophet,
      and none of them was cured by Naaman the Syrian."
28   When the people in the synagogue heard this, they felt deeply resentful.
29   They got up and expelled Jesus from the city and led him to the brow
      of the hill on which the city was built, to hurl him down.
30   But he made his way straight through their midst and went away.

How was Jesus able to walk through the crowd that was going to hurl
him down from the hill? Maybe it was a case of fah jing.

I have read and listened to many accounts of fah jing, and I experienced
it on one occasion. An individual ran at me to fight. I put up my hands
outspread and no sooner did this person touch my hands than his body
catapulted backwards onto the ground. I was truly amazed. In my case, it
was like an adrenalin rush because I have never been able consciously to
project or control an internal power.

Nancy Gibbs' April 10, 1995, *Time* article tells of an incident in which a seven year old girl was blasting down a hill out of control on her bicycle. She started to slip off the seat, but she felt a hand lift her back onto the seat. I think more than likely she experienced a "fortuitous" example of fah jing, and that her hands pushed down and back on the handle bars.

In my efforts to understand controlling consciousness, I consulted a knowledgeable friend, Duane. Duane keeps me abreast of happenings in the world of Yoga and Edgar Casey. He promptly referred me to *The Yoga-System of Patanjali* by Patanjali. I opened the book to levitation. By performing constraints on the relationship of the body to air, the yogi subjugates the relation with the air. This accomplishes a balanced-state of lightness, and the yogi can walk with both feet upon water. Most scientists find such explanations quite vague. I do too.

After walking on water, the individual might be able to walk on a spider's thread. The third test is to walk upon sunbeams. Thereafter, a person can move through the air at will.

I was mesmerized reading *The Yoga-System of Patanjali*. The content itself was revealing enough, but what is of considerable significance is the author didn't consider these acts to be miraculous. Rather they were the efforts of controlled consciousness. Further in *Raja Yoga: Conquering the Internal Nature*, Swami Vivekananda says, "By conquering the current called Udana, the Yogi does not sink in water or in swamps, he can walk on thorns etc. and can die at will." Imagine if Jesus could have died at will before they nailed him on the cross.

Yet, I have the problem that to date there is no documentation of any yoga having accomplished any of these feats. Further, Peter in the presence of Jesus could not walk on water.

Can one control one's consciousness to produce a miracle? When Jesus walked on water was it a consciously controlled effort? Or was he unaware--unconscious--of what he was doing? I think it was a consciously controlled effort. And I propose that what allowed him to walk on water was his complete rejection of the material world. The moral of the story: Don't try walking on water if you are thinking about whether your shoes might get wet. Actually that is when you should be walking on water. That way if you falter, you only sink in water. But if you are walking on sunbeams and you're up about 1000 feet and you start to doubt....

I think Jesus was moving through air at will, above the water. I think he must have come out of the mountains and not from the shore. This might explain his moving past the boat in the Mark version.

Some Christians are concerned that I say Jesus might have moved through the air the night he walked on water. According to the Bible, Jesus already had the experience of moving through the air. In one temptation, Satan took Jesus from the desert and placed him on the pinnacle of the temple in Jerusalem.

One might be able to translate faith as a possible metaphor for control of consciousness. If something is within the boundaries of human capabilities, then should it be considered a miracle? The Yogis say no.

What are the boundaries of human capabilities for controlling consciousness? And more important for me is the matter of whether the boundaries of human capabilities have changed through time. I believe they have. However, something like this is almost impossible to demonstrate. It would be impossible for anyone to live two lives--the first, 2000 years ago and the second in the present--and tell the story. Yet I can appeal to reason. Consciousness had to be different 2000 years ago. There were no industrial noises; there were no transistor radios that everywhere populate the globe today. Quiet is important for the controlling of consciousness. But seeking is the second part. How does one learn to seek? Maybe if Jesus had not died on the cross at the age of 33, and lived 30 more years like Mohammed, he might have provided more guidelines.

Wait a minute! What about Jesus' missing years? One theory is he might have gone to India. There is supposedly a Tibetan manuscript containing reference to someone with a name similar to Jesus. *And* the time frame is close. Could it be that Jesus got some of his ideas from further East? Or did Jesus teach his ideas there? Did he demonstrate walking on water to them? At that time, with anonymous sources and a different geographical framework, Jesus might not have been given credit for his accomplishments.

Regardless of the origins of Yoga philosophy, I can begin to posit explanations to things once thought unexplainable by using information from other spiritual groups. At the bottom of the formula is redirecting our consciousness. Until scientists go out and redirect their consciousness, they will never begin to understand what might have happened during Jesus' time. For the scientist, he or she must live with the yogis for 20 years and then reanalyze the possibilities of the spirit. For now, the scientist and the religious person are coming from different perspectives.

I think I'm mediating the two. Proof of miracles is difficult to manifest. One paradox of miracles is that you need a crowd, but if you perform miracles just to demonstrate you have power, you lose the power.

IF YOU ASK ME

I say Jesus may have walked on water and he may have moved through the air. My belief has nothing to do with divinity but understanding the potentials of human energy. If everything is coming together, adrenalin factor, hypnotic factor and faith factor, anyone can walk on water. Walking on water is like walking on hot coals, but at a higher level.

Granted there is only one "purported" incident of walking on water. However, if I accept the potentials, I also have to understand the limitations.

Most people embrace the material world. As the material world encroaches on our mental state, our ego is continually consumed. In this position, we find it difficult to fathom, much less believe, that feats such as walking on water can be accomplished.

There is a very conspicuous correlation between religious sects, such as the Jainist, and a lack of the material world. Those sects, which try to deny the self, exist in the Third World where there is less material with which to be concerned.

Of course, some Trappists monks live in the United States. However, in 1970 they changed their rules to allow necessary verbal communication. One specific function of speech is to express the self. Now, Catholic priests are permitted to get married. Is this wrong? I'm not concerned with the morality of it, but marriage is a concern with the self and not a denial of it. There's nothing wrong with hedonism--self, self, self--as a far as I am concerned. But it depends on what I want to accomplish. How can I begin to think hedonists are going to believe what those who live in a world of self-denial can accomplish? They won't. These are two different belief systems, two profoundly different realities, and two different states of consciousness.

A control of consciousness can ebb and flow. And Jesus was proof of this. He had his highs and lows of faith, and that is why he went into the mountains to refuel. Where do we mortals go to refuel? Again, this is a concern some have with the Bible; it doesn't give guidelines to develop greater degrees of faith.

I believe it was slower and it was easier to be channeled into a life of self-denial during the age of Jesus. Maybe this explains why there were more miracles and saints in those days. As time went on, the material world encroached on us and we became wrapped up in the desire constantly to express self, thus providing a possible explanation for the diminishing of miracles and saints. I don't believe anyone can walk on water now. No one escapes the material world. Even the most remote jungle people have shirts on which the logo of Coca-cola shines. They want the "medals" of civilization.

As for being religious, many individuals fit into certain ritual molds in our society. All the religious people I know are saddled with trying to fulfill the material desires of this world. They worry about what car they will drive to church where they accomplish weekly rituals. And as for the majority of individuals living in monasteries, I do not see where they have a desire to help make this world a better place to live.

10

WHERE MY TELESCOPE IS AIMED

A predominant theme of the Bible is seeing the future. Were this not true, the Bible wouldn't end with Revelation, a book about events yet to come with the destruction of Babylon. Even the Old Testament book of Jeremiah hints of what is to come in Revelation.

Jeremiah 27:

9   "Therefore hearken not yet to your prophets, not to your diviners, not your dreamers, not to your enchanters, not to your sorcerers, which speak unto you, saying, 'Ye shall not serve the king of Babylon'

10   "For they prophesy a lie unto you, to remove you far from your land; and that I should drive you out, and ye should perish."

The difference in what one knows about and how one prepares for the future is a point of major contention between religions and even between sects of Christianity. But of the latter, there is one point agreed upon: A messiah, from among the Israelites, was prophesied to come into existence. Jesus of Nazareth, an Israelite in the lineage of David said, "Do not suppose that I came to annul or abolish the Law or the Prophets. I came to complete them." (MT 5:17)

The New Testament, a compilation about Jesus of Nazareth, exhorts one to choose to go to heaven and prepare for that option. This can be accomplished by achieving a certain state of mind and doing certain acts (praying and seeking) in the present.

Prophecy assumes predestination. There are two problems. One, does predestination exist? Two, if it does, can one somehow "see" or know it? I am not sure what to make of predestination. On my one completed vision quest, I did have a vision that was about my future, and it did come true. The contents of my vision are something I would have never figured out through my everyday activities.

Many groups in the world believe that the future can be revealed through dreams. While I have worked out many intellectual problems in my dreams, I have never focused on future events of my life in my dreams. Soon, I hope to initiate such a controlled endeavor.

Do some people really have visions of kingdoms yet to come? That is difficult for me to believe. I visited the Museum of Atomic Energy, in Oak Ridge, Tennessee. The first exhibit was about a man who lived in that area and had done a 40-day fast. He had a vision of the great research complex that would one day be built there. This is vague enough that I can say there are probably many visions like this and a certain number will come true.

Personal visions and viewing a vision exhibit didn't really give me much information for determining whether predestination exists. So, I studied the history of prophecy in hopes of reaching some conclusions.

OF PROPHETS AND SOOTHSAYERS

When I was younger and thought of seeing the future, the image of a soothsayer came to mind. (I probably have this image because my father is a big fan of King Arthur, and Merlin somehow entered my mental picture.) The *Oxford English Dictionary* (OED) says a soothsayer is a truth teller, one who is able to see the future. (Sooth means truth.)

A prophet on the other hand, according to the OED, is "One who speaks for God or any deity as the inspired revealer or interpreter of his will." In a popular sense, this generally connotes predicting the future.

Soothsayers

Soothsayers are mentioned several times in the Old Testament, usually in a negative manner by the Israelites. There is a definite theme that soothsaying is not what God wanted. Rather we are presented the scenario of truthful Israelites/Christian prophets versus the untruthful non-Israelites/non-Christians soothsayers. But the picture is not always crystal clear.

Joshua 13:22 says Balaam the son of Beor, the soothsayer, was slain by the children of Israel. "False prophets," that is soothsayers, must die in the Bible. Their death is symbolic of a group's unwillingness to follow God. A background has been provided with the struggle between Israel and the Philistines with Samson and Delilah, David and Goliath.

In Isaiah 2:6, there is another link of hatred between the Philistines and Israel via soothsayers, "Therefore thou hast forsaken thy people the house of Jacob, because they are replenished from the east, and are soothsayers like the Philistines, and they please themselves in the children of strangers."

The only time the word soothsayer is used in the New Testament is in Acts 16:16-19. (Some versions substitute "clairvoyant" for soothsayer.) The story tells of a girl in the town of Philippi who was possessed with a spirit of divination. The girl practiced soothsaying. Paul drove the spirit from the girl. It is too bad we don't get to know what she was seeing or saying. Am I to believe she was seeing something concocted by Satan?

Micah 5:12 sums up who will not be seeing the future with the Lord's statement, "And I will cut off witchcrafts out of thine hand; and thou shalt have no more soothsayers."

Blessed by God

In the Bible, prophets, unlike soothsayers, are somehow blessed by God. In other words, the underlying supposition is they see the future because they are blessed by God. In Isaiah 44:7 we are told, "Could anyone else have done what I did? Who could have predicted all that would happen from the very beginning to the end of time?"

The first individual in the Bible called a prophet was Abraham. God appeared to King Abimelech and told him Abraham was a prophet and that Abraham would pray for him. I've always thought if God went to all the trouble to appear to Abimelech that God would have just endowed Abimelech with the power to pray for himself. After all, there aren't too many individuals in the Bible to whom God appears. But King Abimelech was a Philistine! Nevertheless, I would think if God appeared to him, the king would have been awed enough to convert. Everything isn't crystal clear.

Then comes Moses. God and Moses had direct communication. It was an incident in which God, disguised as a burning bush, could not, or would not, reveal his face. I've always found this a bit strange since we are made in God's image. And moreover, I hope, someday, someone will explain to me why Jesus and God never went face to face, at least in the written version of his life, the Gospels. I understand God was somehow at the Transfiguration, but he and Jesus don't talk. That is strange I think. And what is stranger is that intermediaries of Moses and Elijah had to tell Jesus what he already presumably knows.

God then proceeds to make whatever can be known about the future revealed only through the prophets of Israel. All other prophets must perish. However, God did not have an easy time of getting the label of prophets taken from even those practicing "heathenistic rituals." And among the latter were many of his own chosen people. King Ahab is a case in point.

Ahab was a king of the northern kingdom of Israel for 22 years from 940-918 B.C. He married a Phoenician woman, Jezebel, for a political alliance. Jezebel instituted the worship of two pagan deities; Baal, for whom there were 450 prophets in Israel, and Asherah, for whom there were 400 prophets. Of great bother to the Israelites is the fact that Jezebel used the Israelites' tax money to support these 850 prophets.

Baal's prophets are called prophets and not soothsayers. This appears to be a point of transition in which God has to establish his dominion. Therefore, Baal's prophets are called prophets to be destroyed. After this, any non-Israelite who sees the future will be labeled a soothsayer.

God condemned the worship of Baal and he communicated to King Ahab through Elijah. God will appear to a Philistine king, but not an Israeli king? Of course, this is how all prophets other than those of the house of Israel will become labeled as prophets. In other words, the prophets themselves must go to war in order to prove who has the power to divine the future.

The Battle of the Prophets

Elijah informs King Ahab that there will be a drought and only Elijah will have the power to end it. It is at this point that Elijah hides in Cherith Brook. Once the drought commences, King Ahab looks for Elijah, but can never find him.

While the drought is going on, Jezebel is killing the prophets of Israel. Obadiah, in charge of Ahab's palace, took one hundred of Israel's prophets and hid them in a cave.

In the third year of the drought, God told Elijah, "Go tell Ahab, I'll send rain." Elijah traveled.

At the same time, Ahab talked to Obadiah and informed him they each must go in search of any spring of water. Obadiah departed and encountered Elijah. Elijah told Obadiah to go and inform Ahab, that he, Elijah, wished to meet Ahab. Elijah and Ahab met. Ahab condemned Elijah for causing the drought.

1 Kings 18:

18   Elijah said, "It is you, King Ahab, who caused the drought by disobeying the Lord's command and worshipping Baal.

19   "Order all the people of Israel to meet me at Mount Carmel. Also, bring those supported by Queen Jezebel, 450 prophets of Baal and the 400 prophets of the goddess Asherah."

20   Ahab ordered the people of Israel and the prophets of Baal to meet at Mount Carmel.

21   Elijah confronted the people, "If the Lord is God, worship him. If Baal is God, worship him." The people made no response.

22   Elijah said, "I'm the only prophet of the Lord left, but there are still 450 prophets of Baal."

What happened to the 100 prophets hidden in the cave? And what about the 400 prophets of Asherah?

23   Elijah continued, "Bring two bulls. Let Baal's prophets take one and
      cut it to pieces and place it on wood. I will do the same with the other.
24   "We will each pray and see whose sacrifice is completed."

      Baal's prophets prayed until noon.

27   At noon, Elijah began to poke fun at them, "Pray louder! Is Baal a
      god? Maybe he is sleeping? Maybe he's day-dreaming, or relieving
      himself, or perhaps he has gone off on a trip?"

      So, the idea of American gun-fighters meeting at high noon began in
biblical times? Actually the time setting is so neither gunfighter has an
advantage of having the sun in the other's eyes. I'm not sure how it applies to
the biblical situation.

28   The prophets of Baal prayed louder. They cut themselves with knives
      to complete a ritual.
29   They shouted to the heavens until the middle of the afternoon, but
      there came no answer.
30   Elijah called his people. He began repairing the altar of the Lord
      which had fallen into disuse.
31   He took twelve stones, one for each of the twelve tribes named for the
      sons of Jacob.
32   With these stones he rebuilt the altar. He dug a trench around it. The
      trench could hold about four gallons of water.

      There is the symbolic number four; like that of the characterizations
in the Gospels.

33   He placed wood on the altar. He cut a bull to pieces and placed it on
      the wood. He told his people, "Fill four jars with water and pour it on
      the offering and the wood."
34   He commanded them to do it twice more.
36   Elijah prayed.
38   God sent down fire and it consumed all the sacrifice, including the
      water.
39   The people threw themselves down on the ground.
40   Elijah ordered, "Seize Baal's prophets. Let none escape." They were
      seized. Elijah led them down to Kishon Brook and killed them.

I don't understand. Were the prophets of Baal given a chance to convert? It does say in Isaiah 45:22, "Turn to me now and be saved, people all over the world! I am the only God there is." I would think with a spectacle like fire consuming a sacrifice right before their eyes they would have had immediate faith in God.

41   Elijah told Ahab that there would be rain, and there was.

Jumping ahead, 1 Kings 19:

1   Ahab told Jezebel all that Elijah had done, and how he had slain all the prophets with the sword.

2   Jezebel sent a messenger to Elijah to say, "Let the gods do to me, and more also, if I make not thy life as the life of one of them by tomorrow about this time."

4   Elijah went a day's journey into the wilderness and asked God to take his life.

I don't understand why God doesn't let Elijah square off with Jezebel and kill her.

5   He went to sleep and behold an angel touched him and said, "Arise and eat."

6   There was a cake baking on coals and a cruse of water at his head. He ate and drank. And he laid down again to sleep.

7   And the angel appeared and said again, "Rise and eat, because the journey is too great for thee."

8   He arose and ate and went on the strength of that meat, forty days and forty nights unto Horeb, the Mount of God.

Let's look ahead in Elijah's life. 2 Kings 2:

1   And it came to pass that the Lord would take Elijah into heaven by a whirlwind, and Elijah went with Elisha from Gilgal.

2   Elijah said unto Elisha, "Tarry here, I pray thee, for the Lord hath sent me to Bethel." Elisha replied, "As the Lord lives and as you live, I will not leave you." And they went to Bethel.

3   And the sons of the prophets that were at Bethel came forth to Elisha, and said unto him, "Do you know that the Lord will take your master today?" And he replied, "Yes, I know it; hold your peace."

4   And Elijah said unto him, "Elisha, tarry here, I pray thee; for the Lord hath sent me to Jericho." And Elisha replied, "As the Lord lives and as your soul lives, I will not leave you." So they came to Jericho.

5   And the sons of the prophets that were at Jericho came to Elisha, and
         said unto him, "Do you know the Lord will take away your master
         today?" And he replied, "Yes, I know it, hold your peace."
6   And Elijah said to him, "Tarry, I pray thee, here; for the Lord hath
         sent me to the Jordan." And he said, "As the Lord lives and as your
         soul lives, I will not leave you." And they went on.
7   And fifty men of the sons of the prophets went, and stood to view afar
         off; and Elijah and Elisha stood by Jordan.

The Sons of the Prophets

The sons of the prophets formed a guild-like society of professional
prophesiers. It appears the guild existed in almost every town of any size.
Maybe the sons were the preachers of their day. In which case, I might be
better off looking for sociological reasons why these individuals went into
their professions, rather than assessing a link to God. They are mentioned
several times in the Old Testament, and once in connection with King Ahab.

1 Kings 20:

35   The Lord commanded a member of the group of prophets to order a
         fellow prophet to hit him. The second prophet refused.
36   The first prophet said, "Because you have disobeyed a command from
         the Lord, a lion will kill you when you leave here." And it happened.
37   The first prophet went to another prophet and made the same order.
         The third prophet hit him and damaged his face.
38   The first prophet bandaged his face, and stood by the side of the road
         to await the passing of the king of Israel.
39   When King Ahab passed, the prophet yelled out to him, "Majesty, I
         was fighting in a battle when a soldier brought a captured enemy to
         me and said, 'Guard this man. If he escapes, you will pay with your
         life or pay a fine of 3000 pieces of silver.'
40   "But I erred and the man escaped." Ahab replied, "You have
         pronounced your own sentence, and you have to pay the penalty."
41   The prophet tore the bandage from his face, and the king at once
         recognized him as one of the prophets.

How did the king recognize him? Was he one of the 100 hidden in the
cave?

42   The prophet informed the king, "These are the Lord's words, 'Because
         you allowed the man to escape whom I had ordered to be killed,
         you will pay for it with your life, and your army will be destroyed for

letting his army escape.'"

43   The king returned home to Samaria. He was worried and depressed.

The question remains: How are the sons of the prophets seeing the future? There is some evidence that they mixed and used ointments, but the specifics of the mixing and the use are not known.

Christians will maintain that the sons of the prophets see the future because of a command from God. There are still specifics I want to know. Did God appear in a dream? Or was God a waking vision? Was it only a voice in their ears? Or did it have something to do with the ointment?

With regards to this passage, why didn't the first prophet just bandage his face, rather than going through all the contortions of provoking other prophets to anger? And if the second prophet was a member of the group, why didn't he understand?

The Man Himself

Simeon, a rather unobscure figure, says in Luke 2:34-5 that Jesus will be a "sign that is spoken against," thus providing the first hint, in Luke, of Jesus' destined rejection. Of course, this prophecy is fulfilled in the remainder of Luke, where Jesus is characterized as the savior.

Each fulfilled prophecy gives us the confidence to accept the next prophecy. But there is an inherent problem in viewing Luke in isolation like this. Luke is the third book, and we've been set up by now to accept prophecy unconsciously. By Luke 3:16, John the Baptist prophesied that Jesus will baptize by the Holy Spirit and by fire.

When Jesus was tempted by Satan, what happened next? What was the next thing in Jesus' life besides getting something to eat? Few Christians know that Jesus did not minister until after his 40-day fast. How was his ministry inaugurated? As discussed previously, Jesus read from the book of the prophet Isaiah. Supposedly the book of the prophet Isaiah has been fulfilled with the coming of Jesus. Jesus says, with reference to Elijah. "Verily I say unto you, no prophet is accepted in his own country." (LK 4:24)

So, Jesus' life was a fulfillment of prophecy and he was a prophet.

I'm somewhat perplexed about how Jesus, the prophetic man, had visions of future events. There's nothing in the scriptures that helps me much. Jesus told Peter of his betrayal. Did Jesus see this event as a long drawn-out daydream?

How did Jesus see any future events? Or were they just brief spontaneous thoughts? Or were they dreams at night? How did he experience the Transfiguration? How did he have a vision of all the kingdoms of the world in a moment of time?

Too often a critic demands, "But what Christ saw when he viewed all the kingdoms and the Transfiguration was not a vision; it was real." Who said a vision isn't real? That's what I'm trying to discern. What is a vision? How were all the kingdoms of the world put in one place? The laws of physics that are in everyday existence don't allow for that. And physics does not allow for my one personal vision. More importantly for the issue under discussion, prophecy, when is the content of a vision about the future? I do assume some prophecies in the Bible are owed to visions of an actual "viewing" of future events.

Agabus

Enter Agabus the prophet.

Acts 11:

27   And in these days came prophets from Jerusalem unto Antioch.
28   And there stood up one of them named Agabus, and signified by the
       Spirit that there should be great dearth throughout all the world. This
       came to pass in the days of Claudius Caesar.

Why couldn't the disciples have seen this great dearth? Why didn't Jesus see this? Why do we need Agabus?

Agabus shows up one more time.

Acts 21:

8   And the next day we that were of Paul's company departed, and came
       unto Caesarea, and we entered into the house of Philip the Evangelist,
       who was one of the seven; and abode with him.
9   And the same man had four daughters, virgins, who did prophesy.
10   And as we tarried there many days, there came down from Judaea a
       certain prophet, named Agabus.
11   And when he was come unto us, he took Paul's girdle, and bound his
       own hands and feet, and said, "Thus said the Holy Ghost. So shall the
       Jews at Jerusalem bind the man that owneth this girdle, and shall
       deliver him into the hands of the Gentiles."

The details of Paul's death, presumably in Rome, are unknown.
What about the four virgins? This is their first and last mention in the Bible. But they did make it into the most printed book in the world. Some people insist the Bible is a sexist book. The four virgins lend some credence to this view since there is no record of their prophecies. Only the prophecies

of men are mentioned, not women. The prophesy of Agabus, the man, is presented. But not how or why he was able to do it.

With four daughters prophesying, the evangelist father should know quite a bit about the future. I wonder if he gave the daughters credit for what he was saying about the future.

The four virgins, like Agabus and Christ, are labeled prophets. It seems there was a lot of prophets in those times. Where were all those prophets coming from?

METHODS OR TECHNIQUES

Christians often argue that people not worshiping their God are spoken to through false prophets. There is a profound problem with this. Could Aztec soothsayers really not see into their own future? More basic, can most people accept the possibility that the non-Christian Aztec soothsayers could see anything? The Christian answer would be yes, but that the Aztecs only hallucinated; they didn't really see the future. And any earthly coincidence with what they saw was mere chance. So, then we are left to assume: If the Aztec soothsayers converted to Christianity and became prophets, would they be using the same "T.V." (the mind), but the "channel" (the religious link) would change?

The problem is that we don't know how the "T.V." works no matter which "channel" it is on.

Isn't seeing future events miraculous, no matter who is doing it? Yet somehow prophecies are commonly accepted in Christianity. Well, there are so many prophecies and prophets in the Bible they'd have to be commonly accepted. Why are they so commonplace? My answer: So that when Revelation, a book entirely devoted to the future of the universe, is read, many will believe unconditionally the events will happen.

This brings me back to the vagueness of prophecy. Presumably John wrote Revelation in about A.D. 96. The biggest problem with Revelation as prophecy is that it is a metaphor. Babylon was already a second-rate city at the time Revelation was supposedly penned. Thus, most biblical interpreters accept the idea that Babylon means only a great city that harbors the works of Satan. Now, of course, Babylon is nothing more than a tourist site.

Why didn't John name the city that would have fallen upon the second coming? First, I assume he couldn't. Second, even at the time he was writing, he could have been talking about the destruction of Rome. At that time, Rome controlled the Israelite nation, and 30 years prior had destroyed Jerusalem. But then if Rome fell, which it did in A.D. 476, and there was not yet a second coming, the validity of Revelation would have been in jeopardy. Since Babylon had already fallen in 539 B.C., and since Babylon had conquered Jerusalem in 587 B.C. causing the Diaspora, the writer of

Revelation was safe in using this city for his metaphor.

Some suggest that Babylon is only mentioned in Revelation to remind readers how quick a great city can fall, and how everyone, too, will come to judgment quickly at the end of the world. But if John is really having a vision inspired or directed by God, why doesn't he have any specifics about the end? If he were really seeing the future, I would expect a book more about the future, not the past. I am left with a metaphor of what the future might be like. The message: Believe the end is coming and Jesus will return.

Revelation as a vision brings me back to a main problem with "seeing" or "knowing" the future. Can any prophetic attempt be controlled? Can a prophet, by using certain techniques, go 10 years into the future or 100 years into the future? Revelation leaves me hanging. When will a prophetic insight be limited to personal future events of only the prophet, like Jesus at the Transfiguration? When do prophets only see the future of famous people or entire kingdoms? Or do the prophets see many different aspects of the future and only pick out what seems important?

How is seeing the future accomplished? Can anyone do it? Is there a methodology for it? If I follow some standard formula, can I produce a prophecy? I assume praying is somehow in the Christian formula of prophesying.

If I use my personal context, isolation seems to be a key to seeing the future. One cannot break into another realm, whether it is inside oneself or outside, if one is constantly consumed in verbal communication with someone else. Mohammed had his first vision while in solitude.

In a vision quest, one voids one's self of hunger and thirst also. Talking, hunger, and thirst are all ego-related phenomenon that prohibit one from experiencing other realities. Voiding these may produce visions. Yet, the question I still struggle with is: When and why is a vision futuristic?

Divination

Both the Jewish and Christian traditions are overly ambivalent about divination. In the Bible, Jews and Christians were highly critical of the folk methods for divining such as omen interpretation, dream interpretation, and water gazing.

Scrying involves gazing into water or a crystal until one has a vision. Water gazing was the method of divining used by Nostradamus, the famed Frenchman who lived in the early 1500s. He has become probably the most famous of diviners in European history. I have read most of his writings, but beyond staring into water there is not really much in the way of methodology in his writings. Am I supposed to keep my face "X" number of inches from the surface of the water?

If I just look into water, will I have a vision? Or do I need some psychological predisposition to have a vision? I think the latter may be closer to the truth. This has also been found to be the case with the Native American vision quest. Not everyone who quests has a vision.

Assume I stare into water and I do see something. How can I be certain that any vision is a vision of the future rather than an idiosyncratic image created by my subconscious, much like the majority of my dreams? This is one of the problems with Nostradamus' writings of his visions. His writings are ambiguous enough to leave great latitude for interpretation.

Urim and Thummim

Urim and Thummim were objects which the Jews used to divine the future. Moses, after placing the breastplate on Aaron, put the Urim and Thummim in the breastplate (Leviticus 8:8). There is no precise definition of what they were or how they were used. According to one theory, questions were framed such that the Urim and Thummim, however used, could provide a simple answer of yes or no.

What is of interest is that these objects ceased to be used in 607 B.C. when Jerusalem's temple was destroyed by Nebuchadnezzar. The last mention of Urim and Thummim is in Nehemiah 7:63-65:

> The following priestly clans found no record to prove their ancestry-
> Hobaiah, Hakkoz, and Barzillai. (The ancestor of the priestly clan of
> Barzillai had married a woman from the clan of Barzillai of Gilead
> and taken the name of his father-in-law's clan.) Since they were unable
> to prove who their ancestors were, they were not accepted as priests.
> The Jewish governor told them that they could not eat the food offered
> to God until there was a priest who could use the Urim and Thummim.

Definitions

What is the difference in a prediction, a vision, and a prophecy? A prediction is not a prophecy. A prediction is a statement based on reasoning about the past and present. A prophecy is some type of insight about the future not necessarily connected to the past or present. And a vision refers to what is seen. Visions sometimes take the form of dreams, something most people have experienced.

There is no answer as to which techniques will bring a vision of the future. Unable to know for certain *how* people see the future, I studied *what* they saw.

Dreams

There is an abundance of documentation concerning ancient people who believed that divinities communicated to humans through dreams. Documented dream interpretation goes back to the 13th century B.C. in Egypt. At that time, an interpretation for being plunged into a river meant that one was being purged of evil. Interesting the idea of baptism was around 1,300 years before Jesus.

Two of the more entertaining passages from the Bible are of dream interpretation. God wastes no time getting into dream interpretation in the opening of the Bible.

Genesis 40:

1   And it came to pass that the butler and the baker of the Pharoh offended their lord.
3   And they were put in prison with Joseph.
         [Joseph was a Jew.]
4   And the captain of the guard charged Joseph with them, and he served them. They continued a season in ward.
5   And the butler and the baker both dreamt one night.
7   Joseph asked them in the morning why they looked so sad.
8   Both relayed the point that they had a dream, but there was no one to interpret it, and Joseph said, "Do not interpretations belong to God? Tell me."
9   The butler said in his dream there was a vine.
10   And the vine had three branches, and there were clusters of grapes.
11   And the Pharaoh's cup was in the butler's hand and he took the grapes and pressed them into the cup and gave the cup to the Pharaoh.
12   Joseph said the three branches were three days.
13   And within three days the butler would be reinstalled and serve the Pharaoh.
14   And Joseph said, "When you get out, remember me for this interpretation and tell the Pharaoh so that I might leave prison.
15   "For indeed I was stolen away out of the land of the Hebrews; and here also have I done nothing that they should put me into the dungeon."

The baker also had a dream which he relayed to Joseph. The baker had been carrying three baskets on his head. In the top basket were baked goods for the king, but birds were eating them. Joseph said that the baker would be released in three days only to have his head cut off. His body would be hung on a pole and birds would eat his flesh.

Both dreams came true as predicted by Joseph.

Two years later, the Pharaoh had two dreams, and he called all the magicians and wise men of Egypt together and told them the dream. But there was none who could interpret them. Then the butler, after two years, remembered Joseph.

Joseph was released from prison, and he was permitted to bathe and shave before seeing the Pharaoh. Joseph interpreted the dreams to have to do with the next fourteen years of the Pharaoh's reign. It was an overall good interpretation. The Pharaoh was so relieved to hear the good interpretation that he made Joseph second in command. Not bad for interpreting a couple of dreams, albeit it had to do with the future and the future of the Pharaoh. "And Pharaoh took off his ring from his hand, and put it on Joseph's hand. Joseph got fine clothes and a gold necklace." (Genesis 40:41-42)

The next major dream interpretation comes in the book of Daniel. This scenario begins to tie together many of the concrete definitions of prophets and soothsayers and what is to come in Revelation. In Daniel 1, during the third year of King Jehoiakim, Nebuchadnezzar of Babylon captured Jerusalem. God even let Nebuchadnezzar take some of the temple treasures. Further, Nebuchadnezzar took many members of Israel's royal family and noble families back to Babylon. They were to be taught to read and write the Babylonian language. Four of them mentioned are Daniel, Hananiah, Mishael, and Azariah. This is the Diaspora I began to learn about in Spain in 1970.

Keep in mind God's words in Jeremiah 27:

9   "Therefore hearken not yet to your prophets, not to your diviners, not to your dreamers, not to your enchanters, not to your sorcerers, which speak unto you, saying, 'Ye shall not serve the king of Babylon.'

10   "For they are deceiving you, to remove you far from your land; and that I should drive you out, and ye should perish."

Nebuchadnezzar had a wild dream one night. "Then the king commanded to call the magicians, and the astrologers, and the sorcerers, and the Chaldeans to tell the king his dreams. So they came and stood before the king." (Daniel 2:2)

The king couldn't remember the dream, and he told them if they couldn't reconstruct it and give him an interpretation they would be put to death. Those assembled couldn't do it. So, the king decried that all the wise men of Babylon should be destroyed. They likewise sought Daniel to be slain. (Daniel was one of the people taken as slaves by Nebuchadnezzar.) Daniel, however, spoke with Arioch, the captain of the king's guard assigned to kill the wise men. Daniel said he could interpret the dream.

But he didn't do it right away. He first went to his house and told his friends Hananiah, Mishael, and Azariah to pray to God for the details of the dream. That same night the mystery was revealed to Daniel in a vision. Apparently then, a vision can be of the past.

Daniel was taken before Nebuchadnezzar, and Daniel said, "There is not a wizard, magician, fortuneteller, or astrologer who can tell you what you dreamed. But there is a God in heaven who reveals mysteries. He showed your majesty what will transpire in the future, and I will explain it to you."

According to Daniel, the dream was about the destruction of a large statue. The symbolism, according to Daniel, was growth and decline of empires. The first and largest empire was Nebuchadnezzar's. It would be destroyed and replaced by one of lesser greatness. It too would be destroyed.

Finally God will establish a kingdom that will never be destroyed but last forever. Like Joseph, Daniel was nicely rewarded for interpreting dreams. He was made the head of all Babylonian royal advisers. No wonder some of the Jews never returned to their homeland after the Diaspora.

Dream symbolism with its oft pre-ordained prognostication of future events leads to everyday activities also carrying pre-ordained messages about the future, omens.

Omens

Omens are messages prognosticating future events. The world of omens is complex. Numerology alone, such as the values of 3, 4, 12, 13, 40, and so on, has filled volumes. Much of what I read about omens is somewhat hard to digest, but because of the plethora of bird representations on archaeological artifacts, my own particular fascination is with bird omens.

Before modern science and an understanding of migrations, birds were considered mystical. In a time that the world was believed to be small and flat, people wondered where migratory birds came from. Some thought they came from another world, and were sent as symbolic spiritual messages. Even as a child I was told that robins "brought" spring to the Midwest. That small suggestion provided the foundation for building a greater archaeological/religious complex in my mind.

In cultures throughout the world, birds are seen as omens. In Arabia, al-'Awf was the bird god of omens and divination. In Samoa, there was a god, Ali'i Tu, who took the form of a rail. During times of war, the flight of this bird was closely observed. If a rail flew before a group of warriors, that was considered a prophecy of victory. However, if a rail flew to the side or behind them, the warriors turned back.

Luke 2:

21   When eight days had passed, at his circumcision the name Jesus was given him, as named by the angel before his conception in the womb.

22   When the days for their purification according to the Law of Moses were completed, they brought Jesus to Jerusalem to present him to the Lord.

23   As prescribed in the Law of the Lord, "Each first-born male shall be called holy to the Lord."

24   And according the Law of the Lord, there must be a sacrifice of a pair of turtle doves or two young pigeons.

And that is how Jesus Christ started his life, having two turtle doves sacrificed for him. His life started with rituals of bird sacrifice; ritual, something he later rejected.

When Jesus was baptized (again a ritual), he looked up and there was a dove. Most Christians don't know just how symbolic birds were in the early part of Christianity. Remember Joseph's interpretation of the baker's dream of the birds eating the bread, symbolizing the birds eating the flesh from the baker's head. It is stated in Revelation, when Babylon fell it became inhabited by devils and a cage for every unclean and hateful bird. And then there is Elijah being fed by ravens when he took refuge in Cherith Brook.

Birds have various interpretations in Asian and European traditions.

blackbird   A symbol for temptation and sin because of its sweet and alluring song.

eagle   The symbol of divinity. (Why do you think it's on the dollar bill?)

falcon   A symbol of evil because it is a bird of prey. Once tamed, the falcon is the symbol of the converted pagan.

goldfinch   There was a belief that the goldfinch fed on thorns. Thus it came to symbolize suffering. In later paintings, when the goldfinch is held in the hands of the Christ-child, it symbolizes his passion.

lark   Symbolizes good priests since it flies high and sings as it ascends toward heaven.

owl   A nocturnal bird, once thought to be blind. Thus according to some, it represented the Jews since they did not accept Christ.

peacock   The symbol of resurrection because it was believed its flesh was incorruptible even if buried for three days.

pelican   Represents the sacrifice and redemption of Christ. According
               to one source, this bird becomes angry with its young and kills
               them. Then with its long beak, it tears at its breast, and with
               the blood produced, it brings its young back to life.

sparrow   Symbolizes God's care even for the humblest of creatures.
               Jesus said, "Aren't two sparrows sold for a farthing? And one
               of them shall not fall on the ground without your Father." (MT
               10:29, LK 12:6)

swallow   Symbolizes the Resurrection because it was believed to
               hibernate in the winter and emerge in the spring.

swan   Represents deceit because its white plumage covers black flesh.

EVOLUTION?

There is an underlying assumption in Western society: We always
become more sophisticated than our ancestors. Now we can go to the moon,
something unthinkable to our great-grandparents. Cars most often replace
horses. But in our rush to conquer all frontiers, is it possible that we have
denied ourselves certain accesses to the spiritual realm? Maybe this is why
there is a resurgence of shamanistic studies. Maybe for every two steps forward
there is one step backward.

In ancient times, and for many present day "primitive" cultures around
the world, animistic people appeal to local nature spirits to determine the
future. In the beginning of the Israeli nation, this appeal had to be denied so
that God's will could be accomplished.

The Torah forbids appeals to local nature spirits or the dead for
understanding the future.

Deuteronomy 18:

9   Moses said, "When thou art come into the land which the Lord thy
        God giveth thee, thou shalt not learn to do after the abominations of
        those nations.
10   "There shall not be found among you any one that maketh his son or
        his daughter to pass through fire, or that useth divination, or an observer
        of times, or an enchanter, or a witch,
11   "Or a charmer, or a consulter with familiar spirits, or a wizard, or
        necromancer.

12   "For doing these things are an abomination unto the Lord, and because
        of these abominations the Lord thy God doth drive them out from
        before thee."

        God drove them out for abominations, but did he give them a chance
to repent first?

13   "Thou shalt be perfect with the Lord thy God.
14   "For these nations, which thou shalt possess, hearkened unto observers
        of times, and unto diviners; but the Lord thy God hath not suffered
        thee so to do."

        Maybe that's why Jesus did not make more of a statement against
slavery. God's people were supposed to "possess" other people?

15   "The Lord thy God will raise up unto thee a Prophet from the midst of
        thee, of thy brethren, like unto me [Moses]; unto him ye shall hearken."

        As with many biblical passages, there is latitude for interpretation. I
suppose in this passage the assumption is that the prophet will be Abraham.
But this isn't all well and good because even after Jesus, there is more than
one prophet. In Acts alone, there are four virgin sisters who are prophets. I
continue to ask: Where were all these prophets coming from? And how are
they seeing the future? "Thus saith the Lord, 'Learn not the way of the heathen,
and be not dismayed at the signs of heaven; for the heathen are dismayed at
them.'" (Jeremiah 10:2)
        It seems even the Old Testament cannot deny the efficacy of certain
divinations. The Israelites decry the Diaspora, the carrying away of the
Israelites to Babylon by King Nebuchadnezzar. Yet, how did Nebuchadnezzar
reach his decision to attack Jerusalem?

Ezekiel 21:

21   The king of Babylonia stands at the fork of the road. To discover his
        route, he throws arrows onto the ground and sees their pattern. He
        consults his idols. He examines the livers of a sacrificed animal.
22   His right hand holds up the arrows indicating attack Jerusalem.

        As for seeing the future, the efficacy of appealing to "local spirits" is
also not denied. Samuel died and was buried in his hometown of Ramah. At
that time, Saul, Samuel's son, forced all fortunetellers and mediums to leave
Israel. Later Saul was to enter into a battle with the Philistines.

1 Samuel 28:

5   When he saw the size of the Philistine army he was filled with fear.
6   He asked the Lord what to do. But he received no answer either by
        dreams or by the use of the Urim and Thummim or by prophets.
7   Saul ordered his officials, "Find me a woman who is a medium, and I
        will consult her." He was informed of one in Endor.
8   Saul disguised himself and after dark went, accompanied by two men,
        to see her. He told her, "Consult the spirits and tell me what will
        happen. Call up the spirit of the man I name."
9   The woman replied, "Surely you know that King Saul has forced the
        fortunetellers and mediums to leave Israel. Are you trying to trap me
        and get me killed?"
10   Saul promised her that no harm would come to her.
11   The woman asked the name to be called. Saul answered, "Samuel."
12   The woman screamed, "You have tricked me! You are King Saul!"
13   "Have no fear," spoke the king, "Tell me what you see." She spoke, "I
        see a spirit coming up from the earth.
14   "It's an old man wearing a cloak." She continued. Saul knew it was
        Samuel and he bowed to the ground in respect.
15   Samuel said to Saul, "Why have you disturbed me? Why did you
        make me come back?" Saul replied, "The Lord has abandoned me
        and will not answer me."
16   Samuel said, "The Lord is your enemy as he told you through me. He
        has taken the kingdom from you and given it to David. You disobeyed
        the Lord's command to completely destroy the Amalekites and all
        they had. Tomorrow you and your sons will join me, and the Lord will
        give the army of Israel over to the Philistines."

Saul fell on the ground in remorse. The woman beckoned him to eat.
She killed a calf and fed Saul and his men. I don't know why they ate. They
apparently didn't believe the message; or they wanted to die on a full stomach.
Something is strange about this story.

They left that same night. But we don't know if and what the woman
was paid. Nevertheless, this is another interesting case of calling up the past
to know the future.

The passage 1 Samuel 28 is important since it suggests that God is
not the only source of all truly reliable knowledge. There is another example
of this in 1 Samuel 6. In other words, the Torah forbids appeals to local
nature spirits so that the Jews would rely only on God for their knowledge of
the future, but the Torah does not say that one cannot know the future if one
appeals to local nature spirits, such as birds, omens, dreams, and mediums.

With a background of dream interpretation, symbols and omens, I can understand that the Israelites had to be ambivalent about divination since those are the symbols that have created the entire process of human existence.

After all, how could the tribes of New Guinea know the future outside of God when Christianity has not even been introduced into some of those areas? Can these people, like the woman in 1 Samuel 28, command the spirits of the dead and realize their own futures? Maybe someday someone will find a manuscript in the Vatican library that will give "the key" to prophecies. What am I going to do with soothsayers who are not Christians? Today and in the past, non-Christian interpreters of the future outnumber Christian prophets. Can they or can they not see the future?

Soothsayer Aristander provided Alexander the Great with some of the best interpretations of the future via omens ever in the history of the world. From the existing records, Aristander was never wrong, and he was not linked to the house of Israel.

One of my favorite examples is an occasion when Alexander was asleep in his tent. A twittering swallow circled over his head. It then began landing about on the bed, and chattering constantly and loudly. Alexander waved at the bird, but rather than flying away, it perched on his head and remained until Alexander sat up. Aristander interpreted the event to mean that one of Alexander's friends would soon betray him. It did happen.

Ask individuals like John Maxwell O'Brien, author of *Alexander the Great: The Invisible Enemy*, about Aristander and he will say Aristander's "... revelations were good for morale, and, on *ad hoc* basis, he proved to be remarkably accurate, thanks in part to his patron's ability to turn potential catastrophe into victory." (p.56) I place O'Brien's book among the best five I have ever read, and I hope one day he and I can discuss Aristander.

By using only Aristander's "remarkably accurate" revelations, I have a question. Is it possible that Christians are depriving themselves of seeing other realities because they have often condemned other cultures that tried to peer into the future as heathens? I cannot provide an answer to this question, but I can give one very cogent fact. We who are influenced by the Christian world have somehow been blocked, for some reason, from even discussing dreams as significant on any level.

Dream interpretation fades from the Bible. Why? There is no dream interpretation in the New Testament. Although, three times Joseph received divine warnings in dreams about his family's movements with regard to Herod. And there is one important mention of a dream having to do with Jesus. Pilate was dealing with the matter of whether Jesus or Barabbas would be released from prison. According to Matthew 27:19, "While Pilate was seated on the tribunal, his wife sent him a message that said, "Have nothing to do with that innocent man, for I suffered a great deal today in a dream because of him."

I find it interesting that the dreams in Matthew are actually of Old

Testament individuals. In other words, individuals born before Jesus. I find it of equal interest that there are only dreams in Matthew where we might expect them since Matthew is the first book following the Old Testament. There will be no dreams in Luke, and of course Mark and John don't mention the nativity. My one writer is a crafty fellow.

I have never found a discussion of why dream interpretation dropped from the Bible. I assume dream interpretation or discussion was repressed totally by Christian doctrine because that night-time vision of the world was sometimes controlled and populated by demons of sex, the incubus and succubus. The incubus was the male spirit that would visit females in their dreams for sexual activity. The succubus was the female spirit. The incubus and succubus were recognized by ecclesiastical and civil law in the Middle Ages. Many people continued believing in the incubus and succubus until the turn of this century.

What about the ability to see the future through means other than dreams? In the end, Christians are lead to believe that only through a connection with the Christian God can this be done. Did Jesus ever dream in his sleep?

What is a vision and when is a vision of the future? I'm no closer to answering that question now than when I began. Why are visions only seen by certain people, and why are visions not accepted by modern science?

YOU BE THE JUDGE

Prophecy is a subject that still needs exploring. When is a prophecy a prophecy? According to some individuals, there is an Old Testament prophecy that Jesus would not have any broken bones.

Psalms 34:

19   The good man has many troubles, but the Lord will save him from them all.
20   The Lord will preserve him; not one of his bones is broken.

The fulfillment of that passage is said to be John 19:32-36. The soldiers came, and broke the legs of the first person and of the other who was crucified with him. When they came to Jesus, and saw that he was already dead, they didn't brake his legs. These things were done it is said so that the scriptures could be fulfilled, "A bone of him shall not be broken."

But does the "good man" in Psalms 34:19 necessarily refer to Jesus? If Psalms 34 is the prophecy that some people say it is, I would expect a bit more than just a prophecy that none of Jesus' bones would be broken.

In the meantime, I offer for contemplation the words of Simon and

Garfunkel, "The words of the prophet are written on the subway walls and tenement halls." That graffiti is based on one overriding message: There are those alienated by the material world who do not seek spiritualism, but entry into the material world.

Yet there is for me one compelling characterization about those who see into the future. They seem detached from the world of the present. From what little information I can get about both soothsayers and prophets, they seem to be the ultimate in rejecting the material world to enter the spiritual realm.

Luke 2:

36   There was also Anna, a daughter of Phanuel of the tribe of Asher, a prophetess advanced in years. After her girlhood, she lived seven years with her husband.
37   She was a widow of about 84. She never left the temple but worshipped night and day in fasting and intercessions.

Maybe becoming void of this world is the first step in terms of techniques to see the future. I would believe this from my vision quest. Maybe we don't have prophets anymore because they have all been sucked into the material world.

We should keep in mind that it was not until after Jesus walked out of this world at the age of 30 and fasted 40 days that he began his ministry. I wonder what a 40-day fast will do for me?

11

I WOULD LIKE TO SEE THAT COIN

Raising the dead and walking on water are probably within the boundaries of human capabilities. Divinity need not necessarily be invoked as an explanation of these phenomena. I believe, as discussed by the yogis, that to accomplish any of these acts one must turn one's back on the material world, or at least for a short time, negate the ego, as in a vision quest. A longer negation of ego is a 40-day fast in isolation. Only in this way is the mind free to accomplish feats considered by some as extraordinary. You can't walk on water if you are worried about getting your shoes wet.

The diminishing number of reported miracles through time might be the result of an ever-increasing material world filling our minds with dreams of technological gadgets, with stardom, and with a constant stream of information about a plethora of topics. However, there are those who feel miracles have not really diminished because they never really happened in the past. Rather, we have accumulated a conglomeration of apocryphal tales.

Which is correct? Credibility is a key underlying both suppositions. If there is one event that can be shown to be false in Jesus' life, then we could be faced with challenging the credibility of all his feats.

There is one incident in the Gospels I believe never happened. Exploring the incident in terms of my one-writer theory will give more context to the story. Where would my one writer place such an incident? Matthew, Mark, Luke, or John?

In Matthew, Jesus is a teacher challenging religious law that had existed for a millennia. Jesus' role as a revolutionary has to be established in the first book of the New Testament. It is he who has the ultimate/new authority to interpret the Law of God. Jesus said, "Do not believe that I come to earth to bring peace, rather a sword. I come to set sons against their fathers, daughters against their mothers, daughters-in-law against their mothers-in-law. A man's worst enemies will be his own family." (MT 10:34)

In Mark, Jesus is a man of action. In Luke, he is the savior of all mankind, and thus there is a focus on prophecy. In John, he is portrayed as the eternal word of God.

So, where will my supposed one writer place this extraordinary, questionable event? The feat is in Matthew where it can be forgotten about. Only in Matthew does Jesus pay tribute to Roman authorities.

Now Matthew 17 can be finished. I feel like Alistair Cooke calmly and concisely introducing Masterpiece Theater, "In Matthew 17:23, the Transfiguration is described. Jesus was informed of his death to come. We left our group of four in Galilee, where Jesus told Peter, James, and John, James' brother, to tell no one what they saw or heard. The three were sorrowful."

Matthew 17:

24   They departed Galilee and went to Capernaum. And while they were there a tribute collector asked Peter, "Does not your master pay tribute?"
25   Peter answered yes. And he went to the house where they were staying, and Jesus asked him, "Peter, from whom do the kings of the earth take tribute? Of their sons or strangers?"

How old was Jesus when this happened? He was 31 or 32. He really didn't know who paid tribute? Where has he been? Maybe he was living with the Essenes? Or maybe he was only asking to make Peter think. Or was he asking a rhetorical question? It doesn't appear rhetorical because,

26   Peter answered, "Of strangers." Jesus acknowledged, "Really, then our own sons are tax-free."

No matter where Jesus was from the ages of 12 to 30 (his missing years), my one writer had to attempt corrupting Jesus with the material world. The world he was against. Jesus has come to preach against the material world, but he will have to pay tribute. How would Jesus obtain money? Jesus says to Peter,

27   "But, so that we don't offend the tribute collectors, go to the sea and cast a hook. Take the first fish, open his mouth, and thou shalt find a piece of money. Give it unto them for me and thee."

I first read Matthew 17 as an adult. That day, I made a face just like Richard Pryor, playing the Pharaoh, did in *Holy Moses*. I leaned forward in my chair, pointing to each word as I read them again out loud and very slowly, "....cast...a...hook...Take...the...first...fish,...open...his....mouth, ...and...thou...shalt...find...a...piece...of...money...." My face wiggled all around like Richard Pryor's.

If you have not seen the comedy *Holy Moses*, I recommend it. Briefly, a man in the valley next to Moses' also hears God's voice, and he thinks God is talking to him. But enough humor.

What do I have to say about the coin in the fish's mouth? Until the story is verified from Jesus' mouth, it should be treated as apocryphal. The first writings about Confucius, filled with superhuman acts, have been determined to be apocryphal. What exactly to do about the coin in the fish's mouth? I considered the remaining context of the story.

What happened to the tribute for James and John? Not there. I think my one writer doesn't want people thinking about this incident too much because this is getting very akin to magic. By having it in the New Testament only once and in the beginning, it eventually fades into the background, assuming the New Testament is read from beginning to end. If this incident were in the New Testament more than once, people might begin to ask, "Well, even if it were a miracle, why didn't Jesus just pull the coin from the air, or from behind Peter's ear, or out of his own pocket?"

The answers are simple. If Jesus had pulled the coin from his pocket, it could be construed that he was walking around with money, and the act was neither miracle nor magic. Likewise, I at one time was quite concerned that there was no act of humility by Jesus' making Peter obtain the coin. Why didn't Jesus himself get the coin? One interpretation is that by touching money Jesus would have been corrupted by the material world. But by having Peter fetch the coin and having it in a fish's mouth, Jesus is distanced from the material world. However, this possible explanation is complicated by the house in Capernaum.

WHERE'S THE HOUSE IN CAPERNAUM?

To evaluate my idea of my one writer wanting the coin story to appear only once and to evaluate the idea that Jesus didn't touch the coin because of corruption by the material world, I studied Mark's version.

Mark 9:

30   They departed and passed through Galilee; and Christ didn't want anyone to know about it.

31 He wanted to teach his disciples that the Son of man will be delivered into the hands of men, and they shall kill him. After that, he shall rise on the third day.

32 They didn't understand him, but they were afraid to ask him.

I don't quite understand this element of fear. Why are the disciples afraid to ask Jesus something? The word "fear" does appear in the original Greek Bible, but it is possible that 2000 years ago the word "fear" may have meant "embarrassed." Regardless it is another poor showing by the disciples.

33 And they came to Capernaum, and in the house he asked the disciples, "What did ye dispute among yourselves by the way?"

34 They made no reply because they were talking about which of them should be the greatest.

No wonder the disciples couldn't heal or walk on water. They possessed too much ego.

35 He sat down and called the twelve and said, "If any man desire to be first, the same shall be last of all and servant of all."

Does this mean Jesus could read minds? Or maybe he heard what they were saying, and he wanted to see if they would be truthful?

36 And he took a child, and set him in the midst of them and when he had taken the child in his arms, he said,

37 "Whoever receives such a child in my name, receives me, and whoever receives me, receives not me, but him that sent me."

They are in a house. Where did the child come from?

38 John said, "Master, we saw one casting out devils in thy name, and he followeth not us, and we forbad him, because he followeth not us."

39 But Jesus said, "Forbid him not; for there is no man who shall do a miracle in my name, that can lightly speak evil of me."

It's interesting that once in Capernaum, the "story" becomes completely different in Matthew and Mark. In Mark there is no incident of paying tribute. Is it the different perspective of two writers? I had to remind myself constantly that according to some biblical authorities, Matthew and Luke are copying from Mark. Yet Mark didn't write about something as spectacular as the coin in the fish's mouth? And Luke doesn't mention the story at all?

In Matthew, my writer wants us to deal with Jesus in juxtaposition to the rest of the world. Whereas in Mark, we have a realistic portrait of Jesus with a greater depth of miracles than the other four Gospels. What? A greater depth of miracles and the coin story is not there? The coin story was not a miracle? Very suspect.

For the other writers--Mark, Luke, and John--not to have written about the coin in the fish's mouth supports the idea there is only one writer of the Gospels, especially since John was present at the event, yet he did not write about it. If there were only one writer, wanting us to think there were four, the coin served its purpose in the first book--Jesus standing in opposition to the world by not touching the coin--and then the story fades into the background. And of course, my one writer doesn't even deign to have John talking about the Transfiguration, an event at which he was present, since it too has been covered previously.

The coin aside, why is there a significance of being in a house in Capernaum in both Matthew and Mark? "And they came to Capernaum, and in the house he asked them...." Why would it be important for my writer to have me there inside? I may never know the answers to these questions, but, "the house" is a good insertion by one writer. To have the details of a house in both stories and not the fish with a coin in both stories is too suspicious for me.

If it were a house, whose house was it? I assume it was Jesus' house. In Matthew 4:13, after his 40-day fast and learning that John the Baptist had been arrested, he withdrew into Galilee. "Leaving Nazareth he went to live in Capernaum."

John has more specifics about Jesus' house.

John 1:

35   The next day John was standing there again with two disciples.

John really has an ego just to mention himself and the "the two disciples."

36   He saw Jesus walking and said, "There is the Lamb of God."
37   The two disciples went to follow Jesus.
38   Jesus turned and asked, "What are you looking for?" They answered, "Where do you live, Rabbi?"
39   "Come and see." It was about four o'clock in the afternoon. They went with him and saw where he lived, and spent the rest of the day with him.

Wait a minute! Jesus, the man who had nowhere to lay his head, had a house? Who paid for it? How was it paid for? What is the specific interest about it being four o'clock the day the three disciples visited Jesus' house?

I don't understand why Jesus would pay tribute anyway. Supposedly he was without money, and therefore tribute collectors should have no claim on him. But he has a house; therefore, they might have charged him property tax. Maybe that is how the tax collectors knew to refer to Jesus as Peter's master. They knew he owned the house.

IN THE NAME OF JESUS

Christians search for many things connected with the Bible. Some look for the Ark. Others want Jesus' robe. Imagine if I could find his house in Capernaum. What about the coin? Why isn't there great debate over what coin it was? I would think there should be some great elaborate story spun that whoever possesses that coin would be cursed for life. But then Jesus was just paying *his* tribute. So, maybe the story would go that the holder would be blessed for life. Of course, that goes against Jesus' anti-materialistic message. But Christianity is already far removed from that message.

It's feasible to figure out the type of coin because there are tribute records of the time. If an historian could determine what the average man on the street was paying for tribute in Capernaum, then we could determine which coin would pay tribute for two people. My limited research on the matter shows a *denarius* was "the head tax coin" of the time, but I can't find the coin that would pay tax for two people.

What type of fish carried the coin? No sooner did I ask, than I got information. There is a fish taken from the Sea of Galilee called St. Peter's fish, and why would they name it that? If you think the commercialization of Christmas is bad, get ready. Many tourists, or pilgrims if you wish, visit the Christian Holy Lands every year, and if one could advertise a certain fish involving "Jesus' production of money," one might really boost the economy.

The fish most commonly caught by line and hook in Galilee is Long-Headed Barbel, *Barbus longiceps*. This is a trout-like fish, with a narrow silvery body and pointed head. Since the passage in Matthew clearly states that the fish was caught by line, I would think this is St. Peter's fish. But no!

There is a musht, *Tilapia Galilea*, which weighs up to four pounds and is very suitable for pan frying. It has a detachable backbone and only a few small bones, making it an eater's delight. However, the musht feeds on plankton, and since it is not attracted to other foods, it is not caught with a hook and line. It is caught in large numbers by net. The musht is the fish, never caught by hook and line, called St Peter's fish, and this is the fish served to tourists, all this in the name of Jesus Christ of Nazareth. But it is only a minor detail, so some tell me.

Or as so many have "instructed" me throughout my quest to understand the man Jesus, "Why is it important? He is the Son of God. Don't worry about minor details written after his life." But I'm concerned as to when any detail is a fact or when it is fantasy. It makes a big difference in what and how I believe.

I've often heard, "Isn't it sad what has been done in the name of Jesus?" Yes it is. We need to remember Jesus and the disciples ate grain on the sabbath, thereby breaking the ritual rules. Jesus never promoted any ritual.

Go into any Christian church today, and the first thing you get fed is ritual. Nowhere, but nowhere, in any way did Jesus promote ritual. He rejected the tenets of the Old Testament. Even John the Baptist knew Jesus didn't care about ritual. That's why John said Jesus would not baptize with water. I think baptism is an antiquated ritual with which Jesus tried to dispense.

However, there is a problem with this assertion. On the one hand, there is no passage in which Jesus baptizes; nor does he discuss baptizing with the disciples. One wonders what value there would be in their baptizing since he has ordained them a twisted generation. On the other hand, we are left with the words of Jesus after his resurrection, "Go and make disciples of people of all the nations, baptizing them in the name of the Father and of the Son and the holy spirit." (MT 28:19)

As with the coin in the fish's mouth, I want to hear it from Jesus himself that he instructed anyone to baptize. Why would he only talk about this ritual after his resurrection when he never did it or discussed it in life? I'll contend that the disciples had no powers to demonstrate their connection to Jesus, and therefore, they had to appeal to ritual--baptism.

Did Jesus conduct rituals during his 40-day fast? He went alone in the wilderness. He told the Pharisees, "I want mercy not sacrifice." (MT 9:13) He obviously thought his parents sacrificing two birds at his birth was wrong.

WHAT TO DO?

What to do about the coin in the fish's mouth? I think it would be best if the four Gospels were collapsed into one version of Jesus' life, and the coin in the fish's mouth left out. For me, the coin story is crass. This story implies Jesus could just produce a coin from nothing to satisfy some material need. Furthermore, if this were the case, he could have produced food for himself after the resurrection; he would not have had to ask the disciples if they had any meat. One can't produce something out of nothing. If one could produce a coin in a fish's mouth, one could make one's self grow. Jesus already told the disciples, in Matthew 6, no one, not even he, can make himself grow. Bottom line: Jesus would be disgusted with this story of supposed magic. I believe one of our essences as humans is change, and that we need somehow to control change. So, let's change the Gospels by omitting this story.

A PROBLEM

Every now and then I think about trying to collapse the four Gospels into a single version. However, there are problems I can't resolve. Jesus has a house, but he says he has nowhere to lay his head.

I constantly come back to the three contradictory versions of his last words on the cross. I cannot choose which might be correct. Maybe all three versions could be used as chronological markers of the crucifixion. The earliest statement was probably one of anguish, "My god, my god, why hast though forsaken me." Once Jesus had a recognition that death was imminent he said, "Into thy hands I commend my spirit." And with his last breath of life, he quietly acknowledged, "It is over."

Some people think it is a great sacrilege when I suggest rewriting the Gospels. Why? According to some scholars, portions of the Gospels are copied from each other and/or missing manuscripts. If this is the case, then it shouldn't matter if the Gospels are rewritten into one condensed version.

However, copying is something I contend is not the case. The four Gospels are too perfectly orchestrated not to have been a concerted effort. If John had a genealogy, a coin in the mouth of a fish, or the Transfiguration, and Matthew had a Doubting Thomas, I would be more inclined to believe there is more than one author writing in different times and places.

If my idea of collapsing the four Gospels into a single version is sacrilegious, then the King James Version is likewise sacrilegious. And I believe it is.

ABOUT THE SCHOLARS

Of course, I could only make a collapsed version of the four Gospels if I could prove there was one writer. If I am forced into the shadow-of-a-doubt mentality, I will have to await the "second coming" and get the answer as to how many individuals penned the Gospels. Again, my ego is not tied into my ideas about the New Testament. If God says there were four writers, so be it. But I want to hear it from God.

There will be biblical scholars who say I have not laid out all the arguments they contend about linguistic variation, iconographic variation, and content variation of the four Gospels. They will propose that such information leads to evidence of different dates for the writings.

I know the arguments. They fill tomes.

Furthermore, I know as an archaeologist we could make copies of the earliest documents and then submit them for radiocarbon assays. This would destroy them, but it would give us more definite answers as to the variations in dates. But there is no reason to destroy them since the earliest fragments we have are only copies.

I think the external "evidence" that Matthew was originally written in Hebrew is at best circular. The argument goes that because this Gospel characterizes Jesus as the foretold Messianic Messiah, it must first have been written in Hebrew, and it must have been written before the other Gospels since it does not mention Jesus' prophecy of the destruction of Jerusalem. Thus Matthew is placed at the beginning of the New Testament. I want to see the original, and then I'll believe what we have was copied.

The earliest known fragment of John is the Papyrus Ryland 457. The fragment is smaller than a piece of typing paper. It dates to the first half of the second century after Jesus' death. Therefore, biblical scholars tell me it was copied from an earlier version, presumably the original. I want to see the original, and then I'll believe it was copied as we have it.

There is a bottom line in all of this. None of the original documents have survived--if they ever existed--unless the copies are the originals. This could hold true for Matthew, thus supporting my idea of one writer. Throughout all scholarly explanations of the Gospel's origins, the word "copy" is repeated and repeated and repeated almost endlessly.

The earliest extant version of the Bible, referred to as the Jerusalem Bible was written about A.D. 125. It is written in Greek. So, maybe we could say there was an invested ethnic interest, and 125 years is a long time.

Again, when I say one writer, I will concede that my writer could have been and probably was a director. Even in the present day cases of ghostwritten books, there is a striving for one overall style. In my proposal about the four Gospels, this would not be the case and is not the case. This would allow for the fact that John was written in a dialect different from the synoptics. It was also apparently very poor Greek.

The four Gospels are beautifully orchestrated through necessary contradictions and necessary consistencies. One necessary consistency is the exact figures, in all four Gospels, concerning the feeding of the masses. One contradiction is the two thieves, hung with Jesus, mocking him in Matthew and Mark. However, in Luke, where Jesus is portrayed as the savior, one of them repents and Jesus takes him to heaven.

In evaluating my ideas, most scholars will be the victims of their own epistemological biasing. They already have an ingrained mental ethos for what the Gospels represent. After all "gospel" is tantamount to "good news." To begin to consider my theory, a lifetime of their thinking is in jeopardy. Like the disciples, some scholars have too much ego.

While the scholars are quibbling, I am adamant about one small change. I don't care what dialect John is written in. Nor do I care about the quality of the Greek in comparison to the synoptics. I do care that the fourth Gospel carries the name John. John was at the Transfiguration. It was one of the most phenomenal episodes in Christendom. Yet, the Transfiguration is not in John. The book of John was not written at a different time and place from the synoptics. The Transfiguration was left out because it had already been told three times, by my one writer. In John, my writer has to dwell on having Jesus read minds as in John 4. The scholars don't have to agree on my one writer theory, but they should quit calling the fourth Gospel John.

Mine is an hermeneutics approach dealing only with the New Testament's content. I don't need outside references. By appealing to outside references, the arguments about when and where the Gospels were written become circular. We should always come back to only a comparision of content of the four.

Thus continuing with the case of John, I am left to ponder: The person who wrote John also wrote The Revelation to John? He suddenly went from historical writer to metaphorical writer? Most likely, the scholars are going to say, "But the last book was a great spiritual revelation so a dramatic shift in styles is plausable." The Transfiguration was also a great spiritual revelation, but it isn't in John. Furthermore, in Revelation, John identifies himself, but in "John" he doesn't.

I recently read a controversy that the book of Isaiah was written by one person, by two people, and by more than two people. Who's right? Many of my readers ask me for references. I list some references at the end of this book. I don't want to turn this into an academic debate. Consult any number of local ministers, and they'll give directions. There is enough written that you won't, most likely, reach a decision any time soon.

It would be interesting to know when in history the first fabrication of a text was created. In terms of biblical studies, one of the first falsifications was the Book of Enoch. It was written about the same time as the Gospels. All biblical scholars agree Enoch is not the writer of the Book of Enoch.

Look how the entire content of certain passages was redirected with the King James amendments. As I was finishing this book, a Gideon Bible, with a Korean translation, was presented to me. In the Lord's prayer are words not found in the Jerusalem Bible, "And lead us not into temptation but deliver us from the evil one. *For Yours is the kingdom and the power and the glory for ever Amen.*" (MT 6:13, italics added.) When I see such additions, I know it would have been easy for one person to have directed the writing of the Gospels.

What about Mark 6:11 in the same Bible? "And whatever community will neither receive you nor listen to you, when you leave there shake off the dust from under your feet for a witness against them. *Truly I tell you, it will be more endurable for Sodom and Gomorrah in the Judgment Day than for that city.*" The words in italics were later added to the original text. As for the original passage, when necessary, I'm shaking off the dust.

The arguments will go on, and I will put my theory in the public arena to be tested. My intent when I began this endeavor was only to learn more about how one can balance spirituality and materialism. It had nothing to do with how many people wrote the Gospels. Actually, I still don't really care.

For scholars and non-scholars alike, take a week or two to read the four Gospels from beginning to end a couple of times. And read it with the idea of a one writer theory in mind.

WHERE DOES THE BUCK STOP?

How does one balance the material world and the spiritual world? If we all gave everything up and followed Jesus, where would the world be? Would anybody farm or fish? Or would everybody farm and fish?

I have come to conclude that being part of the material world does not necessarily make one immoral. Confucius expounded on this most of his life. A leader, no matter how rich, should be judged by his deeds. Virtuous behavior has greater effect than laws and punishment. Virtuous behavior by leaders sets the example for an orderly social life throughout society.

I believe a person can be rich and be moral. But I think the more one is attached to the material world, the greater the hinderance of entering the spiritual realm existing within each of us. Jesus was a demonstration of turning one's back on the material world and developing the spiritual realm within.

Confucius, like Jesus, wrote none of his own teachings. Yet when Confucius died, his followers wrote of him doing superhuman acts. These writings were later amended to give the realistic view of the man Confucius. Maybe, 2000 years later, Christians should amend their views of having the only correct religion and inject more spirituality into their own lives.

Deuteronomy 28:

9   If you obey the Lord your God and do everything he commands, he
      will make you his own people, as he has promised.
10   Then all the people of earth will see that the Lord has chosen you to
      be his own people and they will be afraid of you.

Just what I want, all the people on earth to be afraid of me. A Muslim once told me, "If you as an Animist or a Christian do something that you think enhances your spiritual qualities, we are happy for you. But if we do something that we think enhances our spiritual qualities, Christians find that to be negative because they want us to become Christians. Is that fair?"

12

DRIVEN BY THE SPIRIT

As I was about to begin a 40-day fast, I wondered what effect it would have on my life. Jesus' life was divided by his 40-day fast; he did not minister until after those 40 days. The fast was an important event in his life. What was it like for Jesus before and after his 40-day fast?

Prior to his fast, we have his missing years from the ages of 12 to 30. After Jesus was missing for 18 years, we have only the scantiest information. "Then Jesus was led by the Spirit into the desert to be tempted by the devil. After fasting forty days and forty nights, he was hungry." (MT 4:1-2)

Then there are the "details" of the three temptations.

Would I see something on a 40-day fast, assuming I made it until the end? From the experience of my vision quest, I thought I would. I was excited about the prospects of a tremendous spiritual awakening.

MY SPOT

Is it possible that the location of a vision quest could somehow influence the vision? Many people believe in power spots and so do I.

Long ago, I wanted to go to the deserts of Jordan where Jesus did his fast. Just about the time I was ready, the Gulf War broke out. The war was over soon enough, but I chose not to go to Jordan. My choice was not out of fear of being killed, but what if someone interrupted my fast because of war? That would really irk me if I got to day 38, and I was forced to move and stop the fast.

While I was doing research for my fast, I asked several scholars, "What is the latest research on where Jesus might have done his fast?" The answer always came back, "I didn't know anyone was working on it."

"Why not?" I would ask.

The answer would be, "Why is it important? It isn't really important where he did his fast, is it?"

Well, it is to me. Not just the spot, but how did Jesus pick it? Did someone tell him where to go? Finding a spot is not that easy. Besides, it is one additional element to fit into any reconstruction we have of Jesus as a man. How did he perceive the landscape?

Knowing how Jesus picked his spot might help me understand what I am to do in a fast. The absence of food is secondary; the absence of speech is primary. That is why Jesus had to go into the wilderness; otherwise, he could have just stayed in a city and abstained from food for forty days. Everyday from the day we are born, we have an ongoing auditory stimulation. The brain, our consciousness, never gets to experience any alternative existence. The brain is almost constantly busy cataloguing human communication. Most people have never spent a day without speech. Imagine that! Now, imagine going for 40 days without anyone talking to you or you talking to anyone. As the Zen masters ask, "What is the sound of one hand clapping?"

I think I'd know if I walked onto the spot where Jesus fasted. Perhaps ultimate tranquility emanates out of the ground there. Wouldn't it? Doesn't it? But maybe emanating out of that spot is chaos, turmoil, and pain. And maybe nothing emanates out of the spot. Perhaps by design that spot can never be known.

Where would I do my fast? In 1994, I was stuck, more or less, in Hawaii. I was living on Oahu, where it sometimes seems there are more rental cars than trees. Would there be any place on that island that was quiet? It is difficult to get away from urban noise, especially with the ongoing presence of military helicopters.

More importantly, I needed fresh water. Hawaii's streams are contaminated. Mongooses were introduced to the islands to combat rats that were eating the island's sugar cane. Mongoose urinate in the streams and contaminate it with the disease Leptospirosis. Drinking that water is a sure trip to the hospital. I had to find a spring coming from the ground.

For days, I poured over topographic maps to study the headwaters of streams. The problem with the headwaters of streams in Hawaii is that they are located in high recesses of the mountains. Could I make the climb down after fasting 40 days? The ascents are steep and treacherous, and I considered it a bonafide problem.

I asked my friend Paul Malaspina, a soil scientist, his opinion. He thought that the headwaters of the Makaha stream on the west side of Oahu might be a good option since those waters are located in flatter terrain. We got a late start one Sunday, and we were only able to hike about three hours up the stream. We were still far from the headwaters, but one thing was obvious; the marijuana growers would be yet another major problem in finding an isolated spot in Hawaii.

Another option was to filter my water, but still I needed the isolation. My friend Dave Preston, an entomologist at the Bishop Museum, literally knows Oahu like the back of his hand. After hearing my problem, he said, "Give me time to think."

After a couple of weeks, he favored a certain region near the Halawa Valley. He thought it would be best to bring water to me rather than my filtering the water available at the spot. We went to the spot. It was beautiful. But while rather isolated, it was still near a little-used hiking trail. I really didn't want to have to talk to anyone. But I also didn't want Dave to spend too much of his energy on my project. I said okay. But it would mean he and Michelle would have to carry a lot of water a long way.

EXPECTATIONS AND FEARS

I began to have an element of fear about my fast. The fear wasn't over hunger or dying from a lack of food. If I thought I was going to die from hunger, I'd simply get a cluster of grapes and break the fast. But as the time grew near, I began to think about the actual physical effects. My main concern was the stability of my teeth. If they began to loosen, would I call off the fast? I began to regret not doing the fast when I was 30. But during my preparation, an inner voice would tell me, "You are not supposed to be looking back."

My good friend, Eduardo Macotela, once said something similar to me. We were in his car speeding from Tula to Mexico City, and he had forgotten some receipts he was supposed to deal with that day in Mexico City. I said, "Let's go back." He said, "*Nunca, nunca*, never go back, and if it weren't for rear view mirrors, I wouldn't even look back."

I learned a lot from Eduardo. One thing I learned was not to worry about the past. It sounds easy enough, but I still have trouble with it. Eduardo helped me put several bad incidents in my life behind me.

Jesus admonished to look forward; not backward. "And another said, 'Lord, I will follow thee, but let me first go bid farewell to those at home in my house.' And Jesus said unto him, "No man, having put his hand to the plough, and looking back, is fit for the kingdom of God." (LK 9:61-62)

A second fear was what I might see. What I saw during my vision quest became reality. What if I saw great personal tragedies during the 40-day fast?

Maybe better not to fast and not to know?

"Terry, let's get with the Valley of Death," an inner voice said.

"What do you mean?" I questioned in silence.

"You are not supposed to be fearing evil."

Will I "see" "something" after a 40-day fast? Maybe I won't see anything.

Then I asked myself: Am I after a certain experience with my 40-day fast? When I entered training with the Zen and when I did my vision quests, I let those experiences take me without expecting anything. Once I had those experiences of tranquility and vision, I had a basis for expectation. Of course, that basis is what was causing fear of possibly seeing personal tragedy.

Yet, there was the other side of the coin. If I made 40 days in isolation, I might have a vision that would produce an extraordinary spiritual awakening in me. I felt a 40-day fast would somehow negate my ego and put me in touch with the spiritual realm. This became my expectation the closer I got to the fast. If this did not happen, however, I felt I could at least expect some type of profound tranquility to enter my being.

But, perhaps I will only understand myself better. Only?

One day, as I was contemplating my fears of what I might see or experience, the concept of temptations took on a new meaning. After all, Jesus was tempted after his fast. To plan for what might confront me, I thought it best if I again looked at Jesus' fast.

THE TEMPTATIONS

Why did Jesus do a 40-day fast? Was he required to fast to be confronted by Satan? Maybe that is why he was "driven by the spirit" knowing that the confrontation was coming. Perhaps he had to fast so that he would not succumb to Satan's temptations. Jesus' death was revealed to him at the Transfiguration, and maybe Satan's temptations were likewise revealed to him before they occurred. Possibly knowing that the temptations were coming, he had to step out of the material world so he could escape the idea that he could have dominion over all the kingdoms that ever existed.

Matthew and Luke present some details of the fast. Mark mentions it briefly. John does not mention it at all. If my theory of one writer is correct, he focused on other aspects of Jesus since the 40-day fast has already been covered three times.

MATTHEW

In Matthew the Tempter says to Jesus, "Command that these stones be made bread." Why would the devil want all the stones made into bread? One stone would have been enough. But in Matthew, it is Jesus against the entire world, so the Tempter commands a group of stones be changed.

Matthew details the temptations, but he has the vision of the kingdoms as the third temptation. Here again, the message is Jesus against the entire world. He has come to propose a message counter to anything that ever existed. By placing the vision of the kingdoms last, Jesus is then remembered in opposition to the entire world. He rejects what has gone on before. He is new.

MARK

Mark just mentions that Jesus was "driven by the spirit" into the desert for 40 days, but there are no specifics of the temptations. Mark says Jesus went into the desert, fasted 40 days, was tempted by Satan, and "...after...Jesus came into Galilee, preaching the gospel of the kingdom of God."

Why would the fast not be detailed in Mark? Because in Mark, Jesus is more realistically portrayed as a lively man. The emphasis in Mark is on Jesus as a man of action. The temptations are the opposite of action; thus, they are better not detailed in Mark.

LUKE

In Luke, the devil says, "Command this stone that it be made bread." Just one stone? Why not all of them like in Matthew? Because the focus in Luke is Jesus as the savior of all mankind, one stone will do.

The third temptation in Luke is Jesus being levitated up to the summit of the temple in Jerusalem and being asked to throw himself down. (This is covering quite a distance both horizontally and vertically.) Satan tells Jesus "...for it is written, 'He will give orders to his angels to protect you.'" Jesus replied, "It is also written, 'You shall not test the Lord your God.'" Why would this temptation be placed last in Luke? In Luke, many important prophecies are covered. That is what my one hypothesized writer wants to focus on here--it is written and it will come true. And since this is the last time the fast and temptations are to be mentioned in the New Testament, the focus is on never doubting or testing God. My one writer is good.

JOHN

John doesn't mention the fast. This is a major event for John to leave out of a portrayal of Jesus. However, if the Gospels are an integrated whole through well-planned contradictions and inconsistencies, there would be no reason to mention Jesus' 40-day fast in John. Jesus, as he comes out of Luke, is already the accomplished prophet. In John, my one writer needs to spend his time emphasizing the gift of eternal life through Jesus.

ANTICHRIST

If there were four writers, I'd expect more similarity of references to the Antichrist. I would think at least two of the Gospels would use the title Satan. Matthew says, "And when the Tempter came to him." Mark says he was tempted by Satan. Luke says, "...the devil said unto him." This seems to be an example of word variation by one writer, and a good one at that: tempter, Satan, and the devil. There will be those who will argue that this is "proof positive" that the three were written by three different people. Bottom line: It will be a debated point until Jesus returns.

My last look at Jesus' fast didn't help me understand the fast or Jesus any better. But it did make me more positive of my one-writer theory.

THE FAST

In January of 1994, I made a commitment to do the fast. I planned to begin on July 13 so I could finish on my birthday, August 22. However, in April, Michelle and I applied for jobs in Korea. Notification of acceptance would come during the fast. If accepted, we would fly to Korea August 20th. Thus, I had to start my fast on June 19. The silence factor was likely to be disrupted to communicate about our possible move to Korea. Michelle told me not to worry. She could take care of all the administrative duties in preparing for our potential move. I only had to concentrate on the fast.

THE DIARY

While I was on the fast, I had a calendar. The squares were about two inches by two inches. If I had some insight, I made a brief note about it. The following diary was written after the fast.

Sunday, June 19, 1994
I walk through our backyard to the garden on the Kalihi Stream. My new basil crop is doing well. I sit on a terrace wall and I begin to wonder, "Will I make the 40 days? What if I don't?" A quick reconciliation floats into my being. It doesn't really matter. Once I'm into the fifth day, that will be one day longer than my Omaha vision quest. And once I'm in the ninth day, I'll pass the eight-day sesshin I did with the Zen. And once I'm on day 21, I'll be further than I ever have been without food. So, if I only ever get to day 21, there will be a new dimension in my life.

I wonder why I'm having these rationalizations. I never had those types of thoughts before my vision quest or sesshin. Finally, I come to grips with the fact that a 40-day fast is a long time, and there is good foundation for doubt.

Dave arrives early. He finds me sitting in the garden, "Stocker, come look at one last place. There's no water. Michelle and I will have to pack it all in, but I'd feel better since it is closer to my house."

We go to Hawaii Kai. Dave lives on a street that borders wild land immediately ascending into the Koolau Mountain Range. We walk briskly (10 minutes) up to a large grove of trees on a dry stream bed. It will be a great spot. I don't even go into the tree grove. Turning, I look down on Hawaii Kai. I know from the land's contour that once in the tree grove I won't see the city. What an irony; do a 40-day fast looking down on Roy's Restaurant, Hawaii's famed place of haute cuisine.

Dave wants me to go in late in the evening the next day, Monday, since there are often weekend hikers going up on a trail on the terrace behind the grove of trees. Also, he has a family event early this afternoon, so the starting time is postponed one day.

June 20, 1994

I am antsy because Dave is late; it is after 5 P.M. I take stock of myself. For some reason, probably displacement behavior, I take out my billfold and assess the money. I have two dollars. Should I leave it or take it? What does it matter? I take it. I feel so anxious.

Dave arrives at 5:30. We drive to his house, and he shows me some antique toys he recently purchased. He has a tremendous collection. So, I get just one last bit of the material world before departing.

We arrive at the trail about 7 P.M. I take greater notice of the large no-trespassing sign. But Dave assures me the land belongs to the city, and the only time he has ever seen anyone "of city authority" go in there is when the city is working on the power lines, and my tent will not be located in the path of the power lines. But, there is a light trickle of traffic on the road, and I feel conspicuous unloading the packs. How many people go hiking carrying eight gallons of water? Of course, it is between two of us. I try to maintain some humor and lose the feeling of constant worry. But here I am standing with a small folding chair, not something someone would normally carry while hiking. We trek in. Once we are high enough, I look back to see if anyone is watching us. I am having light paranoia.

To reach the grove of trees, we have to jump a small three-foot bank of dirt, cross the dry stream bed of large boulders, and climb another three-foot bank of dirt. The stream bed isn't really much of an obstacle, but I feel good that it should keep out any person simply walking a dog.

There is an old path going through the trees. But it's not really visible. It is at most six inches wide, and it is completely hidden by a thick Guinea grass about three feet high and somewhat difficult to move through. The trees, *Leucaena glauca L.*, also called *Koa-Haole* in Hawaiian, are dense. Most are about six inches in diameter and 15 to 25 feet high. We walk for about fifty yards before there is space large enough to set up the small dome tent. We set up the tent in about five minutes. We shake hands and off he goes.

Dave is gone about 10 minutes when sirens begin going off as though they are right at the bottom of the hill. I immediately think maybe Dave has been arrested for trespassing. I want to run out to the crest and see if that is the case, but I don't want to be seen.

I closely observe my location and decide I want to be more secluded. The small stream bed we crossed coming in is a tributary to a larger stream to the east of my tent. The larger stream varies between 15 and 25 feet wide.

It too is dry. Immediately to the east, across the dry stream bed, is a flat space with extremely high grass and rather dense tree coverage. I trample down the grass and move the tent.

Inside my tent are two-gallon water containers in each corner; a rolled-up, down sleeping bag for a pillow; a yellow double-bed size sheet; one change of clothes in a black gym-bag; a roll of toilet paper; an 8 1/2 by 11 calendar on which to write a daily thought; and a sign that reads: "I AM DOING A 40-DAY FAST. I MAY NOT BE ABLE TO TALK BECAUSE I HAVE NOT EXERCISED MY VOCAL CORDS."

My mind is preoccupied with the sirens and Dave's possible arrest. I decide that after dark I'll go down to his apartment and satisfy myself. I hope to find him there. What a way to start a 40-day fast.

I survey my surroundings in the remaining twilight. Immediately outside my tent, the stream bed is quite wide, maybe 50 feet. There are remnants of a small island, three feet across and fifteen feet long. It is covered with grass and a few shrubs. Upstream the stream bed is almost straight for 80 yards. All the way up are rather large boulders from one to three feet in diameter. Downstream, just past the island, it narrows to 15 feet and immediately drops to a large flat area that during times of heavy rain would have supported a water fall. The fall is a little over three feet.

My mind bounces back and forth between worrying about Dave and the "stark" reality that I'm finally here at one of my life's goals, a 40-day fast. My head aches a bit.

About 30 minutes after dark, I slowly make my way down the hill. Away from the trees, the lights from the city continually encroach so that walking is no problem. Going down, I pass a couple walking a dog. We exchange, "Hellos." Once on the street, I feign jogging a bit because there are people walking, and I suspect they are locals who know each other and not me, a stranger.

Dave's apartment is only five minutes from the exit. I knock on the door. My anxiety level is high. The door opens and there is Dave. The look on his face erases all my anxiety, and I burst into laughter over my own paranoia. After hearing my quick rendition, he chuckles, "No, Terry, everything down here is all right." He emphasizes "down here."

Back I go. I hope no one notices me step over the large chain and into the dirt lane. No one does, but the same couple is returning. Again we exchange, "Hellos," but this time the dog takes an affinity to me, and wants to go with me. He finally follows his family's command to go with them. His name is Oscar.

In the tent, I relax. I place my billfold in one of the corners. I have nothing on my body but clothes. Everything is set. I'm on my way.

The moon is almost full. I sit in the chair and watch it. Another of my missions in life is to watch the full moon as it crosses the entire sky, never taking my eyes off of it.

There are a few mosquitoes, but the persistent breeze keeps them from being a nuisance.

The wind picks up during the night, and the constant flapping of the tent makes sleeping difficult.

DAY 1

I wake up with a mild headache. The headache is from anticipation of the fast and my paranoia from yesterday. I fidget about sitting on this stone and then that stone and looking at another stone. I recall Carlos Castaneda fidgeting about on Don Juan's porch before finding his spot.

I just left a world where I was writing this book everyday. Now there is no writing except my daily encapsulation of my feelings which fit into a two-by-two inch square on my calendar. I decide to write my thoughts at sundown.

Everywhere in my immediate environment I see only nature, but I hear more than an occasional car.

A large Christmas-berry tree, *Schinus terebinthifolius raddi,* on the western bank shades the large flat, water-fall area. I put my chair on the flat area and look downstream. On both sides of me are high sloping ridges. At a height of 1000 feet, they will block any sunrise or sunset. I'm in a canyon.

Early in the afternoon, I find "my" sitting stone. The stone is actually two large contiguous boulders. They form the eastern bank of the stream. The smaller of the two is about three feet high. I can sit on it, swirl around, and lean my back on it and then prop my feet up on the larger one. The boulders are rather comfortable, and they are in the shadow of the large tree. I label them "the sitting stone."

I lie in the tent for about 20 minutes every other hour. The abundant cloud cover keeps the tent cool.

I keep thinking about food, mostly hot dogs. I seem to be drinking water as a form of displacement. The lukewarm water from a plastic container is not particularly refreshing.

About four in the afternoon, I walk up the stream. The gradient is gentle, and the stream bed is straight for about 80 yards. Just before the stream bends, there are two large, smooth boulders positioned in such a way that I can sit on one and recline against the other. The straightness of the channel shores and the gentle blending of the smooth stones one into another creates everything Thomas Merton would have deemed of value for a photograph. I want a picture. I call the boulder I sit on "Merton's throne."

There is no evening wind, and I cannot sit outside because of the mosquitoes. One mosquito makes its way into the tent. I manage to kill it after a couple of slaps on my face.

I drink about half a gallon of water today.

Sometime during the night the wind abruptly begins blowing. The constant flapping of the tent makes sleeping difficult.

DAY 2

I continue to feel stir-crazy, but my headache lessens.

The reality of "the sitting stone" makes itself known. Yesterday it was a novelty, but I learn it is only comfortable for about half an hour at the most. Sitting on a rock has its limits, and I think, "God, it is only day 2!" Nevertheless, I am able to pass a couple straight hours under the shade of the large tree. When the rock becomes unendurable, I move to my folding chair.

I hear two voices talking sometime in the afternoon. It is disconcerting. I finally spot the people. They are on the hiking trail going up into the mountains to the west of me. For a short time up on the trail, their voices are audible to me. But they don't see me. However, I decide to practice my voice a bit everyday in the event someone comes upon me. I decide not to say I am fasting, but to say I am getting away for a day or two. Every now and then I say out loud, "Mind in the present." These four words are one of my old mantra's that my Zen master taught me.

I think about food quite a bit. But my daydreams are not of eating food, but preparing dishes. I think some of them are good enough for my next entries into the Pillsbury Bakeoff. One of life's pleasures for me is cooking.

Again I drink about half a gallon of water.

That night another mosquito finds its way into the tent. I am unable to kill it. It buzzes and buzzes and of course buzzes some more.

Sometime during the night the wind abruptly begins blowing. The constant flapping of the tent makes sleeping difficult. I finally doze off, only to awake with a mosquito bite.

DAY 3

The stir-craziness begins to diminish. I realize I have not built up to this, unlike my prolonged fasts and quests in the late 70s and early 80s. It's likely I'll be fidgeting around for a few more days. It could take a couple of weeks for me to get to a mental state of enjoying being away from the world I just left. I am afraid the book alone has become a part of the mental process of my fast. I'm tied to the material world. Too often I'm thinking of writing about the fast; I am not just experiencing it. When I did the vision quest, I did it for the experience; I did not write about it.

Early in the morning, a helicopter flies very low right above me. I have an initial paranoia, but I stick to my plan to state simply that I'm only getting away for a couple of days; and if there is a problem, I will leave. I practice my voice by saying, "Mind in the present."

There is no cloud cover this day, and it is so hot in the tent that I cannot stay inside from about 11 A.M. to 4 P.M.

I continue to have food-preparation daydreams. It seems that my daily consumption of water will be half a gallon.

This night there are no mosquitoes or wind. My sleep is pleasant.

DAY 4

Already I wish for it to be day 40, but not to go through the process of getting there. I must endure the constant redirecting of my consciousness to reach day 40. It is not good to be wishing day 40 to be here. In sesshin, I never thought about a future day because I had achieved "mind in the present." And this is nothing like the fourth day of my vision quest. I am a long way from achieving anything. I think about a book which Geraldine Dent told me about, but I forget the title. It is about a man who went to live in a Zen monastery and couldn't hack it so he left. I don't really know much about Zen monastic life, but I know that before a monk is accepted in the higher temples, he has to beg for one year. This supposedly instills humility. I image it does. Actually the begging is different from what we know in the west. The monks don't ask people for money; rather a monk walks with his head down, holds a cup in one hand, and a bell in the other. He rings the bell. But I would think that year-long exercise would take the stir-craziness out of anyone. I need that. After a year of walking and begging, one might be inclined to sit for a long time. How do I know Jesus wasn't stir-crazy during the first part of his 40-day fast?

Again, there is no cloud cover, and I can't stay inside the tent in the afternoon. That makes the day rather unbearable. I decide that tomorrow I will move the tent to the other side of the stream where Dave and I had originally placed it. There is afternoon shade there.

A helicopter flies directly overhead in the late afternoon.

I have daydreams of eating some of my food preparations. And I have the weirdest craving for a Bloody Mary. This is a strange sensation since I haven't had alcohol for at least three months before the fast. Nonetheless, the craving is real.

Tonight I manage to keep the mosquitoes out of the tent, and my sleep is rather pleasant.

DAY 5

Dave and Michelle bring water today, Saturday. I don't hear them come up. I am on the sitting stone at the time. I hear Michelle's voice say in a whisper, "He's not in here." I look up to see her looking into the tent. She walks to the edge of the stream and sees me. In a weak voice, I say, "Hi." She is stunned because I am not supposed to be talking outside of purposes of moving to Korea. I explain the dilemma of the hikers.

The three of us slowly converse for about 15 minutes. Michelle updates me on the Korea venture. So that we could become somewhat familiar with the Korean culture before our potential move, we were offered jobs leading tours of Koreans coming to Hawaii. Michelle told them I was off island and wouldn't be back for a couple of months. She couldn't resist saying something about the mystery envelope in the O.J. Simpson murder case. I think she might be joking, and I look to Dave for some confirmation. He just nods. And I came to get away from it all!

I ask them to bring a camera so I can take a picture downstream from the Merton throne.

There is no mosquito in the tent tonight, but the wind blows hard. The constant flapping of the tent is irritating. It makes sleeping difficult.

Lying in the dark, I try to summarize my situation. Here I am on day five, and I'm reflecting on my breaking-records mentality. For a quest, record breaking is stupid and meaningless, but it does serve a comparative purpose. I just passed my first barrier. I'm one day past the four days of my vision quest, but I am so far from the mental state I was in then that the incongruence is baffling.

DAY 6

I have one brief daydream of food.

I find myself just sitting and staring mindlessly.

It rains in the afternoon, and I am confined to the tent. The grass is not as thick here as on the other side of the stream, and I did not put much loose grass under the tent. The hard ground makes prolonged sleeping difficult.

It rains heavily during the night. There is one small leak in the left front corner of the tent.

DAY 7

I have only fleeting glimpses of food in my daydreams.

My mindless staring increases. I think of my Great-Grandfather Richards. He used to sit in a rocking chair and stare for what seemed like hours to me. Maybe that is what we are like when we grow old; the material world is no longer there. I was lucky to have known my great-grandfather. He never called a car a car; he called them machines. And he never called me Terry; he always called me Squire.

A helicopter goes overhead, but I don't even think about it until it is almost passed. I'm used to them already.

I think I understand Joseph Campbell's statement, "I don't need faith, I have experience." I think it is strange that none of the disciples asked Jesus how much faith he had.

The wind blows very hard this night.

DAY 8

Images of food are dissipating.

My prolonged staring is almost like scrying, but without images.

I realize this, my eighth day, is the duration of my sesshin with the Zen, but my mind is not anywhere close to that experience of 1976. I think I should attempt meditating a bit each night.

I wonder why the Zen do an eight-day sesshin. Maybe the units of four are somehow the basic units of human time or capabilities. The vision quest is four days.

The heavy rain from day six produced pockets of water in the stream bed, and the mosquito population drastically increased. This makes going out at night unpleasant, and the mosquitoes manifest themselves in the late afternoon such that I must use large sweeping motions of my arms when I hurry into or out of the tent.

I meditate about half an hour in the tent in the evening.

The tent flaps from the nightly wind.

DAY 9

Today I have gone one day longer than Zen sesshin.

My mind makes a "quantum leap." I finally understand the words "I can think, I can fast, I can wait" from Hermann Hesse's *Siddartha*. I never understood those words before. I thought if one could fast, one could surely wait. But all of my fasts, with the exception of my sesshins with the Zen, were done while walking around. Even sesshins are broken up into discrete segments of time. There are three meals. During a 40-day fast, there is just one segment of time that goes on. One has to be able to wait, and waiting is distinct from fasting.

There is intermittent low buzzing in my ears.

I find the flight of a helicopter extremely obnoxious today.

I meditate about half an hour in the tent in the evening.

The wind makes its nightly arrival.

DAY 10

The novelty of breaking "records" is over. It will be eleven more days before it happens again. I think I won't think much about it, but maybe I will.

Today is lasting forever. Several times, from about noon to 4, I feel like walking out of the fast. Minutes drag on like actual hours.

I develop a routine to make my mind deal with the waiting. I stay on the "sitting stone" for as long as possible. About 20 minutes I guess; I don't have a watch. Then I move to the west bank right under the tree. There is a large rock sloping back into the bank. I lean on the stone for about 20 minutes. Next, I sit in the chair for about 20 minutes. I repeat the routine a second time and then go lie in the tent for 30 or 45 minutes, then back out and repeat the routine. The afternoon is like two eternities back to back.

The buzzing in my ears stops.

I meditate about half an hour in the tent in the evening.

The tent flaps in the wind throughout the night.

DAY 11

You know how you close your eyes really quickly, and you sometimes see flashes of light on the inside of your eyelids? Sometimes those flashes of light take geometric forms. Today I closed my eyes, and there were very vivid animal forms moving. I see a jaguar and birds on several occasions. I am excited about this, and I hope for more.

Today's early afternoon is a repeat of yesterday's. I'm experiencing time differently. I hope it will not happen again, but still the early afternoon lasts forever. I endure the same sitting/standing routine.

I decide to quit meditating. I want this to be an experience separate from meditation.

There is no wind, and I sleep well.

DAY 12

For some reason, I wake with a headache. Not too bad, but bad enough to make the day more miserable. I wonder if Jesus ever had a headache. Do curers, like Jesus, cure their own headaches or do they have to seek out other curers? Or do they ever have headaches? Or do they just endure?

I think my headache amplifies the slowness of time because today's early afternoon is like four eternities blended together. I endure the same sitting/standing routine.

The animal images I saw yesterday do not reoccur.

DAY 13

Today is a water day. I suppose it is the anticipation of seeing Dave and Michelle, but the morning is twice as long as usual. It takes on the qualities of the previous early afternoon. Boyd, a good friend, comes with them. They bring a camera. I want to get a picture of the long, straight channel looking down from Merton's throne. When we get to the throne--which I do not call by that name in front of them--and show them the long straight row of large cobbles, they make remarks that I have fasted too long already. I guess they never saw a Thomas Merton photograph.

I borrow a knife from Dave. I will use it to cut the tall grass and put under the tent to make it more comfortable.

Michelle has a few more details about the move to Korea. When they leave, Boyd looks at me seriously and says, "You do have a tranquil spot, Terry."

Interacting with them for 30 minutes is total sensory overload. When they leave, I immediately go to the tent and, judging by the sun, sleep for almost three hours.

The wind makes its nightly visit.

DAY 14

Maybe the days are dragging on because I gaged the first ten by my "records" of the fifth day and the ninth day. The afternoons become longer each day. That segment of time is becoming excruciating.

I'm amazed by the amount of petty thoughts I continue having. They are diminishing, but there are still too many. The main petty thought is of three individuals in my life who I wish were not there. Actually their existence is only on the extreme periphery of my life, but I hope for the day that I never think about them again. I need to put their past behind me. I remember back to my night with the Trappists and wonder about that aspect of my personality. It is something I don't understand. Nevertheless, for me the essence of life is memories. I want my life to be of good memories, but three individuals represent ugly memories.

The periods of nothingness are increasing. I find myself staring at the ground and having no idea when I began.

The passing of a helicopter almost directly overhead seems acutely obnoxious. I contemplate the noise level of my spot. I hear cars daily in the distance, but they are somehow tuned out. Still there is too much industrial noise at my spot.

I realize the nights are passing without me thinking about time. Even though I am awake and lying in the tent during much of the night, I am not antsy like I am during the day.

This evening I start doing some leg exercises in the tent, mostly just pulling myself into full lotus and seeing how long I can hold it. I estimate five minutes.

Tonight the wind is pleasant. I wonder if there were no mosquitoes, if I could have done the fast without a tent. Maybe Jesus made himself a small shelter.

DAY 15

I slept the entire night. Maybe it was the leg exercises. I have extreme tranquility throughout the morning.

This afternoon, I begin having memories of my past that I never even thought about before. In 1971, my father gave me a 1965 Ford van. Two days after he gave it to me, Nancy and Hans, my son, then six months, and I were on our way to Mexico. I kept smelling something burning, but I couldn't figure out what it could be. The smell grew worse. Finally, I located the source, behind the driver's seat. It was a black box and when I opened it, lo and behold, there was the battery barely functioning without water.

My daydream is only of the battery, not the driving or the trip, but just the odor and finding the battery. The daydream doesn't have any significance I can think of. Why am I recalling this memory during my fast?

My mindless staring increases. My walking is slowing to the point that I am constantly just stopping and staring.

I assess my weight loss. I don't think I've lost more than seven pounds.

I do the leg exercises tonight.

Two mosquitoes are obnoxious throughout the night. I locate them in the morning, and I am not Jainist about their existence.

DAY 16

I begin this day by realizing the time that has passed is twice as long as the eight-day sesshin. The eight-day sesshin seemed like eight days; however, these 16 days do not have a marker for time. Days and weeks mean nothing anymore. There are only minutes that are somehow not made up of seconds, at least not seconds I recognize. Minutes have stretched into unbounded time.

I continue to say, "Mind in the present." But my mind is not in the present. It is all over the place, sometimes in the past and sometimes in the future.

My mindless staring and standing and staring increases in frequency and duration. My walking is slowing to the point that I stop and stare, move a few steps, stop and stare, move a few steps, stop and stare.

Today I begin assessing the idea I might have to move to Mrs. Char's guest house to finish the fast. If I continue at the rate I'm going, I'm sure I might have the spiritual awakening that I am after. But my recovery time could be a couple of weeks or more. Our move to Korea would be around the same time. Could I get on a plane, make a 13-hour trip, begin educational seminars, all after recovering from a 40-day fast? I think if I had done my fast when I was 30, this wouldn't be an issue. But I'm almost 50 years old. My body will need more recovery time. If I move to Mrs. Char's, my sleep will be more beneficial and comfortable without the mosquitoes.

There is another passing of a helicopter and the nightly wind.

DAY 17

I am staring an incredible amount. I stand staring for what seems like long periods of time. I might even be standing and staring for up to 15 minutes. When walking, my steps are tediously slow. I think it might be wise to do the last 20 days in Mrs. Char's guest house and drink juices. If it weren't for going to Korea, I might opt to stay outside. At the rate I'm going now, I think that the 40th day would be like passing the event horizon of a black hole where time and space as we know them cease to exist. Perhaps it was something similar for Jesus.

At one point, I slowly walk down to the joining of the large stream and the tributary. I walk a few feet at a time, then sit on a rock and resume mindless staring. The trip down and back must have taken a couple of hours. When I get back, I see a mongoose near my chair. My body reacts involuntarily, I pick up a stone and throw it at the animal. I miss. The stone no sooner leaves my hand than I think back to watching that animal during my vision quest. Why did I throw the stone today? And what if I had hit the mongoose? I obviously am a long way from where I want to be.

Mosquitoes in my tent make sleeping intolerable.

DAY 18

There is another fleeting memory of the past. There was a family gathering, and we were eating rabbit that day at my paternal grandfather's house. I took the heart and a leg. My grandfather simultaneously talked and reached, "Terry, you should not be slow to eat the heart." His fork quickly snatched it, and away it went into his mouth.

Maybe it is the absence of food that conjures up that image. Today, I am thinking about more of my Pillsbury Bakeoff recipes.

My movements are becoming slower and slower. I estimate that walking up to Merton's throne takes me nearly an hour, a normal ten to fifteen minute walk. I stand staring at the ground and then sometimes I sit on a stone and take more time doing the same activities I've done for 18 days. The walk is now physically demanding. So, I stop a lot, and I sit a lot.

I must make a decision as to stay outside or go inside. Should I switch over to juices? Everything considered, I should go inside. The isolation factor will still be there. I think of the Trappists and the Zen. They're inside. A night of sleep without mosquitoes would be nice.

During one moment of standing and staring, I think: What if someone should walk upon me in this state? It would be difficult to say I was just getting away from it all for a couple of days.

Again mosquitoes and wind disrupt the night.

DAY 19

Should I go tell Dave I am moving inside? About three in the afternoon, I feel I must go. I hope he is there. At first there is hesitancy in my mind about changing my spot. As I walk, I know I am making the right decision. As slow as I am going, 20 more days might render me incapable of walking.

As I step over the chain, there are cars coming and going. Their rapid movement makes me slightly dizzy. I never looked at the world like this before. Somehow, it just seems so meaningless.

I believe in omens, and just before Dave's house is a large garage sale sign tacked to a tree. Dave and I often go to garage sales together. For some reason, I think I will end up at that garage sale.

Dave is not home, but his cousin Al is. I tell him to give Dave a message not to bring water up tomorrow because I will be moving inside. Al remembers seeing me on the afternoon of June 20, and he quickly puts it all together. He asks me if I want a drink of water. I accept. He puts ice in it, and the sensation is the superlative of refreshing.

I think about Jesus saying, "...whoever gives one of these little ones but a cup of cold water to drink because he is a disciple, I assure he will not lose his reward." (MT 10:29) I mention the passage to Al and thank him for the drink.

Al is a Christian and he reads the Bible daily. He was reading when I knocked on the door. He talks about what he calls a natural peace. For him it is a peaceful spiritual acceptance of any given life situation. He is a bus driver in Honolulu. He is often exasperated by many of the situations he encounters on the bus, but through his biblical readings, he is able to put all of the negative emotions behind him. I remember one of Zen Master Kando Nakagima's writings. It was about how to have mind in the present while driving a bus.

I leave. I think to make the day more surreal I should go to the garage sale and see what they have. Maybe a book on fasting? But I cannot see the garage sale from where I am standing, and I can't afford losing more energy. I go back to my spot.

While experiencing the nightly wind and mosquitoes, I appreciate that this will be the last night outside.

DAY 20

I feel anxious this morning. My anxiety is a combination of relief and regret. Pulling the tent stakes I keep thinking, I shouldn't go; I must go. I am moving slowly in packing the tent. Another 20 days is a long time in this state.

The tent down and packed, I sit on the spot where the tent had been. I try to summarize these twenty days. I am living a stupid dichotomy; anticipating a future job and dabbling with a spiritual quest. I should have done my fast in 1977 during my period of no money. At that time, I enjoyed sitting and waiting. I was prepared for an event as important as a 40-day fast. Maybe that is why Jesus had his missing years. Maybe he was preparing.

Now, I have too many materialistic concerns to break free. It is crystal clear how much I am tied to the material world. I fantasize about my book on the Bible being finished. That alone is egotistical. I think that is why Buddha, Jesus, and Mohammed all became the individuals they were. They didn't write, and thereby, they avoided that involvement of ego.

Everyday of our current lives is tied into money. It cannot be escaped, unless one joins a group in retreat, and even then the retreat's survival is somehow tied to monetary transactions.

Thinking about this spot, I realize it isn't that great either. After all, three days earlier I almost killed a mongoose. Why? I'm not sure. But living with the anticipation of hikers wandering into my environment has some subconscious impact. One of the things I can't get over about the industrialized world is noise pollution. Sirens alone are totally obnoxious. What would it have meant to the human mind to have lived at a time when there were only the sounds of nature?

Michelle and Dave arrive. They begin picking up everything while I am still sitting. They seem in a hurry. For a brief moment, I'm offended. I think they might want to talk. But it dawns on me, the fast is still on; I'm just changing spots.

Dave makes a joke, "I hope you haven't packed any water."

I smile.

Dave jerks a water container out of my hand, and lectures, "You shouldn't carry anything." They start out. I can't walk as fast as they can, and they go ahead.

As he is putting the tent and empty water containers in the jeep, I see Dave feels relief I am going. He took on too much of the responsibility for my safety.

Once mobile, I speak slowly and softly, "Hey, Dave, there was a garage sale near you yesterday."

"It's today too, and I got money," and with those words the jeep turns. A couple more short turns, and we are there.

Materials are spread along both sides of a long two-car driveway going to a garage likewise filled with remnants of a life that someone finally wanted to let go of in return for some monetary compensation. I watch as if it is a movie in slow motion.

A young woman lusts over a lamp. But fifteen dollars is apparently too high, even too high to begin bargaining. Her head bobs as she follows the outlines of the lamp imagining it in a special place in her home. I imagine her having a conversation with a friend about finding the lamp at a garage sale. She must sense I am watching her, and she looks at me. I don't look away, and our eyes are locked. In that type of situation, there is usually a sense of time, but today there isn't--at least for me. I simply observe a timeless event. For her, I assume she thinks I am concerned with purchasing the lamp. She breaks the stare and returns to bobbing her head.

I, too, refocus my attention. A man becomes elated with a small, fold-up shovel. I watch him pay fifty cents. I see his pleasure of purchasing a little bit more of the material world. At the same time, I hear, from behind me, the haggling over a price differential of only a quarter.

I see some earrings I want for Michelle. I've bought over 400 pairs of earrings at garage sales for Michelle. Normally, I will say, "How much are these earrings? A quarter?" But today I have no energy for the con. I simply ask, "How much are these earrings?" The woman says fifty cents. I had excatly $2 in my billfold. I buy four pairs. Taking my billfold out and extracting the money, I know my actions are super-slow.

Everything is in slow motion. God, is it surreal. I am trying to reconcile it in my head. Did the world actually slow down, or is it possible for the human mind to perceive normal actions at a slower rate? I assume the slow motion is in my head. I'm back to an old thought: What was a moment of time for Christ and Satan?

I wonder how people perceive me. Do they somehow see me as different? I don't think they do. I think of the last part of the book of Luke. After Jesus' resurrection, some people, including a few disciples, were walking out of Jerusalem to some village. As they walked and talked, Jesus caught up with them, but they didn't recognize him. Jesus asked them what they were discussing. One of them, Cleopas, asked, "Are you the lone visitor in Jerusalem who doesn't know what has happened in the last couple of days?" I've always found that passage intriguing. Are you the lone visitor? I feel like it today. I feel as if I am the only person who doesn't know what is going on in the world. Here I am mid-way in a 40-day fast standing at a garage sale in Honolulu, Hawaii.

Once on the road, Michelle and Dave converse between themselves. I am in the back seat. The windows are down, and with the noise level coming in from the traffic on H-1, I can't discern the content of their conversation. Often they talk about pocket knives. They collect and covet them. I am free to observe the outside world. In my abnormal state, traffic should strike me as obnoxious. But I unobtrusively observe people going by. Where are they going? Some are probably going to garage sales.

I make it into our house without any neighbors seeing me. Michelle gives me a glass of grape juice. An incredible feeling simultaneously oozes throughout my body as the juice trickles down my throat. The word abracadabra finally has a physical counter part for my psyche. My body craves more. Before I realize it, I drink an entire can.

Michelle and I talk about the move to Korea. No papers have been presented, but we have an oral commitment.

Suddenly, I am struck with a sensation of a time warp. It is as if I never did a 20-day fast. I try to articulate it to Michelle. If I go away on a vacation for two weeks, I come back and it seems like the beginning of the vacation was more than two weeks ago. But today it is as if I had never gone anywhere and yet, I hadn't been at home either.

I finally go to Mrs. Char's guest house. I go to sleep immediately.

DAY 21

I appreciate the night without wind and mosquitoes.

I have a bit of a sore throat from talking yesterday, and my stomach is queasy from drinking too much juice. The guest house is clean and orderly. There are only a few things visible: a futon, a single bed, a table, two chairs, and a lamp. There is an adjoining kitchen to the small living/sleeping area. In the refrigerator, there is only juice and water. The guest house is infrequently used.

I have one overwhelming feeling of relaxation about finally being alone. Everyday outside, I felt anxious about the possibility of someone walking upon me. At that time, I thought it was only a minor concern, but sitting here today, I think it was more dominant than I thought.

There is a large clock and I ration myself to a glass of juice every two hours.

The newness of the environment makes the day pass quickly.

DAY 22

I have two fleeting memories of my past.

In one, I'm 12. I'm standing on a corner in Greenville, Ohio, getting ready to go into a movie theater. My Uncle Larry, then 18, pulls up in his 1955 black Ford. His girlfriend, Joy, is with him. They yell to get my attention. I am a bit embarrassed. I don't know why. They ask me what I'm doing. I say I'm going to the movies. The traffic light changes, and they drive away.

That incident happened about 1957. I have no memory of ever thinking about it after it happened until this day.

The second memory was of my first trip to Gethsemane, Kentucky, to visit the Trappists. I was hitchhiking with a lady friend. A man picks us up and says he is just taking the day off and driving around the back roads of Kentucky. It is too good to be true. He drives us to Gethsemane. On the way, I mention eating with the monks in Iowa. We are the only visitors. Inside, I tell the monk of my visit to the Iowa monastery. He tells us the times for chants. We could hear the chants in about 20 minutes. I ask him where they eat and if we can join them. Apologetically, he says, "The Iowa Trappists are well off. Here we are very poor, and we cannot have guests."

We hear the chants and leave. The man drives to the next town, goes to a grocery store and buys a mountain of picnic supplies and then drives us to a park where we eat.

I snap back to the newness of the guest house.

The fact that my fast is now regulated by a clock is somewhat annoying.

DAY 23

I have another glimpse of my past; maybe it is an association with food. When I was about 12 years old, I ran away from home. At 5 A.M. one

Sunday morning, I took my sister's bike and peddled twelve miles in the dark from Bradford to Greenville, Ohio. One of my favorite things in life was going to the 5 & 10 in Greenville with my mother and getting a bag of hot Spanish peanuts. I always wanted a big bag. That day I went to the 5 & 10 and bought a big bag of peanuts. I am standing outside eating them, and feeling so adult that I have the big bag.

Two older boys, maybe 15, walk by and laugh at me because I am wearing my father's combat boots. The boots are original GI, WWII issue. I thought everybody would think they were cool. I snap out of the memory at that point.

Michelle comes over that night. We have official notification of jobs in Korea.

DAY 24

Today, July 14th, I realize things I once associated with the fast are quite trivial and detract from the fast. For example, originally, I was going to initiate the fast on this day so I would finish it on my birthday. I finally realize this is an idea totally unrelated to why I should be doing a fast. I think of the word "stupid" when I remember that idea.

My afternoon is extremely tranquil.

DAY 25

I think about alcohol in my life. I have consumed too much in my life. I question why, but my mind produces no conclusion. Do I want to know the answer? I wonder if this entire thought process is originating in my consciousness or my subconsciousness.

I think I will drink less in the future. Will the fast remove the desire to drink alcohol? What an easy solution that would be. I avoid dealing with part of the reality and focus on something I know, actually hope, about the future. Why am I putting my faith in the external? Because I doubt myself? The answer appears to be yes. I feel strong and weak at once. Then I am angry because I even have to deal with the thought of alcohol consumption in my life.

DAY 26

It is Saturday. Michelle arrives. The Korean authorities require a doctor's statement that we are in "good overall" health.

She tells me Mrs. Char told the individuals she goes to church with I am finishing my 40-day fast in her guest house. One of them blurted, "But what if he dies?" We both chuckle.

Mrs. Char's friends' concern is over whether there might be litigation against her on behalf of Michelle if I die. It just never stops. I had heard enough mindless objections when I began the fast and now this.

Michelle assures me Mrs. Char is undaunted by the comments. She is one of the most devout Christians I have ever met. She was raised a Buddhist, but during high school she joined a Bible study group. After four years of Bible study, she became a Christian. In the late 1950s, Mrs. Char began to buy books from the Seventh-Day Adventists. After a year, she became a Seventh-Day Adventist. She was over 50 years old then.

The last time I ever went to a Christian church was with her. Michelle and I went to church with her on Christmas of 1993. And at the age of 90, she still has a great sense of humor. Often, she, Michelle and I watched Monday night football and ate pizza together.

Michelle talks about leading a tour of Koreans. She mentions going to a Korean restaurant with them. She laughs. She claims whenever she mentions something related to food that my face automatically wiggles.

DAY 27

I begin drinking vegetable juices today. Tomato juice is one of my favorite drinks. My eyes involuntarily squeeze shut as the liquid flows from my mouth down my throat. The solid feeling of the juice causes minor twinges of hunger. The pangs are physically real for about an hour, but my mind has no problem denying the pangs.

DAY 28

I begin taking some vitamins we have lying around the house. A friend, Steve, built a mansion for a vitamin producer, and he gave us a bunch of demo packets. I don't normally take vitamins, yet I think I might as well put them to use. Otherwise we will be throwing them away when we move to Korea. I've heard vitamins are not of much value unless one is eating, but then I don't know what to believe about nutrition news.

DAY 29

My morning vegetable juice is finished. I stare at the empty green plastic glass. It seems as if I have been drinking vegetable juice for months, and yet it has only been two days. I have a blinding realization that my mind and body quickly become habituated to certain situations.

It is comforting to have this realization. I feel the need to have the realization on constant recall for future events in my life. Too soon I can become habituated to anything. I feel a warm glow of satisfaction for having come to this realization. I am relaxed.

I have my first sound afternoon nap inside.

DAY 30

I will go for the physical exam needed for Korea.

Michelle is distraught about me going out in the world after 30 days of fasting. We don't have a family doctor and we don't have a friend who is a doctor in Honolulu. I need a statement from a doctor that I am in "good" health, and I need it quickly. Michelle is convinced that no one in the medical profession would be open minded enough to give me the statement while I am on day 30 of a 40-day fast. She asked advice of everyone in her inner circle. Their combined decision is not to send me to a "regular" medical doctor since fasting is not recognized as anything good by the AMA. One of Michelle's friends had been to a "naturopathic doctor." I don't think about it since I've never heard about naturopathism before.

Via phone conversations with the doctor's office, Michelle informs them I am on day 30 of a 40-day fast, and all I need is a letter stating I am in "good" health. Michelle will get her statement there also, after work today, and she tells the doctor she will fill out my paperwork.

Michelle asks our friend Glen to pick me up this morning. He is a friend we trust and love. Michelle feels comfortable with him "protecting" me. On the way, Glen and I talk. In brief, I tell him I have not yet had the spiritual experience I was hoping for. But I am having continual insights into my own behaviors and the behaviors of the society around me. Glen believes such insights should be included under the rubric of spiritual. But I want something out of the ordinary, much like the vision quest experience.

We arrive at the office, and Glen accompanies me inside. In the front office, the secretary is whispering and using overly-animated gestures, "Oh, come in and have a seat, please. Can I get you a cup of tea?"

We decline.

"Oh, Terry, I understand you are on a 40-day fast?"

I nod. I am not in a talking mood.

"I, myself, am on a watermelon fast." Her face tilts and pushes forward as she lowers her whispers even more.

Glen can't deal with the whispering, and says, "Terry, I'll wait for you in the car."

Finally I meet the doctor. She completes a paper questionnaire. Next she has me sit on an examining table and explains a small machine that is on another table in front of me. Coming from the machine is a type of plug which she places on the top of each of my fingers. Each finger is supposedly an indicator of specific functions of the body. She quickly informs me that the machine is not recognized by the AMA. One of my fingers indicates that my blood is somehow not as good as it should be. Immediately, she mentions a plethora of vitamins she will sell me that very day. I tell her to tell Michelle about the vitamins, that I have 10 more days of my fast to deal with before I am concerned with my blood. She asks why I am doing a 40-day fast.

I reply, "Enlightenment."

She says, "Oh, can you enlighten me?"

I say, "Huh?"

"Oh, it's a joke."

She wants to send me for a blood test. I said, "You mean just prick my finger?"

"No, draw a sample from your arm."

"No, no, and no. You aren't sticking needles in me." She cannot do the procedure herself because she is not licensed.

She tries verbally to coerce me into coming back to the office the next week, on day 37 of my fast. I explain Michelle will arrange any appointments necessary.

I escape the office.

Glen, bless his heart, is pre-disposed to take me by the Hawaii Yacht Club as he picks up his mail. Today is no different. I could object, but I remember some lines of Thomas Merton's: If a friend comes by, you must break your fast. I know I'm not going to break the fast, but I will sit with Glen while he has his coffee. Glen is a retired fighter pilot. For him, the ultimate is going 500 mph at tree top level. Slowing down for a fast he doesn't understand. I am not a proselytizer, and I've never tried to explain it to him. Today is no exception. We have our common ground where we are the best of friends.

In the H.Y.C. restaurant, Glen has his traditional two cups of coffee. I have a glass of tomato juice. I tell Glen about my fleeting glimpses of my childhood. He points out that prisoners of war experience a similar type of phenomenon due to isolation.

Returning home, Glen drops me off at the corner of the Likelike Highway and School Street which means I have to walk three blocks home. He is conditioned to dropping me off there, and I don't mind the walk. However, I don't want to have to interact with any of the neighbors yet. The kind spirits of the universe, among whom I count Jesus as one of the leaders, must somehow be reading my thoughts. No one is home. I have never seen that in the two years I have lived here. I believe in omens. This makes me happy, and I catch myself saying, "It's a small miracle."

I phone Michelle and explain the medical exam. Michelle asks me brief questions, and then tells me not to worry.

She visits in the evening with my signed bill of good health.

What a way to do a 40-day fast: garage sales, physical exams, yacht clubs, and telephone calls. It's not supposed to be this way. Maybe someone wandered into Jesus' path during his fast.

DAY 31

Today I have another fleeting memory of my past. I am about eight years old. Someone in my family is getting married. It might have been my Uncle George and Aunt Pat (now divorced). My mom wants me to take a nap, but I refuse. She says that if I don't, I can't go to the wedding that night.

That's fine with me, and I am prepared not to go. The memory that simultaneously popped into my mind is of my father later saying to me, "I think they would miss you at the wedding, so why don't you go get dressed."

I feel minor twinges of hunger.

DAY 32
My mind is quiet today.

DAY 33
I go out behind the bungalow and sit in the sun for about 20 minutes. How did Jesus perceive the sun? My mind is amazingly tranquil.

The realization that Jesus was devoid of the material world slowly creeps into my daily consciousness. Before it was just an abstract idea for me, but it is becoming a concrete reality.

DAY 34
I write nothing on my calendar today. I'm not thinking about anything. This is where I thought my mind would be somewhere between day 10 and 15. I can't believe it took so long and there are only five days left. Unfortunately, I have to use a portion of them as a transition for getting ready to move to Korea. That means going out a bit each day and becoming accustomed to dealing with daily events.

DAY 35
In the beginning, I was gaging the days according to "records:" the 5th, 9th, and 21st day. I also thought about two sesshins and three sesshins. But somewhere after that, those mental categories broke down. I realize today that I hadn't thought about day 32 being the equivalent of four sesshins. I look at the notes on my calendar for day 32. "My mind is quiet today." I am breaking free of the world I left, but not completely. I knew if I got to day 35, the breaking point, that the next five days would be easy. It's the old, 5, 4, 3, 2, 1 countdown routine.

DAY 36
I write on my calendar, "I'm so focused on the enlightenment aspect at which I am failing, I have to remind myself, 'I just went 36 days without food.'" Today, I realize I could never do another 40-day fast. Physically I could do it, but mentally I could not.

DAY 37
I decide to go out a bit today. There is too much to do to get ready for our move to Korea. I need to readjust a little at a time. I don't want day 40 to be heaped on me. On my calendar, I write, "The ritual of sitting and waiting

is over." I go outside. I will miss the isolation.

DAY 38

Today I walk over to our house. I feel a bit of hunger. I really didn't realize how much weight I lost until I changed from my elastic band shorts and put on a pair of pants. Wow! I look at myself in a mirror. My buttocks are gone. Really gone--all gone--except for the bones of course. I always remember the introduction to anthropology lesson about the Hottentots of Africa storing energy in their butts.

I walk in the yard a bit. Michelle comes out and says there is a long-distance call for me. It must be important, or she wouldn't be telling me. It's Hans, my son. He tells me that one of our best friends committed suicide. I told Hans our friend probably had an incurable disease. He was not the kind of person who would have wanted to "veg-out" in a hospital.

If there is something that would make me believe in predestination, it was learning about my friend's death. For the first time, I had gone out to prepare to reenter the everyday world, and there was the news. I'm glad I fasted 38 days before I received the news. The remainder of the day and into the night, I think: What is it about my friend that I most admired? He was one person I could trust absolutely. I could tell him something and ask him not to repeat it, and I knew it would never get repeated. I never really thought about the quality of trust before, but that is what the New Testament centers on. Jesus couldn't trust Judas, and Jesus confides in us to trust him in his mission. Each day millions of people, with materialistic concerns, touch a piece of paper or metal on which is written, "In God We Trust." My friend is gone, and I wonder where and how one finds people one can trust.

DAY 39

Like day 34, my mind is, for the most part, empty. I think about my friend every now and then.

DAY 40

I make the 40 days. I sit in the small cottage and think. There are those who will criticize me for using a tent for the first 20 days, saying, "Jesus didn't use a tent." And there will be other criticisms, like about my small lawn chair. I know Jesus didn't take a chair, but I don't know that he didn't pile up some type of vegetation making his sitting more comfortable. My final response to anyone is, "You do your 40-day fast the way you want, and then we'll compare notes." I think Bob Dylan said it best, "Don't criticize what you can't understand."

About three in the afternoon, I go over to our house. I sit and observe the details of what is around me. I examine the corners of the room. For some reason, this makes me think about another good friend, Frank, who often looks at the corners of rooms while reflecting.

The same sensation I felt on day 20 is still in my head. It is as if I never did the fast. Yet, I have an overwhelming sensation that it is complete.

I reevaluate my effort. It would have been better if I could have gone on some type of vacation for a week before beginning the fast so that I would have been more relaxed during the initial phase. Perhaps that would have moved the emptiness of mind I felt on day 34 up to day 20. And if that were the case, I might have stayed outside for the last part of the fast. Other than that, there is really not much I could have done given all the variables of time, space, and energy.

It is over. Of all my anticipatory thoughts, there is no tremendous vision, no tremendous spiritual awakening, no profound tranquility. However, I do understand that I am attached to the material world. But it isn't a matter of doing the fast too late in life. I could have been this tied into the material world at 30, but I wasn't. So, age really has nothing to do with it. Rather it was and is my frame of mind.

Jesus said, you can move a mountain if you have enough faith. But how do you achieve that level of faith? By just believing? If that were the case, the original 12 disciples could have done it. Nobody could have had stronger faith than they since they were witnesses to the miracles. No, one would truly have to reject the material world. One can't have it both ways. One can't move mountains and be tied to the material world.

By making that statement, I have arrived one more time at the crossroads. What does it mean to enter the kingdom of heaven? I see the crossroads like this: On the right there are those who take the Bible literally. Jesus really did arise from the dead. On the left are those who look at it metaphorically. Jesus' resurrection should be read as the feelings and dreams of his followers. Jesus' body is the church, and it is the church that is reconstituted, not the physical body of Jesus.

I am going between the two schools of thought. I believe Jesus might have walked on water, but I think the kingdom of heaven is a metaphor for a state of mind. I just experienced a small bit of it. One cannot have a tremendous spiritual experience during a 40-day fast if one is in anyway concerned with the material world. It truly would be easier for a camel to pass through the eye of a needle. However, if heaven is really meant as an afterlife, I don't see why God would want to exclude a moral person because of wealth.

And second, if I really wanted to move a mountain, I would have to keep going in the direction I was going for those 40 days and not come back. However, I'm headed in the opposite direction. I know that, and in knowing it, the fast divided my life as I wondered if it might.

But now I have another problem. What in the Bible is metaphorical, and what is literal, and what is in the imagination of my one writer? It is a complex issue. I wonder what I will continue to think about these matters in the future. I never intended to get involved in biblical research when I set out to do a 40-day fast.

I change thoughts and look at the table. There is a pile of mail. I look at some of it.

DAY 41

What to eat first? Outside Mrs. Char's guest house is a rose apple tree, *E. aromatica*. A large rose apple has a diameter about the size of a quarter. It is gold in color and has a unique aromatic odor, almost perfumy. That is why it has the latin name *aromatica*.

Some religious experts believe the rose apple tree might be the cosmogonic tree, Gambu, of India which bore the golden fruit of immortality. Juices of the fruit created the river Gambu, and the waters of the Gambu have healing power. Buddha is sometimes shown seated beneath a rose apple tree.

I eat one. The pulp is somewhat dry and the taste, and odor, are slightly aromatic. I chew very slowly. The sensation of eating is involuntarily signaled throughout my body. I savor the small fruit for nearly half an hour. I think the automatic refreshment must have been the same for Jesus when he broke his fast and especially when he received vinegar on the cross.

Outside of our house is a mountain apple tree, *Eugenia malaccensis*, and I eat a mountain apple next. It is about the size of a tennis ball, but pear-shaped. The skin is a beautiful crimson color. Unlike an apple, it has only one large seed. The pulp is pure white, and when first ripe, crisp. It is slightly sweet. It is succulent and refreshing. I love mountain apples. As I eat, a sensation of tremendous satisfaction bounces back and forth between my stomach and my brain.

About a half an hour later, I eat a slice of star-fruit, *Averrhoa carambola*. It grows behind Mrs. Char's guest house. The orange fruit is about five inches long, and it is star-shaped in cross section. The outer fruit is quite waxy. The pulp is slightly acidic, and overall, I consider the taste rather bland. This is the first time in my life I have eaten a star fruit. A sensation of novelty registers in my stomach as I swallow.

Finally, I eat a slice of kiwi.

Over the next two hours, I eat half of a banana, a slice of an apple, a strawberry, and a grape.

Our friends Glen and Mary are determined to "take me out" that night. It is a dilemma because I really don't want to go, but again the Thomas Merton line comes to mind, "You have to break the fast for a friend," meaning to me sometimes one has to go against one's original plan because of a friend. Besides my fast is already broken.

We start our evening at the Hawaii Yacht Club. The Kenwood Cup is still in progress and Michelle is volunteering in the gift shop. She broke the all time, one-day sales record. We meet her there and watch her sell. Watching her professional selling skills and the money coming in, I'm instantly and totally immersed in the material world.

In the restaurant, we have a couple of Cajun Onion Blossoms. It is a large onion sliced from the top to give the appearance of a blossom as it folds out. It is deep fried and served with a hot sauce. I eat a couple of pieces. It is good to taste an onion again. I try to drink an O'doul's, non-alcoholic beer, but the alcohol content, little though it is, is still too much.

We go to the Chart House overlooking the Hawaii Yacht Club. I have clam chowder and cheese bread. The fat content of the meal is quite filling. I also have a bite of Michelle's lasagna. The tomato sauce and basil are welcomed throughout my body.

A startling thought permeates my being: I'm already back to minor habituations. Like Siddartha, I'm sliding back to the material world. I recall one of Kando Nakagima's points, "If you want to void yourself of this world, go live in a cave."

DAY 42

Today I ate Mrs. Char's *chook*. It is a Japanese/Hawaiian dish of rice, chicken broth, some chicken meat, and sweet potato leaves. The Japanese/Hawaiians eat this when they are sick to improve their health.

DAY 43 and on

In the following days, I drink prune and apple juice. I eat salads and apples.

TODAY

Today is February 5, 1995, in Naju City, South Korea. I've had time to reflect. In January of 1995, Michelle and I took a three-week vacation to Japan, Taiwan, and the Philippines. That vacation seemed three years long. By comparison, I still have no sensation of time for the 40-day fast, only the intellectual realization that it happened. There must be something to this, but I can't explain it--at least right now.

I am convinced that going to the garage sale on day 20 was a good idea. By going, I had a comparative marker for experiencing time. If I had it to do over again, I would have done the 40 days in one set and then have gone to a garage sale. I had no comparative marker to judge time by coming out slowly in the last 20 days.

I wonder why the garage sale seemed slow. I would have thought that by sitting in once place for 20 days that an activity like a garage sale would seem speeded up. This must relate to the fact that I have only an intellectual realization of the 40-day fast.

Certain critics conclude I really didn't do a 40-day fast since I went to a garage sale. In 1993, Michelle and I did the Honolulu Marathon. En route, we went to a garage sale. Some people insisted, "How can you say you ran a marathon if you stopped for garage sales?" But, we ran the same distance-- 26 miles. In fact, we bought a book and a metal tin at the garage sale and carried them in our backpack the rest of the race. So, the event was that much more grueling.

After finally having written about my fast, I reconcile my thoughts of having wanted to do the fast over again, like so many things in life. If I would have done it in the late 70s when my mind was not chained to the material world, I probably would have been a much different person; I might have been branded a kook, or I might have ended up in a Zen monastery. Outside of my petty thoughts of vengeance, which are diminishing, I like my life just the way it is--good times and mildly hedonistic.

One conclusion I can offer is that fasting won't automatically provide spiritual insights. Fasting for spiritual purposes has to be done with a specific mental framework. In the words of Jesus, one has to be seeking the spiritual. In the words of Swami Vivekananda, one must be concentrating on the spiritual; destroying the ego related elements of pride, greed, fear, ignorance, and desire. This probably answers my question on why the disciples didn't fast.

My fast was a spiritual failure. But, it was a pragmatical success. I had time to think about many things. For one, I hope when I must leave earth, I can fast and sit alone, reflecting. I wonder what my last words will be?

The experience also helped me define what is religious and what is spiritual. Religion is a reverence for supernatural beings and a code of ethics. Alexander the Great, a maniacal killing machine, was a very religious person. He constantly sacrificed to the gods for supplying him victories in battle. For Alexander, the sacrifices must have worked because he didn't lose. As John Maxwell O'Brien said, "...Alexander, a conspicuously religious man,...a brilliant man was spiritually blind...."

Spirituality on the other hand is experiencing another level of consciousness--presumably higher. Two questions are raised: Are there levels of spirituality? What is necessary for achieving the highest levels?

As for the first, I think spirituality equates with tranquility. Thus there are levels. The more one rejects the material world and its manifestations in the ego, the greater the spirituality/tranquility. This tranquility is a result of the emptying of the mind. If the mind is emptied enough, an individual can develop powers beyond the normal. Both Jesus and Swami Vivekananda talk about moving mountains.

In trying to define spirituality, I finally realized what happened to me during sesshin and the vision quests. I was extremely tranquil during those times, and obviously so. During sesshin, I had completed eight straight days of meditation and, when I was done, I looked forward to a year long vacation. No wonder tobacco left my life. Adding to that, I was able to extend the vacation a few months and accomplish a vision quest.

Isolation could help in the development of spirituality. In terms of levels of tranquility and isolation, I compare the Essenes and Jesus. The Essenes rejected the material world and shunned public ritual. They also isolated themselves in monasteries and indulged in silence. If Jesus lived with them during his missing years, he would have been aware of their customs. On the other hand, maybe his missing years were spent in total isolation so he could become the public spiritual being he did. My fast was proof that isolation alone is not sufficient to sustain tranquility. Likewise, many hermits are not tranquil, but apathetic.

We are born spiritual, but we become attached to the material world. Jesus said, "I assure you, that unless you change and become as little children, you will never enter the kingdom of heaven." (MT 18:3) Now of course, the longevity of childhood has been cut shorter with the advent of television and fast food restaurants that promote food with material knick-knacks.

Thus, I have my conclusion about balancing spirituality and materialism. The degree of spirituality is directly proportional to the rejection of the material world and its manifestations in the ego.

As for religious truth, I have come to accept the Unitarian Universalist idea that religious truth should be grounded on universal religious experiences, not the record of historical events such as Jesus' fast. I only attended one Unitarian church service (in Tallahassee, Florida). Maybe I'll make my way back to one when I return to the United States.

I offer this idea to Christians. Maybe Jesus hasn't returned because there is really nothing to come back to. Jesus was a man who wouldn't even touch a coin because it would corrupt his spirit. He said the meek would inherit the earth. If he did come back and squarely faced those practicing weekend rituals in his name, what words would he hear from them? I think the most common statement would be, "Hey, you don't look like your pictures!" Maybe the second most common comment would be, "Money is a necessary evil."

It is possible Jesus will return. If he does, I'll do everything within my power during my judgment to ask, "Jesus, when Satan tempted you and you looked in on all the kingdoms in a second of time, what did you see?"

I still have passing fantasies of finding the spot where Jesus fasted. Subsequent to my fast, I read *Halley's Bible Handbook*. The authors place the location of the fast at the Mountain of Temptation northwest of Jericho. Today this is part of the West Bank. If I could find the spot, I might try to do a vision quest there. But being now immersed in the material world, I don't think I could feel that place. It is a different time in my life.

ACKNOWLEDGEMENTS

I had hoped to avoid writing an acknowledgement section. By not doing such I could avoid the embarrassment of omitting names of those who helped me, and there were very many. There are also certain Christians who may not want to be associated with this book.

However, thank God for Willi F. Moelzer. He read. He edited. He cared. Maybe the best thing I'll get out of this book is his friendship.

I hope I can find a way to repay Heather Bolan in the future. Her work was above and beyond the call of duty.

Pastor Lyle Arakaki and Toney Bradfield constantly helped with scriptural research.

I am thankful for Holly Riffell's and Christopher Small's editing skills.

I have a special thanks for Bert and Anneliese Andrews.

Elizabeth and Kirk Mayer provided meaningful input.

And there is Michelle. She was left out of the backcover photo because there was no one else that day to take our group photo. She forced me to be articulate, and in the end, it paid off.

WANT TO KNOW MORE?

Asad, T.
  1993 *Genealogies of Religion: Discipline and Reasons of Power in Christianity and Islam.* M.D.: John Hopkins University Press.

Boers, H.
  1989 *Who Was Jesus?* S.F.: Harper & Row.

Campbell, J.
  1982 *Primitive Mythology.* N.Y.: Penguin Books.

Duran, D.
  1994 *The History of the Indies of New Spain.* Tulsa: University of Oklahoma Press.

Gitin, S.
  1992 Last Days of the Philistines. *Archaeology* 45:26-31.

Grinnell, G.
  1923 *The Cheyenne Indians.* Vol. 1. Lincoln: University of Nebraska.

Handy, E.
  1930 "Marquesan Legends." Bishop Museum Bulletin 69. Honolulu.

Harris, S.
  1992 *Understanding the Bible.* Third Edition. Mountain View, CA: Mayfield Publishing Company.

Kolchin, P.
  1993 *American Slavery: 1619-1877.* N.Y.: Hill and Wang.

Mack, B.
  1995 *Who Wrote the New Testament?* N.Y.: HarperCollins.

Malina, B.
  1993 *The New Testament World.* Louisville, KY: Westminster/John Knox Press.

Metford, J.
  1983 *Dictionary of Christian Lore and Legend.* N.Y.: Thames and Hudson.

Naisbitt, J. and P. Aburdene
1990 *Megatrends 2000: Ten New Directions of the 1990's*. N.Y.: William Morrow and Co., Inc.

Nun, M.
1993 *The Sea of Galilee and Its Fishermen in the New Testament*. Washington, D.C.: Biblical Archaeology Society.

O'Collins S.J., G.
1995 *Christology*. Oxford: Oxford University Press.

Paris, E.
1995 *The End of Days: A Story of Tolerance, Tyranny and the Expulsion of the Jews from Spain*. N.Y.: Prometheus Books.

Reader's Digest *ABC's of the Bible*. Pleasantville, New York.

Stocker, T. (ed.)
1991 The Problems of Looting and Faking. In: *The New World Figurine Project*, Volume 1. T. Stocker (ed.) Provo: Research Press.

Stocker, T.
1987 Conquest, Tribute and the Rise of the State. In *Studies in the Neolithic and Urban Revolutions*. The V. Gordon Childe Colloquium, Mexico. L. Manzanilla (ed.). BAR International Series 349.

Tenney, M.
1985 *New Testament Survey*. Downers Grove, IL:InterVarsity Press.

Wenham, J.
1992 *Redating Matthew, Mark and Luke*. Downers Grove, IL: InterVarsity Press.

Wilson, R.
1993 "Anchored Communities: Identity and History of the Maya-Q'Eqchi'." *Man* (N.S.) 28:121-138.

Wood, J.
1914 *The Yoga-System of Patanjali*. Delhi: Motilal Banarsidass.